NO CAUSE OF DEATH

IN MEMORY OF JOE FINN,
LEGENDARY *OTTAWA CITIZEN* CRIME REPORTER

NO
CAUSE
OF
DEATH

James Fontana

Midnight Originals / THE MERCURY PRESS

THIS IS A TRUE STORY, based on the investigation and trial of Frederick George Rudderick for the murder of his wife on November 16, 1976. Fred Ruddick's trial began May 24th, 1978, in the Supreme Court of Ontario (Trial Division) under Mr. Justice O'Driscoll. The full, official report of the case is to be found in (1981) Volume 57, *Canadian Criminal Cases* (page 421, the decision of the Ontario Court of Appeal, by Mr. Justice J. Arthur Martin. Official citation: (1981) 57 C.C.C. (2nd) 421.)

Some names have been changed to protect the innocent.

The publisher gratefully acknowledges the financial assistance of the Canada Council and the Ontario Arts Council, as well as that of the Government of Ontario through the Ontario Publishing Centre.

Edited by Beverley Daurio
Cover design by Gordon Robertson
Cover photograph by Doug Forster
Composition and page design by TASK

Printed and bound in Canada by Metropole Litho
Printed on acid-free paper
1 2 3 4 5   98 97 96 95 94

CANADIAN CATALOGUING IN PUBLICATION DATA
Fontana, James A.
    No cause of death
ISBN 1-55128-018-3
1. Ruddick, Frederick   2. Murder — Ontario — Ottawa
I. Title
HV6535.C33077 1994   364.1'523'092   C94-932107-9

Represented in Canada by the Literary Press Group
Distributed by General Distribution Services

The Mercury Press
137 Birmingham Street
Stratford, Ontario
Canada   N5A 2T1

1.

George Broderick was a man who presented many faces.

To his wife and children, he was a loyal family man, a caring provider who attended mass at St. Augustine's every Sunday and who donated his time as a cub and scout leader. To his acquaintances he was a gentleman, honourably retired after a long career in the navy, who stayed lean and fit from his hobby, scuba diving. To his employers he was an engaging life insurance salesman, and, subsequently, an energetic branch manager. To business acquaintances he was a successful inventor of top secret radar improvements, and owner of a thriving flying school somewhere in the Maritimes. A few select intimates understood that he continued to serve his country as a counter-espionage consultant.

On November 16, 1976, two bailiffs discovered Anne Broderick, aged 53, unconscious in the bathtub at the Broderick home in Ottawa's Parkwood Hills. Anne Broderick died 10 hours later in hospital. She had slipped while standing up in the tub. It was not an uncommon type of accident.

Four days later there was a wake at the funeral home, followed by a funeral at St. Augustine's, piously attended by her bereaved husband, children, and many friends. They had little time to adjust to the tragic accident. Anne was gone. The family was left motherless. It was over. Case closed.

But in the opinion of Detective Sergeant Robert Denton Mancuso, George Broderick was a murderer.

Columbo only investigates homicides!

No robberies. No frauds. No drunk driving cases. Just homicides.

This realization presented itself unexpectedly in Detective Bob Mancuso's mind like a kaleidoscope unexpectedly producing a recognizable picture. It was not an answer, he knew, but it was a sliver of confirmation that his instincts were pushing him in the right direction, that his feelings about Anne Broderick's death were justified. These little insights usually came to him when he was not actively thinking about the problem. But he *had* been thinking about Anne's death a lot. In fact, he had been thinking about nothing else for six days.

On the snowy evening of November 22nd, 1976, Mancuso pulled his unmarked Chevy police cruiser into a parking space behind Nepean City Hall and went down into the basement where the police headquarters was housed. By the end of his regular shift, he was convinced that George Broderick had murdered his wife. Mancuso's problem would be convincing anyone else. One or two of his fellow officers were almost convinced, but they lacked Mancuso's certainty that Broderick could ever be successfully tried. And if he couldn't be tried, then why bother?

Anne Broderick's death had all the hallmarks of a common accident, so officialdom was not inclined to spend time or resources on it. Besides, Mancuso's superiors asked, how could a suspect be found guilty of murder if the cause of the victim's death remained an official mystery? It had never been done before.

Mancuso booked off shift, ending another day of chasing elusive fraud artists, "paper-hangers," and endless credit card scams. His time was now his own. He phoned his wife Anita and told her that he would be a couple of hours late. His favourite meal, spaghetti and meatballs, would have to wait. After 17 years of marriage to a policeman, Anita was resigned to disruptions in their home life.

Mancuso retrieved the thin Broderick file from the records room, where rows of green filing cabinets housed the city's unsavoury secrets. It was labelled "Anne E. Broderick, Drowning." He opened it onto his metal desk and lit his 25th cigarette of the day. Then he began to study the file again. The hand holding the cigarette shook a little as Mancuso studied the pages: police reports, witness statements, medical and autopsy reports.

Some of the reports were his own.

A copy of the death certificate attributed Anne's death to "Drowning with profound acidosis and D.I.C. cardiac asystole."

Mancuso had been pulled suddenly from a routine fraud investigation and dispatched to the death scene. Shuffling investigators from case to case was a necessary expedient in the understaffed Nepean Police Force.

The Broderick family home was a modern, modest-sized bungalow at 18 Beaverton Crescent in Ottawa's Parkwood Hills, in a neighbourhood of shade trees and manicured lawns inviting favourable comparison with a scene from *Father Knows Best*.

Uniformed officer Geoff Nichol was already there when Mancuso arrived. Nichol had found George Broderick in the bathroom, crouched over the lifeless form of his wife, Anne, who was lying on the bathroom floor parallel to the bathtub. Broderick, excited and distraught, had thrown a blanket over her naked torso. The water in the tub was bright blue and the shower curtain had been torn from the supporting crossbar. Broderick, stuttering as he spoke, told Officer Nichol that he had warned his wife not to put that "crap" in the water. The "crap" was Anne's favourite, distinctive blue bath oil. She was probably wiping down the tile walls when she slipped and fell, Broderick offered.

There were no major injuries observed on the body at that time.

Officer Nichol quickly put out a call on his portable radio requesting that the Emergency Response Team be sent to the house. Oxygen was needed, fast!

Then Broderick said something to Officer Nichol that the policeman found disconcerting.

"She's been in the water too long and I wouldn't want her to live if she ended up as a vegetable," Broderick said.

The response team arrived, administered oxygen to Anne, and she was rushed to the emergency wing of the Ottawa Civic Hospital. Officer O'Donovan arrived and drove Broderick to the hospital, following the ambulance. Officer Nichol remained at the house to preserve the scene for the detectives. It was a routine, accidental home death, something they might encounter 20 times a year in their day-to-day police work.

The police expected to finish their study of the scene and be out of the Broderick home in an hour.

Sergeant Mancuso and his boyish-looking partner, Detective Murray Gordon, received the dispatch call at 11:10 a.m. and drove straight to the Civic Hospital Emergency Unit. Anne Broderick was still alive but her chances of survival were described by the attending physicians, Doctors Yates and Bourmanis, as being "a thousand to one."

Mancuso spoke with Officer O'Donovan who pointed out George Broderick standing in front of the head emergency nurse's desk. Mancuso joined Broderick, who asked what his wife's condition was. Mancuso told him that she was alive and that there was still "a chance for her." Mancuso casually engaged Broderick in conversation and offered his sympathies. Keeping the tone low-key, he inquired, "What time did you leave home this morning, George?" Broderick replied, "Between 9:05 and 9:10." Broderick went on to explain that he was in a financial bind and that he had left the house to get money for his landlord, the Minto Corporation. He had phoned the bank, he said, and got no answer, so he called his office and spoke with his secretary, telling her he wouldn't be in until later. He decided to return home and stopped for gas and cigarettes on the way. By the time he got home, the bailiffs and the Minto representative were at the door. He asked them, he said, if his wife was at home, and the two men told him "No"; however, they said the bathroom door was locked. Broderick had gone to the bathroom door, called his wife's name, then returned to the kitchen, retrieved an ice pick and jimmied the lock. He said he saw his wife lying in the bathtub and pulled her out with the help of one of the bailiffs and the Minto representative. And then the uniformed officer, Geoff Nichol, arrived.

Mancuso confronted the distraught Broderick in front of the nurses' station, lacing him with a risky question.

"Are you pigging around with any girls these days, George?"

The question, coarse in content and callous in tone, today would get a policeman hauled before a civilian review board for discourtesy and insensitivity to a member of the public. Broderick became nervous and edgy, a condition equally attributable to the shock of his wife's accident.

Broderick stared at Mancuso for a moment in disbelief.

"No way!" he replied firmly and stalked off.

Broderick was then driven back to his home by Officer O'Donovan, after first insisting on retrieving the old blue blanket that had covered his wife.

Mancuso and Gordon arrived back at 18 Beaverton a few minutes later. They had just sent Officers Nichol and O'Donovan away when another car suddenly pulled into the driveway. An exceedingly attractive blonde girl came to the front door. Broderick rushed to meet her. They had a brief conversation— barely audible to the detectives— before she came into the vestibule of the house. Broderick embraced the girl and said to her, "Missy's had an accident. She's in the hospital. She slipped in the bathtub." The girl bolted out the door, into her car, and was gone, as abruptly as she had arrived and without comment to any of the officers.

When Broderick re-entered the living room from the vestibule, he read the quizzical expression on Mancuso's face.

An explanation was necessary. The girl, he said, was an orphan who had been taken in by his family and was a close friend of his wife's. She was like one of the family.

Mancuso thought the explanation was thin. He seized the moment, blindsiding Broderick again.

"You got a girlfriend, George?"

Broderick drilled his reply directly at Mancuso.

"No! I'm not saying I'm a saint! Some time ago when I was in the navy, I was having extramarital affairs with females. But I do not have a girlfriend at all. No way!"

Mancuso remained uneasy with this response.

The girl, blonde and very pretty, had hardly demonstrated appropriate reaction to the news of her friend's "accident," nor had she pursued it with more questions. Equally curious to Mancuso, Broderick had not offered the girl's name. Was she simply Anne's friend, no more, no less? Mancuso entertained a cop's doubt. The girl at the door was young enough to be Broderick's granddaughter, but too much was happening at the house that needed Mancuso's attention. The girl would have to wait.

2.

Death-scene investigators are inevitably confronted with a troublesome human dilemma: the necessity of examining the scene while it is fresh, but often within the disruptive milieu of a grieving family. As the investigator absorbs information, distinguishing the important from the unimportant, business often collides with compassion. Small things can be missed.

But Mancuso had an eye for small things— like the piece of broken fingernail on the carpet.

Mancuso, noticing Broderick's lack of lamentation over Anne's accident, decided to keep on going. He began by asking permission to examine the house. Broderick suddenly became talkative and expansive. Not only could the detective examine the house, but Broderick also said he understood it was Mancuso's job to do so. He understood what it meant to have to perform difficult, distasteful tasks, because during the war he had had to notify widows of the deaths of their husbands.

Then Broderick told Mancuso a story. A few years earlier he had been travelling through Mexico and his jeep had been stolen. He reported it to the local police. Not too long afterward he was notified that the jeep had been recovered and the thief arrested. He was invited to go to the police station, where he retrieved the vehicle. The police officer asked him if he wanted to "look after the accused" or would he permit them to do so. Broderick said that since he was happy just to get his jeep back, "I told the police they could take care of the suspect themselves, at which point the policeman pulled out his revolver and shot the thief between the eyes."

Mancuso looked at Broderick, disbelieving, unsure what to make of this strange tale. He attributed it in part to Broderick's distraught condition. But was Broderick trying to tell him something, or to influence him, perhaps by suggesting some sort of fraternal rapport with law enforcement authorities?

But since Broderick seemed to be in a talkative mood, Mancuso asked him again about the two-hour lapse from the time he said he had left home, at 9:10 a.m., until he had returned to find the bailiff and Minto representative at his house. Broderick backtracked, replying that he wasn't sure if he had left precisely between 9:05 and 9:10, but that he would check with his daughter, Shirley. She had left the house moments before him that morning.

Mancuso noted that Broderick's backtracking was similar to the response he had received earlier that morning in the emergency wing. He let the matter drop.

The investigators' room-by-room examination of the bungalow revealed no overt signs of violence. The interior was neat and tidy throughout, consistent with the Brodericks having gotten up in the morning, washed the dishes, and begun their daily ritual. Cookware, still wet, sat in the sink and clean dishes were draining on the sideboard. The hallway was immaculate. Coats and jackets were in their place in the vestibule closet. The beds in daughter Shirley's bedroom and the spare bedroom were made. On the dining room table, a few Christmas cards had been written out in Anne Broderick's handwriting.

Other investigators would have made a bee-line for the bathroom. It said something about Mancuso's instincts that he concentrated his first observations on the master bedroom. "There are no secrets there," he would say. "That's where it always starts."

The bed was still unmade and the sheets were folded halfway down. Some clothing— a nightgown and a housecoat— lay on top of the bed and off to one side. On the night-table to the left, there was a bra with a religious medal attached to it. There was a pair of ladies' blue panties on a second night-table to the right side of the bed. There was an electric blanket on the bed.

Mancuso noted three false fingernails lying on the night-table on the right side of the bed. On the floor by the left side of the bed he found a plastic cover from the Christmas card box. A few magazines were piled neatly under the bed, undisturbed.

There was nothing in the master bedroom that suggested violence or foul play and yet there was something about the scene that made Mancuso uneasy. He looked around, then walked into the hall where he had previously caught a glimpse of a label attached to the wall beside the hall light switch. The "Energy Saver" label, one of many distributed by the hydro company months earlier, urged conservation of electricity and the turning off of lights not in use. Mancuso returned to the bedroom and examined the electric blanket, taking a close look at its two heat controls. They were both in the full "On" position. He switched them off, wondering whether Anne Broderick would have left them on if her morning routine had not been suddenly disrupted prior to going into the bathroom to bathe.

More questions were lying there on the bed.

The religious medal fastened to Anne Broderick's brassiere indicated that Anne had followed a rather quaint, almost forgotten religious tradition. Anne Broderick must have been a devout and modest woman. Is it likely, he wondered, that she would remove her brassiere, panties, nightgown, and housecoat in the bedroom and then walk naked down the hallway to the bathroom? Mancuso didn't think so. He ordered the police photographer to photograph the scene, including the top of the bed.

Then he noticed what had been teasing at his subconscious since he had first begun to examine the bedroom. The pile of clothing on top of the bed was in reverse order! The housecoat was lying on top of the nightgown, a configuration that told him that Anne might have undressed elsewhere— in the bathroom, perhaps— and that her clothing had been carried back to the bedroom. Or had she been undressed here and dragged naked to the bathroom?

Mancuso returned to the kitchen and casually queried Broderick about this anomaly.

"I may have moved them when I was looking for something to cover my wife."

The significance of the question was not lost on Broderick. From this point onward he would discern that Mancuso was going beyond the obvious questions; the detective was curious about more subtle considerations.

This exchange marked the beginning of a cat-and-mouse relationship that would develop between the investigator and the suspect over the next few weeks.

Mancuso turned his attention to the bathroom. Quite a bit was obvious. Too obvious, he thought.

The bathtub was still partly filled with water.

A plastic shower curtain with double lining had been ripped away at the third ring and three of the metal rings were off the runner. The third ring from the end was bent nearly straight. On the perimeter of the bathtub there was a back scrub brush, a bottle of lotion, a plastic bottle and a rolled up face cloth. The water in the tub was unusually blue, and it was clean, unlike used bathwater. Mancuso ordered samples to be collected and retained. At the rear of the bathroom a clothes hamper held four articles of soiled clothing. Mancuso put his hand into the pile and pulled out a brown electrical cord, five feet long. There were no items of women's night clothing in the bathroom. The bathroom floor and shower walls were dry. There were a pair of pink slippers and a floor mat in front of a double vanity. Everything in the bathroom was neat and orderly. Mancuso told the identification officer, Wayne Holland, to measure the depth of the water, and retain samples. He took the box of blue bath oil beads for fingerprinting. Finally, he directed photographing of the bathroom interior.

Despite the atmosphere of confrontation that was developing between Mancuso and Broderick, protocol required that the detective continue to deal with Broderick on a gentlemanly basis. Mancuso was cautious not to reveal the suspicions his instincts were dictating. Broderick, sensing that the detective's questions were going beyond the routine, adopted the tactic of being disarmingly forthright and cooperative. When Mancuso asked him to describe the position of Anne as Broderick had found her lying in the tub, Broderick was quite specific: she was lying on her left side facing the tile wall, her head at the end opposite the faucets, her face totally submerged in the blue water, and her right leg crooked or bent over her left leg which was straight out. Broderick said that he grabbed her and started pulling her out of the water, yelling for help from the bailiff and his assistant. He and the paramedics had tried to revive her using CPR, without success. When Mancuso asked him about the blue bath oil beads, Broderick replied that Anne always used them. That morning, he said, he had personally run the bath for his wife and had put the bath beads in the water. Then he volunteered the information that he had first taken a bath himself, leaving the water for her, a practice which they frequently followed since they were very energy conscious. Images of the electric blanket in the "On" position and the clean bathwater lingered in Mancuso's mind.

Broderick was being a little too talkative. Worse, he was showing no respect for Mancuso's intelligence.

It was inevitable that their conversation should drift to a television program, one of the *Columbo* series that had aired on television a short few weeks before. The story had been about a man whose wife had been murdered in the bathtub. Columbo, not unexpectedly, had solved the mystery.

"It's a shame they show that kind of stuff on television," Broderick complained to Mancuso. "It might give someone ideas!"

"Is that so?" Mancuso wondered to himself.

The murderer in the television program had done it to be with his girlfriend. A woman named Cynthia.

Before leaving for the day, Mancuso blindsided Broderick with another question from the "obvious" category.

"Were there any insurance policies on Anne's life?" Broderick, exuding cooperation, went into the bedroom, returning with two insurance policies on Anne's life, one for $12,500, written in 1966, and another for $3000 written in 1970. Both paid double indemnity benefits for accidental death.

The policies had been written with Broderick's own insurance company, Canadian Premier Life. The policies were relatively small, as insurance policies go, but if there was the prospect of a double indemnity pay out, then they became significant. The benefits would match Broderick's indebtedness almost to the dollar.

Mancuso tried to avoid an I-thought-so expression.

Mancuso and his young partner Detective Gordon then left the house, telling Broderick they would be in touch with him the next day in order to take a formal witness statement once he had had an opportunity to compose himself.

That night, at 10:00, Anne Broderick was pronounced dead.

Very few criminal investigators are ever confronted with the unique question that troubled Bob Mancuso that night. Ordinarily, in homicide cases, the *fact* of the homicide is not in dispute. The investigator's problem is determining the identity of the killer and the motivation. Bob Mancuso was beginning to sense, even at this early stage, that Anne Broderick's death was a homicide disguised as an accidental death. But his suspicions were just an instinctive reaction based upon nothing more than a few minor anomalies observed at the death scene, coupled with fishy responses and an inappropriate amount of cooperation being shown by Broderick toward him. He had virtually insulted Broderick twice, and had received inappropriate reactions both times.

Why was Broderick stroking him with cooperation and ingratiating stories about the Mexican police? Look for inappropriate reaction. Inappropriate reaction can be excessively *appropriate* reaction. The investigator's credo.

But such ethereal considerations are not the stuff upon which costly murder investigations are launched, particularly against a reputable citizen such as George Broderick.

George Broderick was, to all who knew him, a very congenial business-man who had, by hard work and long hours, climbed the ladder from sales representative to manager of the substantial Ottawa branch of the Canadian Premier Life Insurance Company. He was a family man whose life appeared to be oriented toward his wife and three children and who was active in community affairs. At age 54, he might have passed for someone 10 years younger. He was lean and athletic-looking, with a full head of thick curly hair combed in pompadour style. A few flecks of grey lent distinction to his permanently tanned features, the result of outdoor activities and earlier summers at the lake.

Born in Canmore, Alberta, in 1922, Broderick had signed on with the Royal Canadian Naval Volunteer Service in 1940 at the age of 18, beginning a naval career that was to span 26 years. Starting out as a naval telegrapher, he spent most of his career as a radio technician, continually improving his qualifications so that by 1949 he had become a Chief Petty Officer Second Class Radio Technician. In 1960, he achieved Commissioned Officer status, and in 1963 was promoted to Lieutenant. In the course of his navy service he was decorated with the Canadian Volunteer Service Medal, the Star, the Queen Elizabeth II Coronation Medal, and the Canadian Forces Decoration.

During his career he upgraded his basic grade 10 education through correspondence courses, eventually completing grade 12 and achieving the equivalent of second year university level in accounting and business administration through correspondence courses with McMaster University. In addition to the radio technology and electronics courses which he pursued in the military, Broderick was known to have taken a Russian language course.

He married his wife, the former Anne Edna Pike, in March, 1943, in Ottawa. Anne was a slim, attractive woman with a wistful, melancholy demeanour even when she was happy. She was a practising Roman Catholic and maintained her devotional activities throughout her life. She and George had separated for a short time a few years before, but had, apparently, worked out their differences and re-united. At the time of her death in November, 1976, their two sons, Ryan, 31, who was married, and Gerry, 27, had left home. Only their adopted daughter, Shirley, 21, who was pursuing a degree at Carleton University, continued to live at home.

In 1966, at the age of 44, Broderick was honourably released from military service.

It might have been expected that after an extensive career in radio and electronics, he would have gravitated toward a civilian occupation which capitalized on this expertise. Instead, not unlike many men who seek a complete change when confronted with middle age and their own mortality, George Broderick left the world of radio and electronics behind to become a life insurance representative.

He brought to the life insurance business the same enthusiasm and resourcefulness that had propelled his progress in the navy. He began as a sales representative in the Ottawa office in January of 1966, serving in that capacity until January, 1968. He was described as a better-than-average agent. As a result he was appointed branch supervisor in January of 1968. Within two years he was promoted to manager of the Ottawa branch. His meteoric rise was described by Jack Waldron, a vice-president of Canadian Premier Life, as being the most rapid advance of an employee from agent to branch manager in the history of the company. Broderick's productivity during those four years was looked upon by the company as astonishing, and Broderick continued to build the Ottawa branch until it was ranked as one of their better branches in Canada.

The possibility that this person— a mild-mannered family man, an insurance executive, a man of apparently conservative lifestyle— might have committed murder, tormented Mancuso. George Broderick did not fit the type. But then, they seldom do. The overtly accidental circumstances of the death were not circumstances which gave Mancuso any toe-hold. He knew he would not easily persuade his superiors to start a detailed criminal investigation.

Everything was still in the "uneasy feeling" stage. And uneasy feelings will get you nowhere in a court of law.

The night of November 16th was to be the first of many nights of tangled sleep for Bob Mancuso.

3.

When Mancuso and Gordon arrived at 18 Beaverton just after lunch the day after Anne's death, they found George Broderick home alone. He invited the two investigators in, treated them congenially, and engaged them in light conversation with the confidence of someone who had done nothing wrong and had nothing to hide. But Mancuso noted that he no longer seemed distraught or even emotional, despite his wife's death late the previous evening. Mancuso asked Broderick to describe the events of the previous morning again. Broderick spoke willingly. He described their life in general as being relatively happy and free of any marital or sex problems. He took pride in having taught his wife scuba diving and said that she had taken a Registered Nursing Assistant's course in which she had placed second in the class. He described his wife as a very religious and intelligent woman. The family, he said, was very close knit. He and his wife had recently discussed the idea of getting a bathmat for the tub since the oil from the bath beads made the tub slippery.

Anne was very energy conscious, which was the reason for the "Energy Saver" labels on the light switches around the house. Overall, Broderick's comments were a hodgepodge, an undiluted mixture of the bland and the trivial. When he reached the events of the morning of November 16th, Broderick again recounted the gruesome discovery of his wife in the bathtub. At this stage he displayed the only sign of emotion that the investigators were to see from him that day. He excused himself, went into the kitchen, drank some water and returned, composed.

In the course of this discussion Broderick became self-deprecating, ingratiating, expressing some guilt about collateral things. He "confessed" to not having been a very successful money manager in the home. He had recently agreed with Anne to turn over his pay cheques to her. She would manage the money. Under further probing by Mancuso, he revealed that his overall financial circumstances were bad. Mancuso knew Broderick could hardly deny this in view of the presence of the bailiffs and the landlord's representative at the house when Anne's body was discovered. Broderick tried to explain away his financial situation, saying that he had co-signed a loan in the amount of $15,000 for a friend, to put the friend through college in Toronto. The friend had defaulted on the loan, quit college, and left town. He did not volunteer the friend's name.

The telephone rang and Broderick jumped up to answer it. There was a brief conversation which the investigators could not overhear, but when he returned Broderick said it was just his secretary calling. Mancuso asked, "What's her name?"

"Cynthia," he replied, too matter-of-factly.

Broderick was just completing his statement to the two investigators when his daughter Shirley came into the house. Broderick introduced her to Mancuso and Gordon. Mancuso suggested to Broderick that he would like to talk to Shirley alone. Broderick balked and tried to persuade Mancuso not to, saying that she was too upset. Mancuso became insistent. Broderick relented and took the detective into Shirley's bedroom, but hovered close by throughout the discussion.

Mancuso asked Shirley what time she had left the house on the morning of the previous day, recollecting that Broderick had tied in the time of his departure as being within a few minutes of Shirley's. After some prompting from her father, Shirley replied that it had been about 9:15 in the morning. She said that she had not seen her mother that morning at all before leaving. When asked by Mancuso about her mother's condition on the night before her death, Shirley again relied on prompting from her father, saying her mother had been ill the night before. Broderick corrected his daughter, saying no, Anne had been ill the night of the 14th of November.

This puppet-on-a-string approach was going nowhere. Mancuso decided that Broderick's persistent, continuing interference made it necessary to talk with Shirley at a later date, privately.

Such were the tensions and nuances that Mancuso was picking up in his meeting with Broderick the morning after the death. Nothing was developing yet, nor even beginning to arrange itself into an orderly pattern, nor pointing in any particular direction. Mancuso was just absorbing. It was all up in the air.

It was within this amorphous context that Broderick made a comment that rattled Mancuso.

During their discussion, Mancuso had casually gotten up and wandered in the direction of the bathroom to refresh his memory of its layout. Broderick didn't object, and followed him along to the bathroom where they both viewed the bathtub. It had been thoroughly cleaned.

"It was such a strange death," Broderick offered. "Wouldn't it make a good case for Columbo?"

Mancuso looked at Broderick in wonder, but did not reply. Why was this man, whose wife supposedly met her death as a result of an accident, wisecracking? Why call it a "case"? Broderick's comment would nag Mancuso's subconscious for the next week, but thinking about it later on that day, he detected an element of mischievous challenge in it.

The squad room was strangely quiet as Mancuso sat at the metal desk, flipping through the reports and statements, rubbing his eyes, smoking, and sipping from his coffee mug. He was thinking back to those early impressions of a week before, trying to relate them to the contents of the file. Had anything been missed or forgotten? Had *he* forgotten or missed anything? Sometimes things seemed to be coming together; other times they seemed to be drifting farther apart.

Geoff Nichol, the uniformed officer who had been first on the scene, came into the squad room shaking snow from his heavy police parka. He saw Mancuso going over the file.

"Hey, Sarge, are you still going over that stuff? That thing's a dead horse if you ask me."

"Maybe it is, maybe it isn't. Come on over here for a second and tell me something."

Officer Nichol perched on the edge of Mancuso's desk and took a sip from the coffee mug.

"When you were at Broderick's house, did he say *anything* else that you can remember? *Anything?*"

"Nothing. Everything's in the report, word for word, as far as I can remember it."

"What about your notes? Is there anything in your notes?"

"Didn't make any notes, not at an accident like that."

"What about the *way* he said things, the way he was acting?"

"Sometimes he seemed excited and upset and other times he didn't. Christ, Sarge, you've been to enough of these sudden deaths. People act goofy when something like that happens. You can't hold it against them."

Nichol was right, you couldn't hold it against them. But this one was different. Mancuso pressed on.

"Yeah, I know. But this guy comes out with some really strange ones every now and then."

"Okay, I'll tell you what *was* interesting— but it didn't come from Broderick. It came from Bordeleau, the bailiff."

"What was that?"

"Well, Bordeleau was already there with his assistant Poulin and the rep from Minto when Broderick showed up. They told Broderick that his wife wasn't in the house. They had shouted and no one answered. Then they told Broderick that the bathroom door was locked. Bordeleau said that Broderick acted as if he knew all along that she was in the bathroom. He didn't question it. He didn't bother to look any place else in the house. He just went straight to the bathroom door and pried it open. Now one way or another, that sounds strange to me... I did mention that in my report."

"Thanks, Geoff. I'll have another look at it."

"Go home and get some sleep, Bob, and forget about it. Even if this guy did do her in, you can't prove it. You've got no cause of death, right? You can't say she was murdered if you don't know how she died."

Like an injection that deadens a nerve, Officer Nichol's last comment touched the single factor that neutralized Mancuso's enthusiasm whenever he thought about the case.

He flipped through the file to the autopsy report.

The post-mortem examination of the body had been performed by Dr. Egils Liepa, a well-known, experienced Ottawa pathologist. He had performed a routine, albeit very thorough, non-forensic autopsy. The formal five page report, which would not be submitted by Dr. Liepa until the 29th of December, 1976, a month later, mirrored the informal report now in Mancuso's hands. Doctor Liepa's autopsy was based upon the initial information given to him by the paramedics: that it was an accidental bathtub drowning. To Mancuso, the report read disconcertingly like a litany of body parts, systems, and organs to which the reply was always "Normal." There was no history of pre-existing disease. The only "abnormalities" disclosed were: "Recent bruises over the knees, abdomen, right upper arm, ankles. And recent abrasions over the shins." The pathologist noted that the eyes had been removed for transplantation and that the skin bore needle marks in several areas as a result of medical procedures attempted in the emergency department. The only signs of violence or abnormality were summarized by the pathologist as "small superficial bruises and abrasions." The 60 points in the post-mortem examination all proved to be normal.

The reason for Mancuso's consternation was ultimately found in paragraph eight of the report, under "Cause of Death." The conclusion: "Cannot be determined from autopsy findings."

The pathologist's conclusion hung in the air like a heavy sword of Damocles, threatening to sever Anne's death from further police attention and Mancuso from the case.

Such was the spectre haunting Bob Mancuso: no cause of death, no homicide. No homicide, no case.

He closed the file.

Despite this single discouraging fact, Mancuso continued his inquiries. When he spoke with Doctor Liepa on November 18th, the day after the post-mortem examination, Liepa disclosed to him informally that the deceased was in all aspects a healthy person prior to her death; all organs and systems were normal. While there was some minor superficial bruising, there were no bruises on the skull. He truly could not find a cause of death.

Even with that bleak disclosure, Mancuso kept driving on instinct alone, continuing a hybrid investigation which was not inconsistent with an accidental death investigation. His continued probing, he hoped, would not arouse Broderick's suspicion. That day he spoke with Anne's brother and with her personal physician. The coroner had ruled that there would be no inquest: the death was obviously accidental.

Mancuso recalled Broderick's explanation of his financial situation the day before, and ran a check with the Ottawa–Hull Credit Bureau. Broderick had in fact been glossing over his financial difficulties, which were far worse than he had described. He was heavily in debt and had borrowed sums of money from various commercial lenders. He had been slow repaying his debts, and in some instances hadn't repaid at all.

Mancuso was startled to find that there already were court judgements against Broderick.

Mancuso was beginning to feel that he was not seeing the same George Broderick that Broderick's friends, family, relatives, and public were seeing. There was a dent in the knight's armour, even though it was a small one.

Some things had to be done right away. Mancuso made an appointment at the courthouse to see assistant Crown prosecutor Andrejs Berzins about getting a court order to seize Anne's body.

But there would be no such court order. He was too late. Very quickly after the funeral, Anne's body had been cremated. This too troubled Mancuso, who knew that, at the time, while Catholic practice did not prohibit cremation, it certainly discouraged it.

Later, a relative would describe how George had taken command of the situation, permitting no one to interfere in his handling of the wake or funeral, which he very coolly organized with great efficiency— with military precision. He curtly refused any help from family members.

"I've looked after Anne for 35 years and I don't need any help now. That includes financial assistance."

So no one dared to interfere and Anne was history.
The law had moved too slowly.

In the days that followed, Mancuso conscripted the help of Detective Murray Gordon and continued the investigation, making peripheral inquiries that might give them new perspectives into the enigma of George Broderick. No authorization had yet been given, nor was any anticipated, for a full-scale criminal investigation; so it continued as an accidental death inquiry, "clearing up points."

Mancuso and Gordon sandwiched these inquiries into whatever spare time became available to them in the course of their day-to-day, routine fraud investigations.

It was becoming clear that George Broderick, conservative insurance executive, was actually quite different from the public face he presented.

Mancuso and Gordon turned up more than one curiosity about him.

4.

Ultimately, George Broderick's *persona* would be explained as a remnant from his naval career when he developed an aggrandized vision of himself, or "self-concept," that carried over into his second career. It was the preservation of his symbolic self: a person who was in control of himself and those around him, relying on no one but himself, macho, attractive, wheeling and dealing, successful. George Broderick as he saw himself.

Complete independence and self-reliance were his hallmarks, but it did not end there. He felt that he could make anyone believe anything, convince anyone of anything. And, it seems, he could. It was a talent as fine, genuine, and natural as Joe Dimaggio hitting base hits. As a salesman, he was a "natural," and this was the key to his success as a life insurance representative.

At various times in the years before Anne's death, George Broderick perpetuated stories about himself which had some of his closer relatives and acquaintances convinced that he was, simply, a harmless braggart— a fantasizer and a showman. But others, including his wife Anne, perhaps, accepted these tales at face value.

The two detectives turned up the *fantastic*.

Sometimes, very conspiratorially, George let it be known that his career in the navy was not over, but that he continued in an undercover capacity as an intelligence officer engaged in counter-espionage duties for the government. On occasion, he disclosed, he was under contract with the government as a "hit man" to assassinate various terrorists and Soviet agents. So he was frequently being called away on "short notice" to be briefed and perform his duties, never knowing exactly how long he would be gone or when he might return.

This accounted to his family for his erratic lifestyle and irregular hours.

The two detectives turned up the *bizarre*.

Capitalizing on his extensive training and experience with radio and electronics in the navy, Broderick let it be known that he was also employed by the British government, involved in developing secret electronic weapons and counter-measures. He was not at liberty to discuss these. But he was expecting any time now to be receiving substantial sums of money as a result of the patents taken out on these inventions.

When he fell into financial difficulties, he began to expand on the story, and to use it as an excuse. One of the projects, involving a laser beam weapon, had gotten out of control up at CFB Petawawa. Several men were killed. He was being forced to defend a very touchy civil law suit in which huge amounts of money were being demanded from him for the deaths of the soldiers. Defending the lawsuit was depleting his resources and killing him financially. That's why the bailiffs were at the door!

When some of the creditors questioned him about the Camp Petawawa mishap and the resulting lawsuit, his response was equally fantastic: one day, the deceased man's lawyer, the judge, and a pilot, were flying back to Ottawa from Camp Petawawa when the plane crashed and all of the court papers connected with the case had burned.

The detectives turned up the *curious*.

During the early hours of Christmas Eve, 1973, the Broderick family was enjoying Christmas dinner. Suddenly, around 8:00 p.m. the telephone rang and George grabbed it. He began carrying on a bizarre conversation— completely incomprehensible gibberish to those listening— but what sounded like Russian. He hung up the phone and returned to the table to announce that he had been called away on urgent, official business and would not return until the next night. Then he was gone.

Anne accepted this behaviour without question.

The detectives turned up pure *misrepresentation*.

Broderick had sometimes told his friends that he owned an airfield in the Maritimes, a harmless enough piece of fiction until he decided to borrow money against it.

During the months of April and August of 1975, Broderick persuaded the credit manager of the Bank of Nova Scotia, Carlingwood Branch, to advance him thousands of dollars on the strength of a tale that he had an aircraft for sale at his airfield in Nova Scotia. The sale was about to close and was being handled by a Halifax lawyer called Brian McRae. The proceeds would be used to discharge the short term loans and the money was always to be arriving "within a few days." When the loan came due, no such airport, airplane, or lawyer could be found.

The detectives turned up the truly *sad*.

George had repeatedly promised Anne that he would buy her a new house. Finally, in 1974, he drove her to the swanky city of Kanata on the western outskirts of Ottawa, where he showed her a beautiful, low-level, ultramodern bungalow. He had bought it for her, he announced grandly, even telling her a specific closing date for the purchase. On that day they would be moving into the new house. The day arrived. Anne's brother and his wife had come to Ottawa to help Anne with the move. In anticipation, she had packed all her crystal and china and was beside herself with excitement. George, arriving on the scene in an agitated state, announced that the deal would not be closing that day. The owner of the house had just learned that his wife had developed cancer; the transaction would have to be postponed for three months. When the three months were up, George found another excuse. There was leakage from the swimming pool which was weakening the foundation of the bungalow. He was now involved in a lawsuit over it. He had ordered soil testing to be done and had retained engineers; the outcome would be determined by their reports.

Anne never got to see the inside of the house.

Mancuso looked up from the file. Detective Gordon had joined him and Nichol in the squad room.

"Look, the guy is nothing but a bullshitter, one of the biggest and best I've ever seen," Mancuso said.

"So what else is new," Gordon replied.

"How people buy this stuff is beyond me. The guy is living two different lives."

"So what are we going to do about it?"

"We've got to go after him."

"For what, for handing out a lot of stupid stories?"

"No, for murder."

"You've got to be kidding. We don't have enough to even start an investigation, let alone lay a charge."

Mancuso closed the file and leaned back in his chair.

Gordon knew Mancuso was about to lay it all out.

"Murray, look at it for a minute. The guy has to be lying about the time he left the house. There's a major discrepancy there. If he followed the route he said he took and did the things he told us about before returning to the house, then there's no way that it took almost two hours! I'll bet if we retraced the route and made generous allowances, we'd find that it takes a hell of a lot less time. Then there's that business with Larry Bordeleau, the Sheriff's bailiff. The old guy is very alert as to what is happening when he is evicting people. He's always concerned that somebody is going to get mad and jump him and stuff like that. So he pays attention. Bordeleau says that Broderick came in, just said, 'Hi, Larry,' and headed straight for the bathroom door. As far as I'm concerned, the bastard knew all along she was in there. Then there's the clothing on the bed. You wouldn't expect to find those things there in the first place. A woman like Anne Broderick doesn't strip naked in the bedroom and walk across the house to the bathroom. She would undress in the bathroom and hang her clothes up there before she took a bath. Not only that, the nightgown and the housecoat were reversed on top of the bed as if someone had moved them there from somewhere else. Next we have the water in the tub. My wife uses those bath beads every once in a while and I'm telling you that if the water was *that* blue she would have to put in 10 times the normal amount. And it would be slippery as hell."

"Maybe that's why the accident happened?"

"No, that's what the bastard wants us to think. If Anne Broderick used those bath beads as often as he says she did, she wouldn't have made a mistake like that."

"This is all pretty thin stuff, Bob, for trying to bag an insurance executive."

"What about that plastic wrapping from the Christmas cards? It could've been used to smother her."

"No, it was seized and printed. It came up clean."

"Shit! How about that extension cord from the clothes hamper? Sometimes Anne brought a radio into the bathroom. Could he have tried to electrocute her when she was in the water?"

"I looked at that, too. There was no radio in the bathroom when the four men went in and found her. And the extension cord falls short by a couple of feet when you put it into the nearest outlet. It just doesn't reach."

"Well, how could he have done it then?"

"That's exactly the question that any defense lawyer with half a brain is going to ask you in the witness box... and ask the jury to think about afterward."

"Well, the question we should be asking ourselves is why an insurance company executive making good bucks and collecting a military pension on top of that is renting a house in the first place instead of owning one, and why he's in a financial bind and up to his ass in creditors. And why was he being physically evicted from his home?"

"You tell me."

"There's got to be a woman, Murray. A woman that's costing him a lot of money. The guy is leading a double life. Did you notice how he reacted when I asked him if he was 'pigging around'?"

"He didn't seem to react much as far as I could see."

"That's exactly it. Any normal person with nothing to hide would have been insulted as hell and ready to knock my block off. George just sloughed it off. Hell, Murray, the guy's not normal. They tell me at his wife's funeral one of the mourners showed up wearing a cast on his leg and George was wisecracking at him about breaking it in a skiing accident. At his own wife's funeral, for Christ's sake."

"Just like the Columbo remark he made at the house."

"Same thing. That really bothered me."

"Remember the fingernail from the master bedroom?"

"On the nightstand by the bed?"

"No, those were false ones. I found a piece of fingernail on the carpet."

"It could've come from any place."

"Yeah, but I was reading tonight. The coroner, Dr. Thompson, noticed that one of Anne's fingernails was broken."

"It could've happened any number of ways."

"Yeah, but the body was in the bathroom and the fingernail was in the master bedroom. Think about that."

Mancuso's recitation stalled Gordon's objections. Nichol remained silent.

"Why don't you talk to the chief and see if he'll put you on this full-time?" Gordon asked.

"Do you think I've got enough?"

"I think you've got enough for a closer look. Anyway, Staff Inspector Chaykowski says he'll back you up. He says you have a good nose. He'll put in a good word. Let me know. I'm in if you are!"

Detective Gordon left the squad room and went upstairs. Two minutes later he received a phone call from Bob Mancuso on the internal phone system.

"Murray?"

"Yes."

"That arrogant bastard Broderick is trying me on for size."

"What do you mean?"

"It just dawned on me— Columbo only investigates murder cases."

"Shit! You're right." There was a pause. "I'm in if you are, Bob."

"See you in the chief's office tomorrow morning, Murray. Sleep tight."

It was a small turning point. Mancuso had made his first convert and the spaghetti and meat balls tasted really good that night, even re-heated.

5.

The next morning the chief denied Mancuso his go-ahead for a full-scale criminal investigation. Instead, he tossed the detective half a loaf. He wanted an opinion about Anne's death from Dr. John Hillsdon-Smith, Ontario's chief forensic pathologist. The detectives could take a couple of days duty time to dredge up any further information and prepare a presentation for the chief pathologist. Then the chief would have a fresh look at it.

Mancuso and Gordon assembled their material and flew to Toronto that afternoon, November 23rd, 1976. They took a cab directly to the Centre for Forensic Sciences, anxious to lay out their thoughts. They did not see Dr. Hillsdon-Smith. He was unavailable owing to prior commitments.

Even though Hillsdon-Smith was a leading medical advisor to the police, a cop couldn't just walk in off the street to see him. As the acknowledged leading forensic expert in the province and among the dozen top forensic pathologists in North America, his opinions were widely sought by investigators. Those opinions had been repeatedly accepted by courts of law. Not unexpectedly, his time was meticulously rationed. Mancuso and Gordon arranged an appointment.

The detectives were told that the doctor would be in Ottawa on other business on December 1st. They arranged to meet with him in his suite at the Holiday Inn.

Among his extensive qualifications as a forensic pathologist, Dr. Hillsdon-Smith had considerable experience in bathtub murder cases. He had studied the infamous "bride in the bath" technique and had personally been the pathologist on three such cases in Ontario. His testimony had been accepted by courts both in Canada and England.

Mancuso and Gordon showed up at the Holiday Inn armed with their files, reports, and photographs.

The doctor went over the material in detail, taking his time and questioning the detectives as he moved through the ever-growing mound of paper. He spent several moments going over each photograph, first reviewing those of the accident scene and then the photographs taken of Anne Broderick's body. He paused to examine in closer detail those photographs showing close up views of the few bruises and scrapes evident at the time of death, pausing to suggest in each case how the bruise might have been caused.

After reviewing all of the material, the doctor said that one of the most interesting facts about the case was its similarity to a homicide investigated by the Metropolitan Toronto Police some years earlier, involving an accused by the name of Milligan. Curiously, Milligan was also an insurance man who murdered his wife using the "bride in the bath" technique, to gain access to a large insurance policy on his wife. In that case, however, the coroner had arrived at a decisive verdict of death by drowning. There had been nothing suspicious about it until later when the accused himself started opening up about his wife's death. Only then were the suspicions of the police aroused. Dr. Hillsdon-Smith told Mancuso that with this type of homicide the absence of cogent medical advice and the absence of significant marks or bruising made it very difficult to pursue. He advised Mancuso that Anne Broderick's death might never be solved. From a legal viewpoint, it was a toss-up.

But, oh yes, he felt, personally, that Anne had been murdered. It was almost an afterthought.

At the conclusion of his discussions with Mancuso and Gordon, the doctor made some suggestions, the first being that they get hold of the investigating officer in the Milligan case and pick his brain. The doctor pointed out that in all previous cases where the "bride in the bath" technique had been used, the cases had taken between six months and two years to solve, and the solution came about only because the suspect eventually made inculpatory utterances to other people. He then suggested that they contact the Ontario Provincial Police Homicide Squad in Toronto to enlist their support for a long-term investigation of George Broderick. It was evident to the doctor that the Nepean Police Department lacked the resources necessary to conduct a protracted investigation.

He commended Mancuso and Gordon and the other investigators, saying that the investigation to this point had been remarkably thorough. He could see nothing that had gone untested.

Before the meeting broke up, Dr. Hillsdon-Smith wrote the name of another Toronto physician on a slip of paper and handed it to Mancuso, suggesting that he touch base with him.

Dr. Peter Rowsell, a psychiatrist with a criminology background, specialized in the construction of profiles of suspects for police in homicide cases. This idea was quite novel to the Nepean Police Force and Mancuso

promised to look into it. Before they departed, Dr. Hillsdon-Smith compli-
mented Mancuso and Gordon again on their efforts so far.

On the morning of December 2nd, 1976, the day after their consultation
with Dr. Hillsdon-Smith and 16 days after Anne Broderick's death, Mancuso
and Gordon met with Inspector Walter Chaykowski. Chaykowski had come
up the ranks himself and was in tune with the problems faced by his
street-level detectives. He knew about the instincts good detectives are born
with, and the intuition they develop. Mancuso and Gordon told him the
information they had obtained from Ryan, George Broderick's son, about a
cottage in Quebec and intimations of Broderick's involvement with the
young blonde woman. She was still an unknown quantity and had not figured
in the investigation. Chaykowski was persuaded by these new developments,
and, in particular, by Dr. Hillsdon-Smith's support. He came onside with
Mancuso and Gordon. The death warranted a full-scale homicide investiga-
tion. Chaykowski followed up on his prior commitment that when circum-
stances warranted, he would go to bat with the chief for Mancuso and
Gordon.

In the meantime, Detectives Fermoyle and Champagne were detailed
to go to Buckingham, Quebec, to check out George Broderick's cottage.
That same day, the two foot soldier detectives, working through the Sûreté
de Québec detachment at Buckingham, Quebec, and the local Buckingham
Police, ascertained that Broderick had purchased 15 acres of land and a small
cottage on Lac Sheridan, near Poltimore, Quebec. The cottage and land were
valued for tax purposes at $5000 and had been the subject of a break-in
complaint by Broderick in the month of November, 1974.

The two detectives discovered that the property was difficult to locate
and even more difficult to get to. The unpaved access road was a mile and a
half long up a mountain grade. In the winter it was accessible by vehicle only
for about half a mile. The rest had to be done on foot. The detectives
ultimately found the cottage, a small, comfortable, well-furnished log cabin
on the shore of a misty mountain lake, Lac Sheridan. It was registered to
George Broderick's office in Ottawa.

Mancuso could not fit the cottage into the Broderick puzzle. Ryan, the son, knew about it, but had Anne? Had George ever taken his wife there?

The meeting between Mancuso, Gordon, Chaykowski, and the Chief of Police for the city of Nepean, Chief E.G. Wersch, was quick and successful.

Chief "Gus" Wersch, a man of lean frame and Clark Gable moustache, looked the part of the career policeman whether in ceremonial uniform or one of his preferred double-breasted suits. He surprised the detectives with the extent of his knowledge of the investigation. Wersch's strength was as an administrator. Confronted with having to police a sprawling, mushrooming, bedroom community with an inadequate number of men, inadequate resources and the constant struggle with municipal politicians to find more money, he relied on and placed great confidence in his street investigators. Every day there were new administrative brush fires to put out.

Chaykowski and Mancuso brought him up to date, including Dr. Hillsdon-Smith's recommendations about George Broderick. In the same way that Inspector Chaykowski had accepted Mancuso's instinctive appreciation of the situation, Chief Wersch appreciated and accepted Chaykowski's analysis of the results. He authorized a full investigation and ordered Bob Mancuso and Murray Gordon to get off general duties and devote themselves full time to the investigation. He committed the use of the force's limited funds and resources. Mancuso and Gordon would be free to pursue the case unencumbered by the daily barrage of bad cheques and frauds.

But the chief imposed conditions. The first was that Mancuso would have two months to build a case. At the end of that time, the detectives would have to return to general duties. The second was that Mancuso obtain the support and direct assistance of the Criminal Investigation Branch of the Ontario Provincial Police and the resources of the Centre for Forensic Sciences. The chief felt, quite rightly, that without the resources and experience of these two agencies, it would be virtually impossible to conduct a proper homicide investigation. His final condition was typical of the even-handedness with which Chief Wersch had always performed his duties and which had propelled him to the rank of Chief: the investigation was to be conducted not exclusively with a view to incriminating and laying a charge against George Broderick, but also with a view to clearly exonerating him if the facts so demonstrated.

With this clear mandate, Mancuso and Gordon decided to do more spade work and then return to Toronto.

By the end of the day, Detectives Fermoyle and Champagne learned that George Broderick, contrary to what he had led people to believe, did not hold a P.A.D.I. card— a professional diver's licence. In fact, he was completely unknown in local amateur and professional diving circles. This relatively minor falsehood made Mancuso wonder which further aspects of the Broderick persona were also false.

In preparation for their pending return trip to Toronto, Mancuso and Gordon again met with Broderick's son Ryan, who gave the officers a 15 page witness statement. Ryan was married and living in Aylmer, Quebec. He had been greatly moved by his mother's sudden death and was badly shaken by the prospect that his father was under suspicion. It was obvious to the officers that he loved them both very much, and was torn between his love for his mother and what he felt was his duty in assisting the police. He gave a far more detailed and descriptive account of his father and mother and their family life than Mancuso had received so far from the daughter, Shirley, or the family's friends and relatives. The investigators found Ryan's account to be remarkably balanced and very honest.

Ryan described his father as being a good man and a good father within the context of a family which had had to move frequently because of his military career.

"He placed my mother on a pedestal. He always kept everything from my mother. He said that he was the 'bugger' and she was wonderful. Always, as long as I can remember, he went overboard in front of other people to physically show affection for my mother. He would constantly be calling her pet names and putting her on his knee and asking us boys to show some physical attention. He could never relax; for example, when we would have dinner and even before we finished our coffee, he would be up doing the dishes and telling me to get into the kitchen to give him a hand. My father would say nothing to hurt my mother. I can never remember any argument between my Mom and Dad. As I mentioned before, he never wanted to hurt her."

Ryan's statement concluded:

"He raised us to treat my mother like a queen, to bring little things home, like chocolate bars, or kiss her often. He kept everything from my mother, financial, discipline and others, and I often used this sentimentality my father showed my mother to my advantage."

Then there was the bizarre side of George Broderick, as described by Ryan, which seemed to corroborate some of the earlier rumours that Mancuso had dredged up.

Ryan described how his mother had told him that sometimes George seemed to talk in his sleep in a foreign language, possibly Russian. Or, on other occasions, George would be at Ryan's place, and when they were together, George would get up, making a point of using the phone in front of everyone— even when private phones were available— so they could all hear. After dialling, he would speak a language sounding like Chinese or Japanese.

Ryan remembered his mother saying, "Don't question him about it, he is working on something secret." Ryan said his father would usually be away on Christmas Day for 24 hours or so, announcing in front of everyone that he had work to do. George would say to Anne in a mock childish tone, "Mummy, is it okay if I go and do a few hours' work?" She would reply, "Okay, dear."

"No one would question it so as not to hurt my mother. She knew these were lies, but as I said before, she would do anything to keep him and he took advantage of the situation."

Ryan recited other "lies" that his father had told him: that he had embalmed their grandmother when she died; that he had a brother in jail for murder out west; and, after Anne's funeral, he told a stranger that he had rubbed her coffin to have his "waves" contact Anne's. He even claimed that he had talked to her after she died through these waves which he called "aurora." Ryan described George's stories about the alleged plane trips to Camp Petawawa at all hours of the day and night, curiously always at his own convenience. He had told Ryan of his invention which was going to bring in a large sum of money to buy a house for Anne. He said that the Kanata house purchase was tied up in the courts because the judge was sick, and because his team of engineers was doing work on the pool where a defect caused a problem with the foundation.

"Mom often told me how disappointed she was."

Anne had gone so far as to make a down payment on a dining room set with a furniture firm in Toronto three years before. She had also picked out her crystal for the new home.

"She would say she was afraid to ask my father about the house purchase because he had an ulcer; he would get upset and nervous and go into the bathroom and vomit."

George had also recounted how he had had acid thrown on him at one time, although there were no scars on his body as a result. He said that once he had been co-piloting a plane out west when he spotted a trapper lying on the snow below. They landed and discovered that the trapper's leg was broken. They set the leg, built a fire in the trapper's shack, chopped wood for the winter, killed and skinned caribou, got a fresh supply of water, all for the duration of the winter. When this was done they had run out of time and had to return home. Ryan said that his Dad volunteered this tale more than once.

His Dad, he said, also professed to have degrees in the martial arts and to have won his golden gloves in boxing, but whenever he was asked to produce any proof of this he always had an excuse.

And then the grieving young man, unburdening himself, caught the seasoned detective off guard with a verbal knock-out punch.

His Dad had slept with the young blonde girl on the night of his mother's funeral.

Had Ryan told Mancuso something he thought Mancuso already knew, or did he see it as just another episode in his dad's aberrant lifestyle? Mancuso was unsure. Either way, it was the break he had hoped for. Mancuso hung on every phrase.

The girl was Lisette Martineau, a former girlfriend of Ryan's brother,

Gerry. Her relationship with the Broderick family continued after she and Gerry broke up some years before. Lisette was very close to Anne, whom she had called "Missy." Understandably, she was distraught over Anne's death; Anne was one of Lisette's few friends. Ryan had always entertained misgivings about the relationship because, he said, "At times my father would put her on his knee, and she is 21."

After the funeral, the family had gone to Ryan's house. George and Lisette went to buy a new shower curtain first, and they showed up later. Lisette took two roses from Anne's coffin as a memento. They arrived at Ryan's house about two hours after the funeral and spent some time there, but George avoided the other members of the family. Ryan described his father as being in a "bad state" from the combined effects of liquor and medication. George said that he could not drive. A number of people offered to drive him home but he preferred Lisette driving him. They left between three and four o'clock in the afternoon. Lisette stated that she would return, but she did not. George Broderick phoned Ryan the next day to say that Lisette had spent the night with him at 18 Beaverton. Ryan understood that they had been there alone. Ryan's sister, Shirley, had stayed at his place in Aylmer.

The day after the funeral, at about four o'clock, Lisette came back to Ryan's house with a casserole for supper prepared by one of the neighbours. A dispute broke out over an allegation that Lisette had threatened to disclose one of George's past affairs. The name Eauclaire was mentioned. The argument continued with Lisette running down Ryan's brother Gerry for condoning the affair. There was a general round of name calling.

Ryan ended his session with Mancuso and Gordon with an outpouring of genuine, mixed emotions.

"He was a good father to me and he did everything to help me. It's been a long time since I lived at home, and I feel now, looking over the past years, that I saw my father through rose-coloured glasses. My mother always said that the Brodericks were a cold hard lot."

His father, he said, was a "Dr. Jekyll and Mr. Hyde... In front of people, he would go out of his way to be nice to my Mom, but then take her home and drop her off and leave, saying he had work to do... Though I am very bitter, I do not want to pin anything on anyone or ruin anyone's life. Still, I feel Mom did not die an accidental death. Many things brought out after her death have influenced me a bit, but I feel that my mom died at the hands of my father. My father is two people... He did not want to hurt her but she was going to find out about the mounting problems. After sheltering her all these years, he loved her too much to hurt her, but the second person in him is a liar. The man who wanted everyone to think he was great did this."

Even Dr. Rowsell couldn't have assessed the George Broderick psyche better. At the completion of his statement, Ryan included a final postscript that stated his ultimate feeling with remarkable honesty:

"I have lost a mother and I love my father, as a father, but at this point, I am thoroughly disgusted with him. He brought us up not to lie. I feel though, by revealing what I have, I can either help to convict him if guilty or clear every bit of doubt in my own eyes, so in future years I can look at him honestly and also let him associate with my son. My son idolizes him."

6.

Released from general police duties and unencumbered by the pressures of never-ending fraud cases, Mancuso and Gordon adopted a less hurried, less urgent approach. They took the train to Toronto, making use of the leisurely pace to review events and to ready their presentation for the Criminal Investigation Branch of the Ontario Provincial Police.

C.I.B. Inspectors G. Cooper and A. MacLeod had the power to approve O.P.P. involvement in a full homicide investigation or to squelch it. Mancuso and Gordon laid out the whole story and made their pitch, cop to cop. The O.P.P. brass were impressed with the detectives' spade work so far, but, to Mancuso's dismay, remained noncommittal. They would have to wait a few days for an answer. Exhausted and disappointed at not having received immediate approval, they put up at the Ramada Inn in Burlington. They would put their time to good use while in the Toronto area.

Early next morning, December 9th, they introduced themselves to a surprised Edward Pike at the Toronto offices of Canadian Premier Life. Pike was Anne's brother and had been instrumental in having George Broderick hired by the company after George retired from the navy.

He told them that George Broderick would be terminated in January or February of 1977. He promised to let them know before the termination notice was delivered. Pike made passing reference to George having a girlfriend in 1966 or 1967, some 10 years earlier, a fact that had already been revealed to them by George's son, Ryan. They presumed it was the same affair that had been the topic of dispute at Ryan's house the day after Anne's funeral.

Mancuso and Gordon needed Edward Pike's cooperation in the preparation of the profile on George Broderick. They hoped that when George learned of his imminent termination, he might cooperate with Dr. Rowsell in the preparation of the profile, if it meant he might hold on to his job. After being assured of Edward Pike's cooperation, they left to keep another appointment with Dr. Hillsdon-Smith.

They updated Dr. Hillsdon-Smith with the information they had gathered since the meeting with him at the Holiday Inn in Ottawa the previous week. The chief pathologist had studied the photographs and reviewed the file again, and was now firmly of the opinion that the bruising was inconsistent with a fall or with any exclusively medical explanation. Hillsdon-Smith told them that he had contacted the psychiatrist, Dr. Rowsell, and explained the case to him. The psychiatrist was very interested in the matter and willing to assemble a psychological profile of George Broderick.

Before leaving the Centre for Forensic Sciences on Harbour Street, they located Jack Evans, the Centre's executive officer. Evans had been one of the investigators with the Metropolitan Toronto Police on the Milligan case. What was intended to be a short conversation turned into a long one, as the two investigations were compared. The number of similarities between the two cases was astonishing: both suspects were navy men; there were similar insurance policies involved; both deaths were bathtub deaths; the suspect husbands showed no remorse. In both cases girlfriends hovered in the background and the suspects had engaged in similar bizarre conversations with people both before and after the death of the wife.

Mancuso and Gordon were now moving with the assurance of knowing they were on the right track, but uncertain about where the trail of evidence was leading them.

Dr. Peter Rowsell was a highly regarded psychiatrist practising in Oakville, near Toronto. In addition to his qualifications as a medical doctor, he held degrees from the Royal College of Psychiatrists in London, England, and was a fellow of the Royal College of Physicians in Canada. He held a diploma in psychiatry from McGill University and had a strong background in criminology.

Over the years he had developed techniques and expertise in preparing suspect profiles based upon reliable information provided to him from outside sources. If the identity of a particular suspect was already known to the police, a profile could be assembled to determine if that suspect was the type of person who might have committed a particular offence. Conversely, where the identity of the perpetrator was not known, a profile could be constructed based upon all available information, pointing to the identity of the person who had committed a particular offence. George Broderick fell into he first category.

The two detectives met with Dr. Rowsell on December 10th and went over the case with him. Dr. Rowsell, on viewing the photographs, at once stated that, in his opinion as a medical doctor, the bruises on the stomach were caused by trauma and were consistent with blows or finger marks. He reviewed Broderick's history in Mancuso's notes as it had been ascertained to that point in time.

Rowsell's initial opinion was that Broderick, during his long naval career, had been under steady and unrelenting discipline. Broderick's discharge in 1966 would have had a profoundly unsettling effect. The doctor ventured that this was probably when Broderick's problem started. Broderick, he stated, probably had two personalities, one kind and gentle, the other forceful and cruel.

Dr. Rowsell then demonstrated graphically what he meant to the detectives by splitting a photograph of George Broderick, blocking out first one side and then the other. The two halves were graphically dissimilar; there were two very different sides to the suspect.

After thoroughly reviewing the material, Dr. Rowsell said there was an 80% chance that Anne's death was a homicide and that the characteristics and capability to do it resided in the suspect. He offered to prepare a detailed profile of Broderick which might assist the police by telling them when it would be best to approach George Broderick directly, and how best to interrogate him. In order to accomplish his purpose, Rowsell required Broderick's service records and the factual history that the detectives had accumulated. He also wanted to speak with Edward Pike and Ryan Broderick first hand. A good sample of George Broderick's handwriting would also help in the preparation of the profile. The detectives left, promising to assemble this material for Rowsell as soon as possible.

Late that afternoon Mancuso and Gordon stopped at the Canadian Life Insurance Company on Bloor Street in Toronto to get the details of another case— this one in Simcoe, Ontario— where a man had murdered his wife in the bathtub using the "bride in the bath" technique. Known as the "Gualtieri Case," it had occurred in 1974 and had been widely reported in the Canadian press. The officers were told where they could obtain copies of the trial transcripts. The two detectives were encouraged; the accused had been convicted. The modus operandi apparently involved no struggle and left no signs of violence. Mancuso recognized the parallel with his own investigation and knew he would have to research both those cases before court time. The only anomaly was that in "Gualtieri" there had been an ascertainable cause of death.

Before returning to Ottawa the next day, Saturday, December 11th,

Mancuso spoke again with Edward Pike, mentioning to him that they had been trying to obtain the details of both the Milligan case and the Simcoe case where the suspected bathtub technique had been described and examined.

Pike startled Mancuso by telling him that he had discussed this very same technique with both George and Anne some time in the past. He couldn't remember exactly when, but he distinctly remembered it coming up for discussion.

This revelation stunned Mancuso. Had George Broderick got the idea from his own brother-in-law in the first place? At this stage, anything seemed possible.

On December 16th, 1976, exactly one month after Anne's death, the official homicide investigation was kicked into high gear with the assignment of Detective Inspector W.C. Bowles to the case by the Criminal Investigation Branch of the Ontario Provincial Police. Mancuso and Gordon had done a good selling job on Inspectors Cooper and MacLeod at the C.I.B. in Toronto three days before.

Inspector Bill Bowles was referred to by his colleagues— out of earshot— as "Bulldog Bowles." As an investigator he was uniquely suited to heading up the Broderick investigation. Bowles knew and understood the laws of evidence and had developed a reputation for expertise in the investigation of circumstantial evidence cases. He had, in the past, obtained a conviction in the Donald Turner case, an investigation in which the evidence was not only circumstantial but in which the victim's body was never found. Implicit in Bowles' assignment to the Broderick case was access to resources, manpower, and adequate funding through the C.I.B.

While Bowles would be nominally in charge of the investigation, it was clear from the outset that there would be no turf rivalry between himself and Bob Mancuso. Quite the opposite proved to be the case. Bowles took to Mancuso like a father to a son and admired Mancuso's investigative instincts. He would rely on Mancuso's knowledge of the home turf. Mancuso, for his part, was heartened to see that Bowles was not simply a "desk commander" just issuing orders to the foot soldiers. True, Bowles would be giving order and direction to the investigation, but it was clear from the beginning that he would be doing it in concert and consultation with Mancuso and not from behind a desk. Bowles would be out on the street himself with Mancuso and Gordon, interviewing witnesses, viewing locales, studying reports, and reviewing strategy with them.

So serious was Bowles' commitment to direct involvement that he rejected any notion of working out of the police station. He booked a suite at the Brancombe's Motor Hotel, not far from the police station. It would be both his residence and an off-site headquarters for the team during the investigation. It would permit them to concentrate, free from the tumult of the station-house, and would be less likely to draw attention.

Before Bowles' arrival on the scene, Mancuso and Gordon used the two days available to them to firm up their information to brief Bowles. There were practical considerations. Mancuso was concerned about money to pay for Dr. Rowsell's work on the suspect's profile. He checked with his chief and with the Crown attorney's office and was told that the money would be found somewhere. Mancuso was relieved. He knew that the profile would be a valuable asset to the investigation. Chief Wersch told Mancuso and Gordon that with the assignment of Inspector Bowles, the case was entirely in provincial C.I.B. hands. The two detectives would not have to file the usual daily progress reports with the chief.

Officially, all forensic information about Anne's death had to come through Dr. Jack Thomson, senior regional coroner for the Ottawa area. The detectives had spoken to him before with nothing too specific in mind. Now they wanted to see if he had anything new on the bruising to Anne's body as shown in the photographs. Dr. Thomson suggested that if the bruises were not a result of medical treatment, they might have been caused by either beating or grappling.

But Dr. Thomson had something more important to say.

Broderick was revealing his eagerness to get his hands on the insurance money. He had been pressing the coroner to phone the head office of

Canadian Premier Life in Winnipeg to confirm Anne's death so the funds would be released. Thomson had told Broderick that since the police were still investigating the death, he could not sign any papers, and would not until the investigation was completed. It struck Dr. Thomson as unusual that a person in Broderick's circumstances would bother him about money before the circumstances of his wife's death were entirely resolved.

Dr. Thomson agreed to hold back signing any insurance papers until suspicions about the death had been resolved one way or the other. Finally, Dr. Thomson confirmed that in a conversation with the pathologist, Dr. Egils Liepa, he had been told that the autopsy verdict was inconclusive: "Cause of death unknown."

It would be essential, Mancuso knew, to be able to give Bowles some information about the young blonde woman during their forthcoming briefing. Mancuso remembered the small blue car that had pulled into the laneway of 18 Beaverton on the morning of Anne's death. He learned that it was a 1973 Toyota. Working through the Ontario Licensing Bureau, he further learned that it was registered to Lisette Martineau at an address other than her residence. After tracking down where she lived, Mancuso and Gordon did a drive-by of the address. The blue Toyota was parked in the laneway. Curiously, while her residence was the upstairs half of a duplex, her incoming telephone calls were taken at the residence of a next door neighbour. They later learned that Lisette worked at a flower shop on Rideau Street in Ottawa.

A check with Bell Canada security records disclosed that phone calls had recently been made from Lisette's residence to the Edward Pike residence in Toronto.

Rosamund Jones of Minto Management, the landlord of 18 Beaverton, had taken Broderick's call pleading for an extension on the morning Anne was found. Mancuso and Gordon met with her in an attempt to nail down more precisely the times at which the events occurred that morning.

There were critical discrepancies in the times Broderick said he had left the house and returned. Jones recalled that on the morning of Anne's death, George Broderick had called her at precisely 9:10 in the morning. He had spoken in low tones. She told him that the bailiff would be at 18 Beaverton at 10:40 to evict the family. Broderick promised to be at her office with all of the money by 10:20. At 10:10, Broderick had phoned the bailiff, Larry Bordeleau, who had told Broderick unequivocally that he would be there at 10:40 a.m. to evict him. As an afterthought, Jones mentioned that three days after Anne Broderick's funeral, she received a note from Broderick apologizing for any grief he might have caused her. He enclosed a cheque for $1700 to cover the rent arrears and future rent to December 31st, 1976. He had already applied to Canadian Premier Life for an initial release of $5,000 on the life policies, but the insurance cheque had arrived after Broderick's payment to Minto. Where had the $1,700 come from?

Along with the note and the cheque there were a dozen long-stemmed red roses.

Finally, Mancuso and Gordon returned to the Ottawa Civic Hospital to continue their probing. They were bothered by the bruises on Anne's body shown in the photographs.

Dr. A. Henry, who was then chief of the emergency unit, looked at the pictures and was unequivocally of the opinion that the bruises observable on the knee and abdomen were inconsistent with any medical steps that his staff might have taken in the I.C.U. He authorized the officers to interview the nursing staff who had attended Anne Broderick on the morning of November 16th. The nurses insisted they did nothing to cause bruising to Anne Broderick. They could easily distinguish those puncture marks done in the emergency unit for medical purposes from the suspicious bruising. There had been a blood clotting problem, they said, and the bleeding would not stop immediately.

They thought that the situation was somewhat odd. The nurses wondered why George Broderick did not go to the hospital in the ambulance with his wife and they were incredulous that he had failed to notify his daughter about Anne's condition.

He hadn't bothered to ask the nurses about his wife's condition. They had never before seen a case where the surviving relative did not wish to notify the next of kin and where inquiry was not made of every person present about the condition of the loved one. One of the nurses passed on a seeming tidbit of hearsay: she had heard that since Anne's death, George Broderick had given one of his wife's wedding rings to "a friend." It was the kind of gossip not uncommon to small town Ottawa of the 1970s.

The detectives pursued the question of the bruising with Dr. Tom Estall and Dr. Ian Yates. The doctors confirmed that the general bruising was not caused by the emergency room staff, although some bruising did occur on the arm while they were looking for a vein. They also pointed out that there was a small amount of bleeding from Anne's mouth while they were working on her. It was the opinion of the doctors that the bruising could be attributed to a condition called D.I.C., disseminated intravascular coagulation.

Four weeks had passed since Anne's death.

Detectives Mancuso and Gordon now briefed Inspector Bowles on each and every element of the case that had been ascertained to date. They stressed that, until now, the investigation had continued as an accidental death investigation, and, although suspicions existed, no one outside the circle of investigators was yet aware that they were looking at it as a skilful homicide.

After assimilating the wealth of information that Mancuso and Gordon had dredged up since the 16th of November, Bowles expressed his admiration at the results of their legwork so far— all under the guise of an accidental death investigation.

"But it's all pointing to suspicion, fellas. There's still no hard evidence."

"We know it, Bill. That's what you're here for, isn't it?" Mancuso chortled. Bowles looked grim.

The time had come to open up the investigation a little. Bowles wanted to interview the bailiffs, Bordeleau and Poulin, personally. They also decided to see Landrigan, the landlord's representative. The time had come, Bowles said, to start taking formal witness statements from these people. In other words, to start nailing things down.

That night Mancuso had the team over for dinner. Anita worked her magic in the kitchen. After dinner they hashed and rehashed the investigation into the small hours. Bowles was happy to see he had a home away from home for the duration of the hunt.

That same night, in another part of the city, George Broderick entertained friends over drinks at one of his favourite haunts, the lounge at the Carleton Towers Hotel. He, too, was in a good mood. Things were beginning to look up.

The next four days were long and hectic for the police.

Between December 16th and December 20th, Bowles, Mancuso, and Gordon re-interviewed all the people who had been at the home on the morning of November 16th, ensuring that no detail had been overlooked or recalled since then. This time around, formal written statements were taken.

On the 20th, Bowles went back to Toronto to confer personally with Dr. Hillsdon-Smith. The chief pathologist's opinion remained the same: the abrasions to the knees and shins on Anne Broderick's body were inconsistent with a fall in the bathtub, and suspicious enough to point to homicide.

But this was not Bowles' main reason for returning to Toronto. He knew that the inevitable confrontation with George Broderick must soon take place. He wanted to know more about the man he would eventually have to interrogate.

Bowles had been notified that Dr. Rowsell's psychological profile of George Broderick was complete. The document, which ran 15 single-spaced typewritten pages, analyzed George's psychological makeup in detail and was supported by fact and observations from the people whom the doctor had interviewed. The conclusions, though not unexpected, were nevertheless enlightening: George Broderick was a highly intelligent, self-reliant, hardworking fellow who would be the first to help you if you were in trouble. A strict disciplinarian, he maintained his home well and, until recent years, had met his moral and financial obligations. He would never take advice. He had been described by a relative as the type of individual who could "take out his own appendix." In recent years, he had developed a reputation as a "bullshitter and a showman." When he had had a few drinks he was inclined to become cantankerous. He had come into contact with psychiatrists who had been treating his wife following their brief, three month separation several years earlier. He had no use for psychiatry.

Psychiatrists, to him, meant weakness. His reputation as a braggart and a liar was amply demonstrated by the litany of fanciful stories that had come to light.

If Broderick had read the profile, he would have been amused and puffed up at the same time.

The investigation team dispersed to spend a few days with their families over Christmas and New Year's, but they were anxious to get back on Broderick's trail. (But even New Year's Eve would be a productive evening for Mancuso.)

On January 5th, 1977, they met in Toronto before re-grouping in Ottawa. Bowles decided to move their task force closer to the action. They booked rooms at the Talisman Motor Hotel in downtown Ottawa. This would be their "headquarters" for the duration of the investigation.

A direct confrontation between the investigators and George Broderick, it was recognized, must necessarily take place before too much additional time had elapsed. With each passing day, the risk increased that Broderick would discover the extent of the investigation and that it was now a murder investigation. There was also the chance that if he learned of it, he would run. On the other hand it was necessary for the investigators to be fully prepared for the confrontation, and to be holding as many of the aces as possible without showing them to Broderick. The next few days were spent pursuing more of the interminable medical aspects of the case. Opinions were elicited from Dr. D. Levene of Toronto's Sunnybrook Hospital and from John Funk, the assistant director of the Centre for Forensic Sciences. The investigators met again with the psychiatrist, Dr. Rowsell, at his Oakville study, and went over the psychological profile with him. During this Toronto excursion, the investigators were introduced to Ivan Yip, a chemical analyst with the C.F.S. who agreed to conduct a test on the bath oil, applying expert, professional standards. In a controlled setting, using the same amount of water at an approximation of the same temperature, Yip would attempt, by gradually adding and mixing the distinctive blue bath oil beads Anne always used, to reproduce the colour of the water disclosed from the photographs that Mancuso had ordered on the day of Anne's death. The chemist's controlled tests would be photographed for comparison purposes in court. Ultimately it was determined that it took three-quarters of the entire box of bath beads to duplicate the colour of the water. The result was water with a very slippery texture. The directions recommended one or two bath beads at the most.

On the same day, Rod Williams, an O.P.P. wire-tap expert, accompanied prosecutor Harry Black to the chambers of Justice John Holland of the Supreme Court of Ontario. Canadian wire-tap laws required that the investigative agency seeking to install a wire-tap must get written authorization from a judge of the superior court, either provincial or federal, and that the officer tender a sworn affidavit satisfying the statutory criteria before the wire-tap is authorized. These criteria include reasonable and probable grounds that an offence has been committed, the reasons for so believing, the extent of the investigation to date, the reasons why it is necessary to tap rather than employ alternate means of investigation. There are other considerations. The hearings are held *ex parte*, that is without the target of the wire-tap knowing or attending the hearing which is held in secret in the judge's chambers. The authorization, once granted, remains valid for a specific length of time, usually three months, and may be extended by another application. But the application isn't a cakewalk.

This time the government's attorney was successful. Justice Holland granted authorization to perform electronic eavesdropping on the specifically named targets— George Allan Broderick, Lisette Martineau, and Cynthia Eauclaire— all targeted at their respective residences. The authorization recited prospective charges of murder, conspiracy to commit murder, and accessory after the fact to murder. The authorization gave them one month, from the 5th of January to the 3rd of February, to turn up something useful.

Once it was approved by Justice Holland, O.P.P. Officer Gerry Chapman, the technician, surreptitiously began putting the system in place. Six days later it was functioning.

The rest of the week was spent catching up on paperwork and preparing reports, a nettlesome obligation for any policeman in full flight on a murder investigation. And each night there were strategy meetings.

On the 11th of January, Bowles decided to "surface" the investigation of George Broderick. It would coincide with the start of the wire-taps and might shake the tree a little. So that day Mancuso and Bowles applied to Justice of the Peace Lynn Coulter for search warrants to search for evidence at 18 Beaverton, at the Ottawa office of Canadian Premier Life, and at Cynthia Eauclaire's residence in Vanier. The search warrants were granted, again on *ex parte* application.

The investigators met one last time for a council of war, preparatory to confronting George Broderick.

Mancuso called local Assistant Crown Attorney Mac Lindsay, to alert him that the investigation would be "going public" the next day.

From this point on, Lindsay would spearhead the case from the prosecution's side.

7.

Investigators closing in on a suspect work cautiously and with circumspection. They must remember at all times that improper tactics, trickery, or breach of a suspect's constitutional rights could result in a case being jeopardized in the cold, hard scrutiny of the courtroom.

It was agreed that Inspector Bowles and Detective Gordon would set up a meeting with George Broderick. Mancuso had been confrontational with Broderick before, so Bowles was warned that Broderick might react negatively— he might clam up. They agreed that, during the meeting, Mancuso would make himself scarce.

Although the investigators were personally convinced that Broderick had murdered his wife, without hard evidence to support a charge it would be foolhardy to confront Broderick head-on. They had no idea what Broderick's reaction was going to be. More important, they did not know who else might be involved: Cynthia Eauclaire, Lisette Martineau, or one of George Broderick's sons. It was conceivable that any of them could have been implicated as accessories.

Any concern the investigators might have had about Broderick being reticent was dispelled quickly after Detective Gordon phoned him to set up the interview. No, it would not be necessary for them to come over to his home. He would accommodate them by coming over to Bowles' headquarters at the Talisman Motor Hotel. He would be happy to talk with them. He believed in cooperating with the police; they performed a valuable, difficult service.

When Broderick arrived at the Talisman on the 12th of January, 1977, he was clearly under the impression that this was still an accidental death investigation. If he suspected otherwise, he gave no indication of it to the investigators.

For their part, the investigators did nothing to suggest to him that a full-scale murder investigation was under way or that he was the prime suspect.

Broderick presented himself as the fully cooperative, anxious to please, nothing-to-hide, bereaved widower. After the exchange of a few pleasantries, he participated wholeheartedly in an interview that lasted one hour and 15 minutes. The investigators had given Broderick no police caution, no "right to remain silent." If they had, they would have alerted Broderick to his true position as a murder suspect.

This approach was legally risky business. By not giving Broderick the standard police caution before questioning him, any incriminating statements he might make would not meet the common law test of voluntariness and would likely not be admissible in evidence. At trial, the prosecutors would be forced into the argument that no police caution was necessary at that stage because the police had nothing more than suspicion with no hard evidence to place Broderick in the suspect category, and because the case was still in its early investigatory phase with no reasonable anticipation that Broderick might incriminate himself.

It would be a tenuous argument at best.

In fairness, the police at this time were governed by the common law. The constitutional obligation to inform the suspect of his right to counsel and his right to remain silent was still in its formative stage. The Charter of Rights and Freedoms would not be proclaimed for another five years.

They went over a lot of old ground with Broderick, rehashing bits and pieces, hiding the important under the trivial. He had already given Mancuso a lot of it in his verbal statement the day after the death. Bowles and Gordon silently noted that, again, there were discrepancies in Broderick's account of the events.

Now he said that after getting up that morning, Anne had run the bathwater and put bath oil into the water. He had taken a bath before her and left the bathwater for her. He then left the house, around 10:00 a.m., he said, to go to his downtown office. Before arriving at the office, however, while downtown, he realized that he had forgotten his glasses, so he phoned his office to let them know that he was going back to the house for them. Bowles went over the route Broderick said he had taken that morning. This time Bowles produced a map. Be specific. Broderick traced the route for Bowles, marking the spot where he had stopped for cigarettes and gas.

George Broderick was a model of cooperation. If anything, it was difficult to get him to stop talking. He answered the officers' questions willingly and expansively and appeared to be never at a loss for words.

Again he categorically denied any involvement with any other woman either before or since Anne's death, a denial that by now they knew with certainty was not true. More important, they realized that by persisting in the lie Broderick was not aware of their real suspicions and purpose.

Broderick was not aware that the interview was being taped. A James Bond type of hard shell briefcase sat innocuously off to one side in the room.

At the conclusion of the interview, Bowles casually mentioned to Broderick that they had obtained a search warrant for the house at 18 Beaverton. Broderick expressed some surprise. A search warrant was not necessary, he blustered. Could the officers not see that he was ready to cooperate fully? He was a law-abiding citizen. He would even accompany the officers to his home. No problem.

They arrived at 18 Beaverton late in the afternoon, accompanied by two experts, John Funk and Bill Towstiak, from the Toronto Centre for Forensic Sciences. Towstiak was a blood examiner with special expertise in locating and reading blood droppings and spatters. They searched every part of the house, square foot by square foot.

Nothing. Absolutely nothing.

Later, all the reports filed by Towstiak would state unequivocally that there was no evidence of blood or body tissue in any part of the house or on any articles of clothing in it.

More photographs were taken by the identification officer, and Bowles seized a fistful of documents, including Broderick's income tax returns for the previous two years and a curious invoice showing that George Broderick had paid for the storage of household furniture owned by his secretary, Cynthia Eauclaire. Among the papers were two court documents, Directions to Garnishee, against George Broderick's salary. One was from the Bank of Nova Scotia and the other from the Department of National Revenue, totalling approximately $15,000.

Before leaving, the ident officers removed the lock from the bathroom door to be held as material evidence.

That day the wire-taps picked up two nuggets.

The first would cause Bowles and Mancuso to shuffle their plans. Broderick, they learned, was scheduled to leave in four days to attend a conference of Canadian Premier Life managers in Winnipeg. He would be there all week. They decided to escalate the cat-and-mouse game by beating him to Winnipeg. They would check into the same hotel and let their presence be known. They wanted to see his reaction. Would he make any incriminating moves or noises? And they had some digging to do at Canadian Premier Life's head office anyway.

The second gem was a long, rambling conversation Broderick had with an unidentified person. He re-told the story of his wife's death and this time gave a version that was clearly inconsistent with what he had told the investigators just a few hours before at the Talisman.

The next morning the detectives took the map and drove a police cruiser around Broderick's traced routing. It took 50 minutes.

When they arrived back at the Talisman there was another call waiting for them from the wire-tap team. During the past 24 hours they had struck gold. Broderick and his secretary had been exchanging phone calls. The calls were very guarded, which tended to make them appear incriminating, but they revealed one thing.

George Broderick and Cynthia Eauclaire were lovers. It wasn't Lisette after all. The night with Lisette must have been a one-time opportunity.

Broderick had cheated on two people, his wife and his girlfriend.

Mancuso let out a low whistle. Things were developing faster than he had expected. But at least they had found "the woman."

But the erupting mountain of information satisfied the investigators only that there was a dark side to George Broderick, and that they were on the right track. During their nightly get-togethers in the Mancuso rec-room they were forced to acknowledge that the legal membrane separating suspicion from hard evidence had not been penetrated.

The man was a liar and a cheat. So what?

With this realization hovering over them, Bowles and Mancuso flew to Winnipeg on January 16th. At the last minute they changed their plan, arranging instead to leave two hours after George Broderick rather than before. They wanted to be certain that he actually left. They brought their search warrant with them, to be "backed" by a Manitoba Justice of the Peace. It authorized them to search the head offices of Canadian Premier Life at 360 Broadway Street in Winnipeg.

They checked into the Holiday Inn where Broderick was staying. The psychological war games would now begin.

The next morning in the coffee shop, George Broderick looked up from his bacon and eggs and went pale when he saw Bowles and Mancuso nonchalantly having breakfast and chatting in the booth across from him. They didn't seem to notice him. He stopped eating, gulped the remainder of his orange juice, and left abruptly, saying nothing to the two detectives. He had been shaken by their unexplained and unexpected presence.

"Imagine that," Mancuso mockingly complained to Bowles. "He didn't even say 'Good morning.'"

They presented the search warrant to the Canadian Premier Life head office, and were given immediate access to the Brodericks' records and files, both George's and Anne's. The company's vice-president of marketing, Jack Waldron, praised George Broderick and confirmed Broderick's history with the company.

The Broderick saga was already well known to the detectives, but they listened patiently. This was a new, more authoritative perspective. And there were some new tidbits of information: unfortunately, Waldron continued, a deterioration in George's performance had set in early in 1975. So pronounced was it that the company had considered a change of management. Broderick had tried to explain away his problems in terms of personal financial pressures. He had even raised the often-told story about inventions sold to the British government which he had produced in his laboratory at CFB Petawawa. The story was, by now, wearing thin. He told his company he had $75,000 coming to him but some legal difficulty prevented him getting the money out of England.

He was being sued as well, as a result of a laser beam experiment that had gone wrong in which a soldier in the Canadian Armed Forces had died. George said that all his money was tied up in the courts. When the Direction to Garnishee arrived at head office in October 1976, George said it was a mere misunderstanding which he would clear up quickly. A manager of life insurance funds with garnishees outstanding against him has no credibility. Waldron had given George an ultimatum: if these things were not straightened out soon, there would be little alternative but to remove him as Ottawa manager.

As of November 15th, 1976, one day prior to Anne's death, Waldron still had received no satisfaction from Broderick that his financial problems were resolved. A letter of termination addressed to Broderick was prepared by head office and Waldron had been given the unpleasant task of delivering it. George Broderick was to have been terminated as branch manager on November 18th, 1976. Waldron was in Toronto with the letter in his briefcase when the news of Anne's death reached him on November 16th, just two days before the termination was to take effect.

While Bowles and Mancuso were digging in Winnipeg, parallel events were going on in Ottawa.

Detectives Gordon, Fermoyle, and Champagne executed a search warrant at Cynthia Eauclaire's home in Vanier. For two hours the search team scoured Eauclaire's residence, seizing and meticulously recording documents which they initialled, dated, and inventoried for later examination by Bowles and Mancuso. Eauclaire was present and cooperated with the officers. She agreed to go with them to the police station for interrogation and to provide a written statement.

This was the first inkling Eauclaire had that the police were having a look at her as well as George Broderick. Not surprisingly, she was shaken by the experience. Nevertheless she gave a lengthy statement to the officers, who began the questioning without any police caution or warning. The officers were careful not to reveal what they considered to be important or unimportant.

She identified herself as George Broderick's secretary at Canadian Premier Life's Ottawa office. She said she remembered the date of Anne's death well since it was the same date as the district manager's birthday.

The officers wrote the questions and answers in their notebooks:

Q: Did you personally hear from George Broderick on the day of his wife's death?
A: Yes, he called first thing in the morning and said that he had an appointment and things to do. He said that he would be in to work around noon.
Q: What time did he call you?
A: It was before 9:00 in the morning.
Q: Do you know where George Broderick called from?
A: No, I don't know. It sounded like a shopping centre or outside. I could hear noise.
Q: Did George Broderick talk long on the phone when he called you?
A: No, just long enough to tell me he was going to be delayed.

She said that Broderick's son Gerry phoned afterward, trying to locate his dad, and it was only then that she learned what had happened to Anne.

Q: Did you hear from George Broderick after Gerry placed the call?
A: Yes, about 20 minutes later, George Broderick called. He was broken up, crying. He told me he had come home and found the repairman at his house, that he asked the repairman where his wife was and he didn't know. George called out his wife's name, checked the house, found the bathroom door locked, forced the bathroom door open and found her lying face down in the bathtub.

What did Eauclaire know of the Broderick family?
She described Anne Broderick as being "a very fine person." She said that George talked about Anne quite a bit and everything he said was good. "She was very intelligent and all over Mrs. Perfect." She described George as being a moderate drinker. She had no knowledge of his involvement in any businesses outside of the life insurance company. She was unaware of any

financial problems he might be having, although she said, "He is very secretive." She described him as being a family man, a good father and husband, and a good provider. About her own relationship with George Broderick, Cynthia Eauclaire was remarkably candid:

Q: Are you having an affair with George Broderick?
A: No.
Q: Are you in love with George Broderick?
A: Yes, I am.
Q: Does George Broderick love you?
A: I think so, yes.
Q: Have you ever slept with George Broderick?
A: Yes, I have.
Q: Have you ever been intimate with George Broderick?
A: Yes, I have.
Q: Have you ever had intercourse with George Broderick?
A: Yes, I have.
Q: How long have you been intimate with George Broderick?
A: Years? Oh Lord, I don't know, maybe five or six years.
Q: Have you ever been to a cottage owned by George Broderick?
A: Yes, I have.
Q: Where's the cottage situated?
A: Notre Dame de Lasalette, Quebec.
Q: Did Anne Broderick know about George and you?
A: No.
Q: Has George Broderick ever asked you to marry him?
A: Not in so many words.
Q: What do you mean, not in so many words?
A: He has never come right out and asked me.
Q: Has George Broderick told you that he loves you?
A: Yes.
Q: Have you told George Broderick that you love him?
A: Yes.

Eauclaire disarmed the officers with her forthrightness. They switched to less sensitive questions. She told them about George's daily routine and admitted that he had helped her out financially from time to time. She believed he was moving from 18 Beaverton to an apartment although she was not sure when. She said that she knew Lisette Martineau, describing her as "a friend of George's family."

During the course of the questioning, the officers said nothing to suggest that their inquiry was anything more than a follow-up to the accidental death of Anne Broderick.

8.

George Broderick phoned Cynthia three times while en route to Winnipeg and again while in Winnipeg. The detectives learned from the wire-taps that George and Cynthia discussed personal matters. Nothing incriminating was said, nor anything that would indicate fear over the investigation. There was no suggestion of a cover-up. Curiously, George Broderick made no mention to Cynthia that Bowles and Mancuso had turned up across from him at breakfast in the coffee shop of the Holiday Inn. But in a telephone conversation between Cynthia Eauclaire and her son, taped the day following her interview with the police, Eauclaire showed that she was quite shaken. She described the police as having been rough on her. She believed that the police were suspicious that a murder had been committed. She came to this conclusion completely on her own; the subject of murder had never come up during the interview with the police.

The day after the interview, Officers Gordon, Fermoyle, and Champagne executed a search warrant at the Ottawa offices of Canadian Premier Life at 251 Laurier Avenue West. By this time, Bowles and Mancuso had left Winnipeg, flying on to Calgary and Chilliwack to develop background information about George from Anne Broderick's relatives.

Cynthia Eauclaire was in the office when the detectives arrived with the search warrant. George Broderick's son Gerry showed up unexpectedly and stayed there throughout the search. A specialist from the Royal Canadian Mounted Police was brought in to open some of the locked drawers and cabinets, and a large number of documents were seized after being inventoried and shown to Gerry Broderick. The search lasted two hours. Some of the documents revealed that George Broderick had, in the past, entered into a lease with the plush Juliana Apartments at 100 Bronson Avenue in Ottawa.

During the search Gerry Broderick phoned his father in Winnipeg to let him know what was going on. He said the police were still searching and had all his cabinets and drawers open. They had found everything including the "Juliana things" and the papers for the garnisheed wages.

Broderick replied, somewhat cryptically, that he would now have to make a clean breast of everything. The officers would subsequently ascertain that George was referring, not to Anne's death, but rather to financial anomalies and income tax problems.

He was not on the point of confessing to any crime.

Meanwhile, the wire-tap information kept coming in.

On the same day, Lisette had a telephone conversation with her landlord, K---- B----, in which Lisette's own difficult financial situation was discussed. The content of the conversation would lead the investigating team to speculate that if Lisette were in financial difficulty, she might be the sort of person who would have use for a sugar daddy like George Broderick. This was the first the police knew that she was suffering financial hardship.

Later that day, January 21st, after searching the Juliana apartment, the Ottawa team drove up to George Broderick's cottage near Notre Dame de Lasalette, Quebec. Cynthia had named it, appropriately, "Dreemcumtru."

One of the neighbours at Lac Sheridan told the officers that he believed George Broderick had bought the cottage around 1970 and that George came up there quite often with a woman named Cynthia. The neighbour said that George Broderick had introduced Cynthia as his wife, saying that they had not been married long. It was not until after George's arrest that the neighbour would learn the truth.

On their swing through British Columbia, Bowles and Mancuso decided to make one last stop and talk with Ray Broderick, George's brother, in Victoria. It had been intimated that part of George's financial problems were attributable to his having assumed financial responsibility for the care of their aged mother, who was living there. Ray was incensed by this suggestion, calling it "bullshit." He told the officers that he had been taking care of his mother quite exclusively. George had contributed little or nothing.

By January 25th, Mancuso and Bowles were back in Ottawa and Murray Gordon brought them up to date on what had been accomplished during their absence.

Direct, hard evidence was still lacking, but the major elements in support of motive had clearly emerged. George Broderick was in serious financial difficulties, and was being pursued through the courts and his income garnisheed, just prior to Anne's death. He was at the point of being evicted from his house with the attendant embarrassment to his wife, who had not known about the arrears of rent. He had probably been aware that Jack Waldron was on his way to Ottawa with a letter in his pocket from head office, terminating him as the district manager of Canadian Premier Life. George was in love with Cynthia Eauclaire and wanted to marry her. They had continually professed their love for each other by phone when George was away and had exchanged rings two years before. George had, on more than one occasion, introduced Cynthia as his wife.

Taken altogether, these details tipped the motivational scale, pointing to one question and evoking one answer.

What single event could solve every one of these problems for George Broderick and prevent his life, his world, and his house of cards from collapsing?

Anne's death.

It did not require any great investigative insight or deductive leapfrogging to see this. The double indemnity insurance policies on Anne's life would solve George's personal financial difficulties; the house would be saved. He would be free to marry the woman he loved. And all of this without going through the heartbreak, expense, embarrassment, and legal maelstrom of divorce.

But there was still no hard evidence. Not even a cause of death.

The unknown element in the equation continued to be Lisette Martineau. To date, the detectives had taken a hands-off approach with her.

But something in the pretty blonde girl's demeanour had triggered Mancuso's instincts and curiosity from the beginning. Had it been the quick, almost furtive embrace in the foyer at 18 Beaverton on the morning of Anne's death? Or was it the impression she gave that she was somehow involved, yet not involved, that she was on the periphery of the action but not part of it?

Mancuso felt she knew *something*. Being so close to the Broderick family, she *had* to. But she was saying nothing, even though the life of her only confidante had suddenly been snuffed out.

Lisette was the Cosette of *Les Misérables*, a young girl-woman without roots or close relatives, clinging to her only friends. It had been this waif-like quality that led Anne Broderick to befriend her, take care of her, and be a mother and advisor to her.

Mancuso had spoken with Lisette just once, in the early stages of the investigation. The interview proved abortive when Mancuso, again trying the verbal sucker punch, had asked her a pointed question about her sex life. Lisette had jumped up and stormed out of the police station, indignant at the suggestion implicit in the question. From then on, in her eyes, Mancuso was clearly the tough cop and she avoided him. She related very well to the boyish Murray Gordon, however. He was the good cop. So Bowles detailed Gordon to deal with her exclusively, if and when necessary.

By the 26th of January, they decided that it *was* necessary. Lisette was brought down to the police station in the morning and interviewed by Detective Gordon. Mancuso was present, but remained quiet.

She began by mentioning her relationship with George's son Gerry about six years earlier and how she had been "adopted" by the Broderick family. Her relationship with the Brodericks continued after she had broken up with Gerry. They exchanged gifts, had her over for Christmas, and were concerned about her well-being. But she hadn't seen Anne Broderick for about three months before November 16th, 1976. When she showed up that morning at 18 Beaverton, she said she saw the two police cars, knocked on the door, and was met by George Broderick.

"Missy's had an accident," he told her.

She described George's face as being puffy and as having marks on the right hand side. She asked him what the marks were and he replied, "It must be nerves." He seemed very upset. She said she returned later in the afternoon, some time between 4:00 and 4:30. George Broderick was trying to call his son Ryan. George told her that he couldn't get out of his mind how he had found Anne. He described taking her out of the water and giving her mouth-to-mouth resuscitation.

Then Gerry Broderick, George's other son and Lisette's ex-boyfriend, showed up. Lisette left.

She had gone to the funeral home every night, keeping company with the family. After the funeral service, she and George went to a department store to buy a new shower curtain, new window curtains, a new clothes hamper, new bathmats, and some non-skid pads for the bathtub. George had told her that he wanted these articles to help his daughter, Shirley, psychologically. After that, she said, they went to Ryan Broderick's home in Aylmer, Quebec, where they talked, had a couple of drinks and something to eat. They stayed there until George suggested that they leave because he had taken some medication and had been drinking. She drove him to 18 Beaverton and she offered to stay.

"I slept in Shirley's room and he slept in his room. We did not sit up and talk, but went right to bed. I got up first, had a shower, made some tea, and he got up shortly after. He had a shower and we sat in the kitchen and had a cup of tea."

Later on that morning, the day after the funeral, they cleaned the bathroom, washing the walls, the sink, the bathtub, and the tile wall. When George left to answer the telephone, Lisette said she was left alone in the bathroom and wondered how Anne could have fallen and ended up face down in the tub.

"I couldn't figure it out." She asked George about this when he returned and he reiterated that there was no bruising, broken bones, or bleeding. But he did say that there were nerves on certain parts of the body, where, "if you are hit, you die instantly."

"I wasn't satisfied with this answer," she said simply.

After the clean-up session George gave her a few of Anne's things, then threw out the rest. She said he promised her Anne's fur coat, since Anne would have wanted her to have it, "but I never got it." Later that day they were invited back to Ryan's house, but George would not go, saying that he had to attend to "navy business." She went anyway and she and Ryan discussed Anne's death long into the night. It was so late she stayed overnight.

In the course of conversation that evening, she conveyed to Ryan what George had told her: that if the police learned of George's affair with Cynthia, they would become suspicious and would suspect foul play. Lisette decided to confront George Broderick. She told him that she thought he had hurt Missy.

He replied, "You know, Lisette, I've never hit her or hurt her before."

Before? Mancuso, listening, wasn't sure what to make of it.

Lisette was suddenly scared to be with him, she said. When she saw the police at 18 Beaverton she had wanted to go back into the house and say, "Bullshit, you killed her."

"But I didn't."

Then George told her that he had bought a diamond ring for Cynthia. He planned to marry her, but only after a year or so, "So that no one would be suspicious."

Lisette ended her statement on this cryptic note: "Gerry told me that George was involved in espionage and that he had a black belt, third degree.

Mr. Broderick was always talking about killing people and hitting them in certain parts of the body where special nerves were. The art was called Polynesian nerve killing or something like that."

Mancuso, watching from the other end of the room, caught the "Mr. Broderick" instead of the usual "George." Nice touch, Lisette, he thought.

She hadn't told the investigators very much that they didn't already know, but she gave it a new perspective. It was a straightforward statement, given in narrative, without questions or excessive probing by the officers. While it didn't provide many new answers, it focused on a few old questions.

If George Broderick had killed his wife, how had he done it? He was accurate in telling Lisette that there was no blood, broken bones, or significant bruises on the body. But why was he continually tossing out the references to nerve killing? Why had he been so anxious to get rid of the items in the bathroom and most of Anne's personal belongings so soon after the funeral?

The investigators did not fully realize it, but with this initial interview with Lisette they were about to travel down an investigative path with many bumps, curves, and switch-backs.

The first of these curves would occur five days later, on January 31st, when Lisette phoned Detective Gordon. She wanted to make another statement.

After her first interview, she had agreed to let Mancuso drive her home. Detective Gordon followed in a police cruiser. At that time, they retrieved the pink laundry clothes hamper from her residence together with some of the other things George had given her.

After her first statement she began to experience pangs of conscience. Mancuso always felt that she was holding something back, that some dark secret was churning inside her. He sensed that it had a lot to do with George Broderick. But no confrontational questions had been put to her on the 26th. They had been cautious, recalling that she had stormed out of the police station when Mancuso brought up the question of her own sexual involvement. Now they didn't want to risk frightening the little bird away.

But this time she sang like the proverbial canary.

"The reason for this statement being given at this time is that I felt guilty at the time I first talked to the police about my relationship with Mr. Broderick. After I had concluded my statement, I told the police the truth about my relationship with Mr. Broderick and then arrangements were made for me to give this statement."

Lisette, the waif, had been actively intimate with George Broderick. She recounted how it had begun in 1971, while she was still going out with Gerry. George had invited her up to the cottage at Lac Sheridan, where he was going to do some work.

"While going to the cottage in his car, he started to fondle me. I didn't know what to do or say. Before we even got to the cottage, he parked the car on a hill and then we had intercourse."

She said they had intercourse again later that day after a session of nude swimming. She was frightened of him, she said, and he knew it. He warned her not to tell Gerry. They then returned to Ottawa. George had not done any work at the cottage.

Another time, in 1975, Anne had invited her over for dinner. Afterward, George offered to drive her home. He stopped outside her apartment and begged to come up, but she refused.

"He made advances to me and we had sexual intercourse in the front seat of his car. At this time I was not going with Gerry any more. During the time I had been going out with Gerry, I had become very close to Mrs. Broderick and was invited over on many occasions."

Lisette confirmed the episode that left the seasoned investigators shaking their heads.

She told them that after Anne's wake on November 18th, George asked her to come for supper at a restaurant on Baseline Road in Ottawa. He tried to get her to drink more than she wanted to. They left and he started driving aimlessly around the city. He said to her, "You know I never laid a hand on her." Meaning Anne. He suggested that she had been washing the tiles around the bathtub and that she fell and hit a nerve on the right side of the face just below the cheek. He said, if struck there, "it would kill you and this is what happened to Missy." Eventually, he stopped at a construction site in the west end of Ottawa. Just to talk, he said. He made advances and they had sexual intercourse in his car. Then he drove her home.

Lisette was disgorging memories that had been choking her for years, memories she could never have revealed to her only friend and confidante, Anne Broderick.

On November 20th, the day of Anne Broderick's funeral, she and George bought new things for the bathroom. She had told the officers this story before. But this time she indignantly pointed out that she had had to "lend" George the 60 dollars to purchase these items.

After the funeral and after spending the evening at Ryan's home, they returned to 18 Beaverton where they had sexual intercourse in the master bedroom. In Anne's bed. Right after her funeral. George promptly fell asleep and Lisette went into Shirley's bedroom.

Lisette was clearly trying to purge her guilt over this desecration.

But it didn't end there.

She described two more occasions of sexual intimacy after Anne's death. On one of these occasions, it was after he had a disagreement with Cynthia Eauclaire.

"He talked to me about how much he loved me, about marrying him, about him getting me pregnant and having a baby girl. He repeated this quite often. He made advances to me and we had sexual intercourse on the chesterfield."

With these revelations, the investigators were left to wonder about the new dimension that Dr. Rowsell's profile of George could take on, a profile of a man who would cheat not only on his wife but on his mistress as well. What kind of man would be so insensitive as to have intercourse with his son's ex-girlfriend in the matrimonial bed on the same day as his wife's funeral?

Soap opera plots paled by comparison.

Lisette ended her second statement by disclosing that George had recently warned her about talking to the police. On the morning of January 26th, before she had gone to the police station to give her first statement, he had called her and chatted casually for a few minutes before warning her.

"The police may be around to talk to you. They're still investigating. Don't tell them anything, except that you knew Missy and the family. Nothing else."

After these two statements, Mancuso and Bowles believed that Lisette knew even more than she had told them. But she was not the type to give it up easily. Nor would the information be sweated from her. She would reveal it in dribs and drabs, adjusting to any twist or turn in events and according to her emotional state at the moment. Lisette was clearly a person to be treated with kid gloves.

From this point on, the investigators would be particularly accommodating to her. And that was Detective Murray Gordon's department.

9.

Lisette Martineau's revelations to the investigators, though startling, did not add greatly to the evidentiary package weighing against George Broderick. But it was obvious that Lisette was privy to whatever discussion and bickering had been going on in the family since Anne's death.

People in the inner circle had been talking with her and she, in turn, had started talking to the police.

This prompted the investigators to bring Lisette to Justice of the Peace Coulter, where she swore under oath that the contents of her second statement were true. All future written statements given by Lisette would be sworn, as a precaution, to protect the officers, and to prevent backtracking later. This procedure was unusual. Swearing of ordinary witness statements is a formality generally considered unnecessary. A witness who is not seen to be either a suspect or a party to criminal proceedings is unlikely to change her story later. Ordinarily it is sufficient if the statement is written out either by the witness or the police officer and simply signed by the witness after reading it over for accuracy. Witness statements are uncautioned statements.

The revelations in Lisette's second statement raised the very real possibility that she too might be a suspect in Anne's death, either alone or in concert with George Broderick. Her statements introduced new elements of complexity and new possibilities. Fresh avenues had to be explored.

The police barely had time to catch their breath. Inspector Bowles and Detective Gordon decided to talk with Lisette again the following day.

In tandem with these events, the "second team" of detectives— Fermoyle, Gordon, and Champagne— had completed their inquiries with the Royal Canadian Mounted Police, the Canadian government, and the British government. They confirmed that George Broderick was not involved with intelligence work for them, nor had he been involved in any clandestine experimentation with electronic warfare or laser beam technology. The entire story was nothing more than a dismal piece of fiction concocted to prop up an aging ego.

The Russian government would neither confirm nor deny.

Lisette called Detective Gordon the next day, February 1st, to tell him that she wanted to speak with the investigators again. They decided that only Bowles and Gordon would see her. If she wanted to make a further statement, Gordon would write it out for her. She liked Murray Gordon.

Her third statement to the police was given on her own initiative and instigation. It was as powerful as it was short. She had been thinking.

Lisette's third statement altered the entire course of the investigation and resulted in George Broderick's arrest.

"I did not reveal what I am about to say before because I was afraid of Mr. Broderick and because I was involved with him," she began.

Then came the break that Bowles had been hoping for. She continued:

"On the morning of November 16th, 1976, I arrived at the Broderick residence around 10:30 a.m. I pulled into the laneway. I got out and walked up the front steps, checked the mailbox and saw mail in it. I peeked through the front door window and saw Cindy Lou barking and running around. I had not knocked on the door. At the same time I heard Cindy Lou barking, I heard Mrs. Broderick screaming and shouting, all mixed in with the dog's barking. I knew there was trouble, so I did not stick around. I went to my car and got in and went to my girlfriend's place. I don't remember whether Mr. Broderick's car was at the Brodericks' or not. I stayed at M--- D----'s place a while and came back to the Brodericks'. I saw the police there and hesitated before going in. I was scared and didn't know what to do. I went to the front door and spoke to Mr. Broderick. The conversation was short, and when I went out, I felt like saying, 'Bullshit, you killed her,' because of what I had heard previously."

The membrane between suspicion and evidence was close to being pierced with this narrative.

When Mancuso saw Lisette come to the door and speak with George Broderick on the morning of Anne's death, he had no way of knowing that she had been there earlier. The time frame for her earlier visit was in the ball park, but it would require more definition.

Besides, Cindy Lou, the Brodericks' dog, was ordinarily quiet and was accustomed to Lisette being in the Brodericks' house. Was Cindy Lou upset by something going on *inside* the house?

The officers didn't doubt what Lisette told them. There was no reason to doubt. The revelations in this third statement were volunteered. There was no obvious motive for her to concoct a story, unless she was trying to incriminate George Broderick, a prospect that the investigators considered remote.

Lisette's response to Broderick's announcement— "Missy's had an accident,"— had been that she felt like saying, "Bullshit, you killed her." Why should Lisette react that way?

But the investigators were convinced that she was still not telling them everything she knew. She was serving it up to them in dribs and drabs; perhaps feelings of guilt were the sporadic, compelling force.

She seemed to be under great pressure and somewhat at a loss as to whom she could trust and where her allegiance lay. The investigators recognized the delicate position they were in. They would have to treat her with great deference and compassion, refraining from any improper influence upon her, yet remain encouragingly receptive.

After completing this short third statement at the Talisman Motor Hotel, Lisette phoned George Broderick with the officers present. She suggested to him, forcefully, that she did not believe Anne had had an accident. They ended the conversation. Nothing further was said at that time and the matter was left hanging.

Lisette's third statement gave the investigation new momentum. The time had come for Bowles and Gordon to confront Cynthia Eauclaire again. The next morning, February 2nd, Gordon called for Cynthia Eauclaire and drove her to the Talisman where she was questioned.

By now the police were less interested in her relationship with George than they were in the intricate details of what had taken place on the morning of November 16th. Eauclaire spoke willingly and freely. She gave another long, rambling statement outlining the events of that day.

But her meetings with the police were the equivalent of migraine headaches for her. She would sooner have been anywhere else in the world than in a room at the Talisman talking with two police officers about George Broderick. By now she was aware of their suspicions and that the "accidental death" investigation was no longer *just* that. Her lover was under investigation for the death of his wife. Not a comfortable thought.

Nevertheless she talked long and freely. The police let her go on. They did not know how much she knew or whether she would cover for George if she did know anything.

Did she, for example, know about George's involvement with Lisette, and, if so, would Cynthia try to hang him?

It was all very much up in the air. So they listened.

Cynthia had divorced her husband in 1970 and fallen in love with George. He in turn had separated from Anne for a period of time after Cynthia's divorce, renting an apartment with a view to establishing divorce grounds— three years' separation. But George could not see it through. He returned home to Anne after three months.

In 1975, George gave her an engagement ring and a wedding band. They exchanged promises to get married some day.

Cynthia offered to turn the rings over to the police.

George bought the cottage at Lac Sheridan for $12,500. It was for both of them.

She said, curiously, that George made frequent periodic trips up to Camp Petawawa and remained away overnight. It had nothing to do with insurance work. The investigators could understand George giving his wife this story, but why hand Cynthia the same line?

Finally her narrative came back to the day of Anne's death:

"I arrived at the office between 8:00 a.m. and 8:30 a.m., my usual time of arrival. I put the coffee on and did my filing. This normally takes about 45 minutes, give or take 15 minutes. I was filing, somewhere around 9:00, when George Broderick called in (I didn't think it was from his home, as I could hear traffic or machinery noise in the background). He said, 'How are you today, I won't be in till noon, I've got things to do and I have an appointment. If anyone calls, I'll call them back this afternoon.' He seemed to be speaking in a normal tone of voice and appeared cheerful, like any other day."

George's son Gerry came in around mid-morning, did some chores and then tried to reach his father at home. There was something wrong with the telephone so he called a neighbour. The neighbour told Gerry that an ambulance and the police were at the residence and Gerry left to go home.

"Twenty to 30 minutes later, George called me. He was upset and crying. He said, 'Anne had an accident in the bathroom... they've taken her to the hospital and I don't know how serious it is.' Some time after, Gerry came into the office and said his father had come home because he had forgotten his glasses."

In a parallel concerted blitz, during business hours of February 2nd, the second team, led by Detective Fermoyle, executed search warrants on the Toronto-Dominion Bank, the Bank of Montreal, TransCanada Credit Corporation, and the main branch of Birks' Jewellers at the Sparks Street Mall in Ottawa. The documents seized from the various financial institutions confirmed George Broderick's debt crisis. The receipts from Birks' Jewellers confirmed the purchase of rings for Cynthia in 1975.

On February 3rd, Shirley Broderick was brought to the Talisman to make her statement. She was downcast, forlorn, and serious beyond her years. She told the police officers about their family life and her love for both her mother and father. She provided some insight into the jousting that plagued the family. She was objective and non-partisan, taking neither her mother's side nor her father's. As with Cynthia, the police let her talk.

Bowles noted some of her more specific comments. Her mother very seldom had a bath in the morning. Even though Anne bathed every day, it was usually in the evening before retiring. She always used the same distinctive blue bath oil beads. Shirley described her mother's ritual on those days when she did bathe in the morning.

Anne's routine consisted of entering the bathroom with her PJs and radio, and placing her PJs on top of the hamper. While she was soaking in the tub, she would listen to the radio which she sat on the bath ledge. She washed the bathtub while the water was running down the drain or after she got out. She used cleanser. "I have never seen her wash the tiles after or during a bath. She usually did that when she was cleaning the sinks and toilet. The radio is a transistor with four small, long batteries."

Shirley said that her mother had never had a fainting spell at home or at work, but occasionally she complained about stomach pains. The doctor could find no reason for this. Within the last two or three weeks of her life, Anne had told Shirley that she didn't think she could go on much more with her belief in the "new house" situation.

Shirley described her relationship with her father as being good but not close, even though they had occasional close moments. He was looked to as the breadwinner; "He was and still is overprotective," she said.

Shirley's recollections about November 16th were very specific.

"The day of the accident I got up at approximately 8:00 a.m., left the house between 9:00 and 9:15 a.m., and caught bus number 77, I think at 9:31 a.m. Prior to leaving, Dad didn't offer me a ride like he usually does when he asks me what time I'm leaving. I thought that deserved an explanation.

"I heard Dad run the bathwater for Mom that day. Mom would not walk from the bedroom to the bathroom unless she had something on, and since it was morning, she would have had her PJs on. Her undergarment pants would be on the floor, on the left side of the bed if you were lying in bed."

Shirley then left for school by bus and spent the entire day there. She knew that something was amiss when her brother Gerry picked her up at school at 6:50 in the evening. He told her about the accident. She immediately expressed reservations about the "accident." She could not reconcile the idea of her mother drowning— which she believed would be "quick and final"— with the fact that her mother was still, at that time, alive in the hospital. When she reached home her Dad met her at the front door and took her in his arms. Lisette was already at the house and George was upset and worried. He repeatedly told Shirley that Anne was too intelligent a woman to be left a vegetable, and that he hoped it wasn't a violent death.

She specifically remembered his use of the word "violent." This comment was, at least, suspiciously ambivalent if he believed she had slipped in the tub.

When the investigators asked about her recollections of the night before, she said that she had come home and had dinner. After dinner, she had invited her mom to a prayer meeting at St. Augustine's Church, scheduled for 8:00 p.m. Anne begged off because "she felt ill in the stomach." Shirley came straight home after the prayer meeting, arriving between 10:30 and 11:30 p.m. Anne said that she felt a bit better and that the pain was gone.

There was no explanation for Anne deciding not to have her usual evening bath on the 15th but rather to have a morning bath on the 16th of November. There was no explanation as to why, that morning, George Broderick had decided to draw his wife's bath and to put the bath beads in the water for her. There was no explanation why George Broderick chose not to drive Shirley to school that morning, nor why he stayed on at the house after she had left to catch the bus. There was no explanation as to why Anne's PJs were found in the bedroom when it was clear that she had had no opportunity to return there.

Shirley and the officers had at least one thing in common. They all felt that these things "deserved an explanation," as she put it.

At the conclusion of Shirley's interview with Bowles and Mancuso, Constable Holland was brought back into the picture. The investigators wanted an independent witness to be in a position to testify about the bathwater temperature.

Bowles explained to Shirley that he wanted her to fill a bathtub containing the same amount of water, approximating the same temperature that her mother preferred. Shirley complied, using the bathtub in the Talisman suite, gradually increasing the amount and raising the temperature of the water until the desired temperature was reached. Constable Holland took periodic readings. The right temperature turned out to be 105 degrees fahrenheit.

10.

Later that day, Detective Gordon met with Cynthia Eauclaire. She handed him the two diamond rings that George Broderick had given her in 1975. Before he left, Gordon asked Cynthia to slip the rings on. Like other pieces of the puzzle that were beginning to come together, they fit.

Lisette had complained about nuisance phone calls she had been receiving at her apartment. She could not identify the caller. Nothing was said by the caller, but the repeated calling was making her edgy. So, late that afternoon, Bowles and Gordon drove over to see her. They discussed the calls and gave her their comfort and reassurance. She was, after all, their prize witness.

In the interim, the second team had dredged up more documentation from the Bank of Nova Scotia and the Household Finance Corporation, showing that Broderick was into those lenders as well. During the months of April to August, 1975, Broderick had borrowed several thousand dollars from the bank on the strength of a promise to repay the amount from the sale of an airplane he said he owned. The detectives' search for both the elusive aircraft and the mysterious lawyer who was supposedly handling its sale would later add to the investigators' arsenal of ammunition against Broderick. But they were curious why a seemingly prosperous insurance company manager would need bank loans totalling nearly $7,000. That was a lot of money in 1975.

On February 4th, Constable Holland, having ascertained the preferred temperature of Anne's bathwater the day before, returned to the bathtub at 18 Beaverton and began a series of experiments. The distinctive blue bath oil beads were dissolved in the same amount of water at the same temperature, until the same colour was achieved as had been seen on the day of the death.

The results of this experiment startled the investigators. Holland had to empty three-quarters of the box of bath beads into the tub to achieve the same colour.

The wire-tappers were still vigilant.

On February 3rd, 1977, Justice Garrette extended the interception authorization to March 5th, 1977.

The interceptions were causing the police to think that George's son Gerry might be implicated as an accessory after the fact. When he was questioned on February 7th, he gave a page and a half, recounting things the police already knew. He said that he knew about the affair between his father and Cynthia and that he condoned it. He was aware of the exchange of rings. He was not outraged about this but expressed it matter-of-factly.

On January 26th a call from George Broderick to Lisette had been intercepted. He alerted her to the fact that the police were still investigating Anne's death and that they would probably be around to see her. He admonished her to say that they were "just good friends." He phoned her again on other occasions, but the exchanges were innocuous.

After her blockbuster revelations of February 3rd, 1977, the police treated Lisette with a lot of attention, responding to her calls and attending to her wishes. They were protective, ensuring that no harm came to her.

Early in the morning on February 7th, she phoned Detective Gordon. She had received another call from George Broderick. She was agitated. She wanted to talk to the investigators again. Now! Bowles and Gordon went over to her house. Mancuso stayed away.

Lisette repeated her earlier observations about her first trip to 18 Beaverton the morning of Anne's death. Lisette wanted to talk again.

Bowles and Gordon accompanied her back to the Talisman Motor Hotel.

If Bowles, Mancuso, and Gordon were still recovering from Lisette's statement of February 1st, they were about to be really knocked out this time. What she had to tell them would make the February 1st statement pale by comparison.

But she would do it her own way, in her own time. She was composed, resigned to unburdening herself once and for all of the knowledge that was clawing at her conscience. Bowles and Gordon settled in to hear what she had to say. Gordon wrote as she spoke.

Lisette began on a sorrowful note, explaining that each year, on her birthday, November 14th, Anne gave her a birthday present. On Tuesday, November 9th, seven days before the death, Lisette drove over to see Anne but there was no one home. She decided to come back on her next day off from work, November 16th. She arrived there in the morning.

Lisette paused. The officers refrained from any prompting, content to simply let her speak when she was ready.

"I drove into the laneway of the Brodericks' house. I don't remember seeing Mr. Broderick's car. I walked up to the house and looked in the mailbox. I opened the storm door, stood on the step, looked through the window, and saw Cindy Lou barking and running around. She seemed very excited. I opened the door and stepped in. The dog stopped barking. I looked down the hallway and saw Mr. Broderick holding her. Mrs. Broderick was on the floor in the bathroom. She had no clothes on. She was half sitting up, on an angle. Mr. Broderick was behind her, holding her under the arms. I don't recall what he was wearing, but they didn't seem to be the same clothes he was wearing later on when the police were there. He might have had on a sports jacket and dress pants, a belt. I'm not sure because I didn't stay. I don't believe Mr. Broderick saw me because he wasn't looking in my direction. I ran back to my car."

Bowles and Gordon exchanged looks. There it was. All wrapped up in one, long, loose sentence.

Lisette sat prim and downcast, awaiting their inevitable questions.

"Time, Lisette?"

"I recall looking at my watch. It was 10:20. I thought of taking my watch and leaving it in the house so I could prove I had been there."

"Where did you go, Lisette?"

"I was sore and I didn't know what to think, so I went to my girlfriend's and stayed there a while. I didn't tell my girlfriend M— D—— what I saw. I decided to go back later to find out what had happened. The police were there. I hesitated before going in and talking briefly to Mr. Broderick. He said that Mrs. Broderick had had an accident. I knew he was responsible. I left there and told Tom Stott that Mr. Broderick killed Mrs. Broderick. I didn't tell Tom Stott what I saw." Tom Stott, the police learned, operated a service station off Hog's Back Road, not far from 18 Beaverton. Lisette had dated him once or twice in the past.

Lisette described her return to 18 Beaverton:

"I was curious and went back. A guy by the name of Mark Deslaurier was already there. (In fact, this person was Michel Deslaurier, a sales representative with Canadian Premier Life.) He had arrived at the Broderick home to pay his respects at 4:30 in the afternoon after he had heard of Anne's death."

The balance of Lisette's fourth statement was a close repetition of what she had said on earlier occasions:

"... Broderick told me that Missy was washing the bathroom tiles and she slipped and hit her face on the tub. I asked if there was blood or bruises or broken teeth or bones. He said there were none, but that there were certain nerves on your face, that if you were hit there or fell, you would die instantly and this is what happened to Missy, she hit a nerve. Deep down inside I knew this was not true. While I was there, he went to do the wash. I didn't see what he was washing, but when I went to the bathroom, the pink bathmat was gone. While I was there, he called a doctor who's a personal friend of his to see what the chances of her living were, and each time he talked to the doctor he seemed relieved because he told me that the doctor said that her chances of living were not very good. He said that he hoped she would die because she would be a vegetable for the rest of her life, but I felt that he was afraid that she might come to and say something."

Then, with a foretaste of things to come, Lisette volunteered a modification to her earlier statement. She had not heard screaming coming from inside the house.

"When the police talked to me then I was scared. I told them I heard screaming, but that was not true. I felt I had to tell them something because I didn't know whether or not one of the neighbours saw me drive up, but as far as looking in the mailbox and seeing the dog, and all the rest of it, that is true."

Detective Gordon, who had been furiously taking down the statement, arranged to have it typed up immediately.

It was late by the time the typing was completed, so Gordon drove Lisette home. They arranged for her to go with them the next day to a Justice of the Peace to swear the statement.

With Lisette gone the investigators got together for their ritual evening drink and council-of-war. They wondered what had prompted her to finally break down and tell what she had seen.

The wire-tappers, Williams and Chapman, would soon provide a partial answer.

The day before, on February 6th, M---- B----, owner of the house where Lisette lived, phoned the Ottawa Police Department to report a break-in at the house. At about 5:20 in the evening on that day, an unknown person broke into the residence through a window, rummaging through the house, and searching through personal papers. The intruder was scared off by K---- B----, his wife, who was the only one home at the time. The investigators were satisfied that the intrusion had been committed specifically to frighten Lisette and to dissuade her from speaking with the police. She had no valuables or tangible incriminating evidence. The police decided it was intimidation, pure and simple.

The next day, before Lisette contacted the police in preparation for making her final, formal statement, she got a call from George Broderick. He wanted her to come over. She said no. He backed off, then casually asked her what she knew of the progress being made by the police. She said "Nothing!" Finally he said that he was getting tired of the police investigation and reiterated that the death was accidental. His voice was heavy with frustration and impatience.

The nuisance phone calls continued to plague Lisette, everything from silence to immediate hang ups and heavy breathing. While the police had suspicions about the identity of the caller, they were in no doubt as to the purpose of the calls— to frighten and upset Lisette so badly that she would refuse to testify.

It could have been that call from Broderick that finally sent Lisette back to Detective Gordon.

Promptly at 11:40 the next morning, Gordon and Lisette sat in front of Justice of the Peace Lynn Coulter in her private courthouse office on Nicholas Street in Ottawa. Lisette's statement from the day before had been typed up and she read it over slowly in the presence of the J.P.

"Have you read the statement and do you agree with the contents?"

"Yes, I have and I do."

"Are you prepared to swear to it?"

"Yes."

The Justice handed Lisette a bible and administered the oath. "Do you swear the contents of this statement to be true so help you God?"

"I do."

Lisette set the bible back down on the desk and signed the document.

The Crown attorney's office was half a block away. Bowles, Mancuso, Gordon and Lisette all showed up together to talk with prosecuting attorneys Lindsay and Berzins. The prosecutors went over her statement with her. It was clear, in law, that Lisette's testimony as evidenced by this sworn statement was more than sufficient to issue a warrant for the arrest of George Broderick.

That evening at 9:09 p.m., Detective Gordon tried phoning George Broderick on the pretext of discussing the investigation, but Broderick was playing it cagey. Then, just after 11:00 p.m., Gordon phoned Lisette, saying they would like to speak with her again. She agreed and Gordon picked her up and drove her to the Talisman. It was 11:30 p.m. The investigators had Lisette phone Broderick from their room, to confront him with what she had seen. They wanted to gauge his reaction. She complied, telling Broderick that she was still afraid to come down to see him because she had been at the Broderick home about 10:30 a.m. on the day of Anne's death. She said that at that time she heard Anne screaming and the dog barking in a crazy way. Broderick just laughed it off. He and Anne had only been discussing the recent Quebec election, he said.

There was nothing else of significance in the conversation. But it caught the officers' attention that Broderick did not deny being there at that precise point in time, which was inconsistent with what he had said in his previous statements to the police.

The phones were busy that night.

Cynthia Eauclaire received a telephone call from her daughter and expressed the view that she thought she would not be working at Canadian Premier Life very much longer. She ventured that George Broderick was going to be arrested very soon. Cynthia thought she might like to pick up two suitcases from her daughter's but was afraid that if she was being followed by the police, they might think she was leaving the country. She expressed fear their names and reputations would be damaged when all this became public in the press. Lastly, she worried that George Broderick would get 25 years in jail.

Then there was another phone call from Lisette to George Broderick. She confronted him about the nuisance calls she had been getting. Broderick denied any responsibility for these calls. She then asked him what he wanted her to say about her attendance at the house at the time of the murder. Broderick replied, with consistency, "Tell the truth."

During this telephone conversation, Lisette and George Broderick talked about the morning of Anne's death again. Broderick did not vary from his original story. The only thing that upset Broderick at all was Lisette's admission to him that she had told the police about going to bed with George two days after Anne's death. With that, George cut off the conversation and abruptly hung up on her.

11.

The investigators were now sprinting toward an early arrest of George Broderick.

Most of the next day was spent huddled with the prosecutors. Dr. Hillsdon-Smith came in from Toronto to look at the medical aspects of the case again.

Gordon spoke with Lisette during the day to reassure her that she was in no difficulty with the law, and to reassure her that the nuisance calls would soon stop. The police were masking their concern, however. She was being subjected to ever-increasing pressure and harassment from the phone calls. They suspected too that the calls would probably not end, at least until Broderick was arrested.

But the investigators' troubles with Lisette were far from over.

In the early morning hours of February 10th, after everyone had gone to bed, Inspector Bowles was awakened by a call from Lisette to his room in the Talisman. She wanted him to meet her in the bar. She sounded desperate. Before Bowles could finish dressing, there was a knock on his door and she was standing there, forlorn, upset, and sobbing. She begged him to allow her to spend the night there, saying that she would sleep on the chesterfield. Bowles replied, "Absolutely not." He left the door open and then phoned Constable Rod

Williams, asleep in another room, who arrived within seconds. Lisette was still crying and muttering that "Gerry was going to get her." She kept repeating that the police did not understand what a madman he was, that he idolized his father and would do anything for him.

Bowles shared Lisette's anxiety. He noted that she had not been drinking.

In the midst of her wailing, Lisette attacked the bed, punching it with her fists, saying "I saw her little feet, I saw her little feet."

Bowles was trying to make sense of this while trying to calm her down. But Lisette would not stop wailing.

Bowles understood her to say:

When Lisette was looking through the window, she saw George Broderick dragging Anne through the kitchen and down the hallway towards the bathroom, with his arms under Mrs. Broderick's arms. Broderick was wearing a sports jacket, dress slacks, a shirt and a tie— not the same clothing that she saw him in later that morning, a grey suit.

Bowles grabbed it fast! The unexpected, graphic description of Broderick dragging Anne's body down the hall was dynamite stuff. And it was detailed down to what he had been wearing.

When Lisette showed up in Bowles' room, he had instantly told Constable Williams to reach Murray Gordon and get him there. Gordon arrived within the hour. His presence had an immediate settling effect on Lisette. Bowles then recounted out loud to Gordon, so Lisette could hear, what Lisette had just told him about seeing George drag the body down the hallway.

Lisette nodded in agreement with Bowles' recitation.

Detective Gordon sat with Lisette, talking with her, calming her down. She sobbed that she was terrified of going to court and very much afraid for her life.

Bowles interjected, asking her *how* George had been dragging the body.

"His arms were under hers," she replied. She then demonstrated what she meant.

Bowles probably wished he had never asked her the next question, because ultimately it did not advance his cause.

He asked her how she could enter into a sexual relationship with George Broderick, after the death, knowing as she did that he had killed Anne?

The imprudent question drove Lisette back into her shell.

It was obvious that she was consumed by guilt and fear. She became frantic. Abruptly, she changed her story. She took it all back! Everything she had just told them was a lie, she said. She had *not* been there earlier that morning and she did *not* see or hear anything. What she had said about hearing Anne scream was not true.

But the short, explosive retraction was not delivered with the conviction of her earlier statements.

The retraction was seen as an emotional response, unrelated to the truth.

Detective Gordon settled her down again and there was more gentle discussion. Then she switched back, retracting her retraction. She painfully confirmed that everything she had told the officers was true. And yet, she said, she was not entirely sure in her own mind whether she was imagining it or not.

Bowles asked Gordon and Williams to drive her home. Now wide awake, they returned to the Talisman to make their notes and to commiserate.

Then they all went back to bed to rest up for the coming day.

At 1:00 that afternoon, the investigators met with Mac Lindsay and Andrejs Berzins for a last-minute review of these developments and the evidence. The prosecutors were unanimous. There was now adequate evidence to support a charge of first degree murder. Three hours later, Mancuso, accompanied by Bowles, went to Justice of the Peace Coulter and swore out a charge of first degree murder against George Broderick. An arrest warrant was issued immediately.

For Mancuso, it had been a long, winding road. But in many respects, the journey had just begun.

The arrest of a known, identified suspect on a serious charge can range from a very formal, courteous meeting to a parking lot punch-up. It is always a time for caution. People have been known to react strangely while being arrested for murder.

Since Mancuso had been investigating Broderick for quite a few weeks under the guise of accidental death, the arrest would be the equivalent of Mancuso calling Broderick a liar to his face. He would be rejecting the explanations that Broderick had given him. He would, in effect, be disclosing what his true purpose had been all along. It was highly unlikely that Broderick would react with warmth to his arrest and the accusation of murder.

Mancuso and Bowles decided to take no chances.

After their meeting with the prosecutors broke up late in the afternoon, they began a search for George Broderick to serve the murder warrant and to arrest him. Broderick could be anywhere and the officers wanted to avoid violence and avoid provoking Broderick into flight.

Constable Chapman, the O.P.P. wire-tap man known as "The Duck," tried unsuccessfully to get a trace on Broderick's whereabouts from the "bird dog" tracking device he had installed in Broderick's Cougar. No luck. (Chapman would later learn that because it was a very cold night Broderick had been using the heater in his car. This confused the bird dog, making it ineffective.) The police were left to rely on street procedures. Nothing helpful was coming in on the wire-taps, so Mancuso began making the rounds of places where he knew Broderick hung out. By 7:00 in the evening, after several visits, he found Broderick's Cougar parked behind the Canadian Premier Life office on Laurier Avenue West. But Broderick was not in his office.

Three and a half hours later they found him in the lounge of the Carleton Towers Hotel on Albert Street.

Broderick was seated at a table with a group of people including the lounge's good-looking blonde singer. George was preoccupied, regaling them with stories. Mancuso couldn't hear what was being said and Broderick could not see Mancuso.

It was a stand-off. Wait. Avoid violence. Avoid a scene. The lounge was half full.

Mancuso went to the front entrance and spoke with Bowles and Gordon, who were waiting there. They called the assistant manager over and flashed their badges. Mancuso pointed out George Broderick seated in the lounge. He asked the assistant manager to tell Broderick that some people wanted to speak to him at the front entrance. As a precaution, Mancuso sent Gordon around to the back of the hotel to cover the rear entrance in case Broderick was spooked and tried to make a run for it out the back way.

The manager whispered discreetly to Broderick.

Reluctantly, Broderick left his group with the feigned exasperation of someone who is constantly being interrupted for important consultations. At first he had some difficulty suppressing his surprise at seeing Bowles and Mancuso there. They had never bothered him this late at night before.

Broderick's attitude was unconcerned and breezy.

"Hello, Bill! What are you doing out so late at night?" he addressed Bowles. "More questions?"

Mancuso jumped in, pulling the blue Warrant of Arrest from his pocket. He was all business.

"George Broderick, I have here a warrant for your arrest on the charge of first degree murder in the death of Anne Broderick, under Section 218 of the Criminal Code. I caution that you are not bound to say anything, but whatever you do say may be taken down in writing and given in evidence at your trial."

"Oh, shit!" was all George Broderick could manage.

Mancuso reached out and took George Broderick by the arm, establishing the physical contact which many old line detectives believed was necessary to make a formal arrest.

If George Broderick was initially surprised, he quickly overcame it. Consistent to the end, he tried to schmooze the police.

"Look, fellas, I've had a few drinks and I'm with some people here tonight. Can I just go to my room? I'll see you tomorrow. I've made some appointments for the morning, but I'll see you at the station around noon. We'll get this business cleared up then."

Broderick was treating his arrest as a minor annoyance, like a parking

ffort

ticket, flies to be brushed from his shoulder. He'd explain it all to his good friends the police later, okay?

But Bowles wasn't buying it, and administered a secondary caution to Broderick about saying anything more.

Mancuso deftly spun George around, snapped the handcuffs on him and hustled him into the back seat of the police cruiser. Detective Gordon sat in the front seat next to Bowles, who drove.

Once in the police cruiser, Bowles activated the ubiquitous tape recorder hidden in the briefcase. It stayed on until they arrived at the station, but the officers were careful not to engage Broderick in any probing conversation at this stage, so nothing of significance was recorded.

Broderick was searched and placed in a holding cell. Within the hour he voluntarily provided two breath samples to a breathalyzer technician. Two readings of 100 mgs and 110 mgs in 100 mls of blood respectively put him over the limit for driving, but hardly drunk. The breath technician observed that the effects of alcohol were slight.

With the arrest, Mancuso's quadrille with Broderick was essentially over. The ballet of the lawyers was about to begin.

Bowles and Mancuso spent the next couple of days getting ready for the bail hearing, which had to be scheduled quickly. Canadian courts are reluctant to hold charged persons in custody for long periods of time before their trials, and the prospect of George Broderick being released pending trial was very real.

The officers renewed their resolve to resist bail for George Broderick, partly as a result of a phone call from Lisette four days after Broderick's arrest. She had continued living with the B—— family. The harassing phone calls had not subsided after Broderick's arrest. There were never any overt threats, no words spoken. Just the aggravating, fear-instilling interruptions of phone calls coming at all hours of the day and night, with no one on the line. It conveyed a message to Lisette. She became extremely fearful that Broderick was going to be released on bail; her earlier fear of him was now greatly multiplied.

As a result of this torment, her own doubts about what she had seen or heard on the morning of November 16th intensified. Bowles recognized this and proposed that she be seen by the psychiatrist, Dr. Rowsell. She agreed. It would help her to assemble and distinguish, in her own mind, fact from fiction.

The officers continued to give her support, consolation and reassurance. To help matters, Bowles suggested a little experiment.

The next day, at 4:30 in the afternoon, Bowles and Detective Gordon— Mancuso again being deliberately absent— drove to the B---- residence, picked up Lisette and brought her to 18 Beaverton. Bowles parked the cruiser in the driveway in the same location where Lisette said she had parked on her first visit to the house on November 16th. Alighting from the car, she re-enacted the event, proceeding along the walk up the front steps. She peered into the mailbox momentarily, then opened the screen door. She hesitated as if re-living something too painful. She paused on the steps and looked through the window of the front door. Lisette was trying to remember. From her vantage point, she could see the kitchen and the dining room area.

"That's where Cindy Lou was running around and barking," she said.

Lisette then drew back from the window. It was obvious from the look on her face that she was puzzled.

"I'm still not sure that I was here that morning," she repeated. "But something in my mind tells me I was." She glanced back through the window, swinging her gaze first to one side and then the other. "I am sure I saw George using his foot to push the bathroom door open when he was dragging Anne. I'm sure."

Bowles and Gordon watched and listened in silence.

"But if I saw that, then I must have been *inside* the house and I don't think I was."

The detectives were satisfied that she was trying very hard, and in the process going through considerable torment. She might have seen what she described so graphically in her third and fourth statements, yet, in the mental maelstrom, she could not *accept* that she had seen it. As a result, she thought she might not have seen it, and she now merely *imagined* that she had.

Her confusion was complete. The experiment was inconclusive.

In her earlier statements, Lisette had specifically described the clothing that George Broderick was wearing when she saw him dragging Anne's body. The day after George Broderick's arrest, Detective Gordon and Constable Holland conducted a warranted search at Room 101 in the Parkway Hotel where George Broderick had been staying after he was finally evicted from 18 Beaverton. The officers seized a number of items, including George Broderick's clothing.

The day after the abortive experiment at the house, the officers, as much to allay Lisette's fears as for any other reason, went to the B---- residence and put a recorder on her telephone. They hoped to find out who was making the harassing calls. Then they drove her to the station where she was told that she would be entering a room to observe some items of clothing. She would be asked if she could identify any of George's clothing, from either the first or second time that she had seen George Broderick on the morning of November 16th.

Lisette entered the room, looked over the array of clothing and immediately picked out George Broderick's grey suit.

"This is what he was wearing the second time I was there," she said with certainty. She continued her examination, spending a few minutes before she selected a pair of rust-coloured slacks. In her statements she had described Broderick as wearing rust-coloured slacks when she saw him on her first visit. The police waited for her identification.

"All I can say is that they look familiar." The sight of George's clothing was causing her distress. She quickly left the room.

George Broderick's bail hearing was on March 3rd, 1977. Although the case was entirely circumstantial and despite a nine-to-12-month backlog in the courts before trial, Justice Holland of the Supreme Court of Ontario was sufficiently impressed with the strength of the prosecution's case that George Broderick was denied bail. Mancuso was the principal witness for the prosecution. Broderick's lawyer, Richard Bosada, argued with great reason and passion, stressing that the total absence of any evidence of Anne's cause of death must inevitably result in an acquittal and that Broderick should therefore not be held in custody. But bail was denied. George Broderick became a permanent resident of the Regional Detention Centre, pending his preliminary hearing.

His incarceration seemed to lift some of the burden from Lisette, who again changed her story and agreed to go to Toronto to be interviewed by Dr. Rowsell. Lisette wanted her landlady, Mrs. K---- B----, to accompany her. Mancuso would make the necessary arrangements.

12.

With the announcement of George Broderick's arrest for the murder of his wife Anne, other witnesses with something to offer started coming forward. Tom Stott, the operator of Brookfield Garage, had been one of these.

Kaspar Stauffacher was a Swiss who had emigrated to Canada and become a citizen. Although employed as a bush pilot in northern British Columbia, Ottawa was his home. He started taking out life insurance policies with Canadian Premier Life in 1955 when it was known by the name of Continental Insurance. He had come to know George Broderick, and had been forwarding his annual premium cheques to George since 1973. George, in turn, was supposed to have been forwarding Stauffacher's premiums to head office in Winnipeg. On one occasion, George had told him that he sent the cheque to Winnipeg but that they had lost it. Stauffacher said that Broderick always made it a point to inquire when he would be going north for the summer, but he expected this as part of the business. In January, 1976, he called Broderick to inquire about the value of his insurance policy, which had by now matured. Broderick persuaded him to leave the money with the company in an annuity plan at a favourable interest rate. Stauffacher agreed, subject to confirmation from head office as to the present value of the policy. Three months later, Stauffacher called Broderick since he still had received no confirmation. He had to leave soon to go north for the fire season, and would be gone until September. Broderick promised him that the confirmation would be at his house when he returned in September. When Stauffacher returned there was still no confirmation. He phoned Broderick to find out what was going on. Broderick instructed him not to come to the Canadian Premier office any more; he would visit him at his home instead. On September 7th, 1976, about two months before Anne's death, Broderick went to Stauffacher's and wrote out a letter on Canadian Premier letterhead, confirming that the proceeds of the insurance policies had been received and the proceeds re-invested in the annuity plan.

Stauffacher had misgivings about all this cloak-and-dagger stuff. He told Broderick he wanted confirmation of the amount and further confirmation that it had been properly invested.

At the beginning of November, 1976, before Anne's death, Broderick went to Stauffacher's workplace. Stauffacher described what happened:

"He came to my place of work with a form from Canadian Premier Life Insurance head office in Winnipeg with a breakdown of the amount of money that my matured policy was worth, totalling $7517.79. This document looked real and I was satisfied with it. Then Broderick told me that he could invest the money in his company at 10% interest if it was in his name. He further explained that if I did it on my own, I would only get 6% the first year and 9 1/4% the second year. I briefly discussed possibly investing another $10,000 at this interest rate, as well as turning over to Broderick the money my matured policy was worth. A few days later, prior to his wife's death, he contacted me again about this investment, and I told him to give me a few more days. I wanted to think about it."

Stauffacher called him back "around the middle of November" and found out that Broderick's wife had died. Then, "I waited a couple of weeks and he called me at work and came to see me the next day."

Broderick gave Stauffacher yet another version of the events surrounding Anne's death.

"He said he had got up in the morning, his daughter had left for university, and he had left around 9:00 a.m. for work. He said his wife told him she was going to have a bath and be ready by 10:30 to go shopping with him. He went to his office and phoned home to see if she was ready and there was no answer. He then went home to pick up his wife. When he arrived, he found the door unlocked. (He had told his wife to leave the door open as the neighbour had to do some repairs in the kitchen). When he found his wife in the bathtub, he ran to check with the neighbour to see if he had done the repairs. The neighbour said no and Mr. Broderick told him to call an ambulance. He told me he had given artificial respiration and had managed to get her heart beating until the ambulance arrived. He told me that she must have slipped in the bathtub. He had been after her for years to get those skid mats, but she always forgot to get them."

But Stauffacher wasn't swallowing this.

"The whole thing sounded funny and I was somewhat suspicious. I had seen a movie on TV about eight years ago, where a woman was murdered in the bathtub. I said to Mr. Broderick, 'Do you mind if I ask you a rude question?' He told me to go ahead, and I said, 'Did you put your wife away?' He said nothing for a couple of minutes, then stood up and became slightly emotional. He said, 'Why should I do that? I've been happily married for over 30 years.' I said, 'What about your girlfriend?' 'My wife has known about the girlfriend for over four years.' I told him at this time that I wanted a couple of more days to think about it, and to give me a call later."

The last thing the police needed at this stage was a totally new version of the events of November 16th, served up by George Broderick.

But the best was yet to come.

"Somewhere around the 12th of December, he again came to see me at work. He told me at this time that his wife had been cremated and that the autopsy showed nothing. He said I had put him in a bad spot with the insurance company. He said he had made arrangements to invest the $10,000 by December 15th, 1976, with Canadian Premier Life Insurance Company. I asked him about security for the $10,000. He said if he died, it would buy $55,000 paid to his estate, and I said, 'What if you go to jail?' He said, 'If I go to jail, the cash value will be $26,000.' He then agreed to draw up a collateral agreement on his life insurance."

These discussions with Stauffacher occurred four weeks after Anne's death, at a time when George Broderick believed the police were investigating an accidental drowning.

A little knowledge is a dangerous thing. Mr. Stauffacher decided to invest his money as George Broderick had persuaded him to do.

"In Switzerland, a body is cremated only if the police are satisfied that nothing is wrong. I told him that I would let him invest the money for two months in his company and if everything went well (and if he wasn't arrested for murder), I would keep the money invested longer."

Not very good for Mr. Stauffacher.

Three days later, George Broderick drove Stauffacher to Montreal. They went to the Royal Bank at Belanger and Delormier Streets. Stauffacher took out a bank draft for $10,000 payable to George Allan Broderick personally. Broderick drove Stauffacher back to work in Ottawa. A month later, Stauffacher was still demanding his collateral assignment and receipts for his investments. Stauffacher said he would go to Broderick's office to get them but Broderick protested. He would rather deliver them personally the following day. The next day Broderick did deliver the collateral assignment and two receipts for a total amount of $17,517.79, backdated to November 1st, 1976. He promised that on his return from Winnipeg he would bring the completed collateral assignment from the insurance company's head office.

In early February the prophetic Mr. Stauffacher learned that Broderick had been arrested for his wife's murder.

When asked why he would enter into this unorthodox arrangement for the re-investment of his funds with Broderick, Stauffacher replied that since Broderick had been a manager with Canadian Premier Life for over eight years, "I believed that I could trust him with investing the money with the insurance company as he had suggested... During the time that I knew Mr. Broderick, he told me he had a consulting firm in South America with four or five electronic engineers. He also told me that he had $30,000 coming in from this company, which he would be getting in January, 1977. He also said that he owned a Super Cub plane on floats worth $12,000 to $15,000. He said he owned his Mercury car and a cottage in Quebec that someone had offered him $55,000 for."

But the Stauffacher revelations, as revealing as they were, did not greatly advance the prosecution's case in the evidentiary sense. They showed Broderick to be a cheat and a liar, something the prosecution already knew, and knew that it could demonstrate to the jury. More evidence was needed.

On March 31st, Detective Gordon picked up Shirley Broderick and took her to Kanata where they did a drive-by at the bungalow her dad said he had bought for Anne. It was a sad event for Shirley, as she looked at the beautiful home with its setting of trees, shrubs, flowers and the dreams which were never to come to fruition.

On the same day, Mancuso and Gordon met at the station and conscripted Donna Wallace, a civilian employee with the police force. Donna was about the same height, weight, and build as Anne Broderick.

She got her swim suit and the whole team— Mancuso, Gordon, Wallace, Constable Holland and Sergeant McGarvey, the ident men— went to 18 Beaverton. They did not go to re-enact the "accident," but rather to take measurements and observations.

Donna Wallace would be the corpse of Anne Broderick.

The bathtub was filled to the same level measured on the morning of November 16th by Constable Holland. Donna Wallace, clad in her two piece bathing suit, took a position in the water on her left side, face down in the water with her feet tucked underneath the faucet and her head at the opposite end.

Officer McGarvey took colour photographs of the scene from a variety of vantage points, viewing the body as someone might see it on approaching the partly opened bathroom door. For the model to fit entirely inside the tub of water, she had to adopt a serpentine condition, her knees together, drawn up in a fetal curl.

In a second position, she lay flat on her back in the water, feet underneath the tap, body out straight. This posture put her head and shoulders out of the water with the back of her head resting on the rim of the tub, unsubmerged. Then photographs were taken of her standing in the corner next to the faucet, demonstrating the position of the faucet and the taps relative to her knees and thighs, where bruises had been observed on the body of Anne Broderick.

While this was being done, Mancuso was systematically nosing around the house. The interior of the house, while still tidy, had not been cleaned since the date of the death, except for the bathroom. After George Broderick had moved out, the house had been sealed and re-keyed. No one else had had access since that time.

Mancuso stood in the doorway of the master bedroom, looking from the bedroom to the bathroom, trying to imagine what had taken place the morning of November 16th. He imagined Anne Broderick asleep in the bed. He imagined her going from the bedroom to the bathroom wearing her robe and night clothes. And then the question that continued to confound: how did the clothing get back to the master bedroom and why was it in reverse order on top of the bed?

As he surveyed the scene, assessing the route from the bedroom to the bathroom, Mancuso speculated that Anne Broderick had been taken forcibly in her half-dead, half-alive condition from the bedroom to the bathroom. Every other explanation was either too lame, improbable, or self-serving.

What had happened to her then, here in this bedroom? Had she been throttled unconscious? Had she put up any fight? He tried to picture Broderick grappling and groping with the terror-stricken woman. A speck embedded in the carpet on Anne's side of the bed caught Mancuso's eye. He could not tell immediately what it was. It was obscured by the nap of the carpeting and the overhang of the bed. Had something been missed on the first go around? Mancuso got down on one knee and separated the pile of the carpeting: It was one of Anne's fingernails! Mancuso remembered the three false fingernails that had been found the morning of Anne's death and the other piece he'd seen that first morning, embedded in the carpet.

Shirley had told him that her mother always put her false fingernails away after taking them off. But those had been found in plain view on the nightstand. Mancuso remembered the autopsy photographs of Anne's body. Two fingernails had been broken on one hand— not the false fingernails but the natural fingernails!

Mancuso gently lifted the fingernail from the carpet by the bed and examined it. It was a natural fingernail, and broken, not cut.

The question in Mancuso's mind became clear. Had some act of violence taken place here in the bedroom during which, in an act of desperate resistance, Anne had broken her natural fingernails?

Constable Holland, the ident officer, bagged and tagged the broken fingernail.

A date of June 24th had been set for the preliminary hearing. And while the legal test at a preliminary hearing is weighted in favour of the prosecution, the investigators recognized that the evidence ultimately presented at a trial was usually no better than what was available for the preliminary hearing. Time was running out and there was still work to be done.

Shower curtain hooks and rings comparable to those at the death scene had to be obtained for testing. More interviews had to be conducted.

They interviewed Anne Broderick's cousin, who had spoken with George Broderick after the funeral. By now it was not surprising to the officers that George had given Anne's cousin a version of events which contained more new, minor, variations. Again, he tried to explain why he was having her quickly cremated. He did not want Anne put in a grave where there was dampness and water and where it would have the same effect on her as on drowned sailors during the war. Curiously, he also told the cousin that he found it odd that Anne's clothing was found in the bedroom and none in the bathroom. She was a modest person, and would never go into the bathroom without some clothes, he said.

In early April, Inspector Bowles received a letter from Drummond and Company, a firm of lawyers and notaries in Edinburgh, Scotland. The letter had been written on March 29th, 1977. The solicitors represented a Mrs. Anne Frew. George Broderick appeared to have defrauded Mrs. Frew in the amount of $15,000.

Mrs. Frew was quite elderly and had been a Canadian resident until the death of her husband, at which time she had returned to her native Scotland. She did not wish to travel to Canada to testify, but did provide a statement.

Her husband had taken out insurance with Canadian Premier Life and George Broderick was the acting agent. They had never socialized with Broderick. Mrs. Frew's husband died in 1973, and George Broderick had taken care of all of the papers for her claim under her husband's insurance policy. Subsequently, Broderick proposed to her that some of the money be re-invested. In 1974 or 1975, she had written him out a cheque for $15,000, on the understanding that she was investing it with Canadian Premier Life and that this was in the normal course of Broderick's duties as an insurance agent.

She had written to Broderick on July 10th, 1976, asking why she had not received any reply to an earlier letter: "I had been wondering about the money you were going to invest for me." She pointed out that the $15,000 had been withdrawn from her savings account rather than her chequing account. She was curious to know what was happening.

In response, Broderick had telephoned her, she said, saying that he had been very ill and hospitalized for some time but would now tend to her affairs.

During this time, the investigators were also contacted by a firm of Quebec notaries, in Pointe Gatineau, Quebec, on the road to "Dreemcumtru."

Their complaint was simple. A Mrs. Adrienne Tremblay had received monies from an estate and had loaned $10,000 to George Broderick. The loan had been processed through their law firm. Broderick had used the cottage as collateral and Mrs. Tremblay was still owed nearly the full $10,000.

It was one more weakness in the house of cards that Broderick had constructed.

The next individual to surface in this parade of claimants was the elderly Mrs. Alice Pilon, whose story was almost identical, although she had lost a lesser amount. She had been a client of Canadian Premier Life for many years. She knew and trusted her agent, George Broderick, so when, in 1972, he asked for a loan of $2,200 to be paid six months later at 10% interest, she had no qualms. In December of that year, she advanced him a further $2,000 to be repaid within six months at 12% interest. Broderick had made small payments to her in cash, but as of the date of Anne's death, more than four years after the initial loan, Mrs. Pilon was still owed $1,300. No interest had ever been paid.

By the middle of April, 1977, eight weeks before the start of the preliminary hearing, the police located a supplier for the same hooks that had been on the shower curtain at 18 Beaverton. The firm, Trend Notions and Novelties, was located on historic St. Hubert Street in Montreal, and was headed up by a cooperative gentleman, Albert Moyse, who oversaw the obtaining of identical hooks and the making up of shower curtains for testing and for court purposes. The results of these tests were to prove crucial when the prosecution built its circumstantial case in the course of the trial.

Then new problems surfaced with Lisette.

In another of her quixotic cycles of cooperation and non-cooperation, she agreed to speak with the psychiatrist, Dr. Rowsell. The prospect of testifying at the preliminary hearing was forcing her to confront her dilemma. She volunteered to see Dr. Rowsell. She would cooperate.

13.

Detectives Fermoyle and Champagne were assigned to escort George Broderick back and forth from the Regional Detention Centre to the courthouse for his court appearances. It was about a 20 minute run each way. They were under instruction not to question or engage Broderick in conversation, but if he had something to say, to just listen. By now his lawyer, Dick Bosada, would have prudently advised his client not to make any more statements, so it was unlikely that Broderick would open up again anyway.

As time passed, however, and Broderick adjusted to being in custody, he became more expansive with the escorting officers. The need to give some form of explanation was still gnawing at him. At one point, about 10 days before the bail hearing, he gratuitously offered that since he had believed the investigation was an accidental death inquiry, he had not felt any obligation to tell the police *everything*. The implication was that since he hadn't told them everything, they had discovered things on their own which now cast him in a bad light. Broderick told the escorting officers that he now knew that Bowles and Mancuso had discovered both his extreme financial indebtedness and his philandering. He said that he was telling the officers this because he felt that he should be re-interviewed in order to give a more accurate account.

Subsequently Broderick telephoned the police station, trying to contact any one of the principal investigators. He was unsuccessful. They avoided him. Finally, he spoke with Detective Gordon, who said that he would try to arrange for Broderick to be re-interviewed once Inspector Bowles returned from Toronto. An appointment was set up for this specific purpose, but was never kept by the police. Whether they failed to re-interview Broderick for some tactical reason or to prevent cluttering their own case is unclear. But at this stage, since the police were aware Broderick had retained counsel, it would be improper to conduct further interviews unless invited by his lawyer. Broderick at this juncture told the escorting officers that the whole thing was just a bad mistake. He was confident that he would be cleared in the end.

Inspector Bowles was back in Toronto, busy with other cases. With Broderick in jail and the true intent of the investigation publicly revealed, it was left to Mancuso and Gordon to continue with the "mopping up" portion of the investigation, re-interviewing specific witnesses, filling in details and loose ends. Even before the bail hearing on March 3rd, they re-interviewed the Pikes, a good number of the Brodericks' friends and acquaintances, the parish priest, and their daughter Shirley, who asked to be interviewed.

Throughout all of this, the officers lavished attention on Lisette, their critical witness, who was always present in the background.

Mancuso and Gordon also contacted Emile Zidichouski, a supervisor at Canadian Premier Life who had been at Broderick's office at the material time the morning of November 16th. He could offer nothing factual which might assist the police.

Tom Stott recalled Lisette having come into his garage around the date of Anne Broderick's death. Lisette had told him that she had just come from the Brodericks' place and that something had happened there. There were police cars in the driveway, she told him. She described speaking with George Broderick, whom she said had a frightened look on his face.

"She told me that there had been an accident involving Mrs. Broderick and although I don't remember the exact words, she told me that she thought he was responsible for his wife's accident. I told her not to jump to conclusions."

This was the extent of Stott's recollection, but it confirmed the feelings that Lisette was having that morning.

On March 8th, Mancuso spoke with Dr. Rowsell to make final arrangements for the interview with Lisette. They wanted Rowsell's opinion on her ability to recollect events and on her state of mind.

Mancuso and Gordon squeezed in a fast trip to Montreal to collect the duplicate shower curtain hooks and shower curtains from Albert Moyse.

Were the pieces beginning to come together?

On March 21st, Mancuso and Gordon accompanied Lisette and her landlady to Toronto, where they checked into the Oakville Holiday Inn. Mancuso called Dr. Rowsell to confirm that the sessions would begin the following morning. He also let Inspector Bowles know that they were in the city.

For two days, over March 22nd and 23rd, Dr. Rowsell interviewed Lisette. Inspector Bowles was present at these sessions, with Lisette's consent. In fact, she said that she was more comfortable having him present. Bowles was a silent observer at these sessions.

Incredibly, the two days of meetings between Lisette and Dr. Rowsell proved completely unproductive when she again reversed direction. She either could not or would not cooperate with the investigating psychiatrist. She was unable to say what she had seen. This was followed by the contradictory statement that she "wanted to keep it to herself."

The next day Mancuso and Gordon drove Lisette and her landlady back to Ottawa. The whole trip had been a waste of time, but on the way back to Ottawa, Lisette agreed to talk to Mac Lindsay, the prosecutor. Lindsay wanted to meet her personally to assess her effectiveness as a witness, but the investigators doubted that she would be any more cooperative with him than she had been with Dr. Rowsell.

Unexpectedly, Detective Gordon was contacted by Lisette. It was a double-reverse.

Now she wished to speak with Dr. Rowsell again. No, she insisted, she was not wasting their time. The changeable Miss Martineau now promised her full cooperation. She had the detectives spinning and they had no time to lose.

Another appointment was made immediately and the same evening

Mancuso and Gordon flew with her to Toronto. They put her up for the night at the Holiday Inn in Oakville. They treated her courteously, buying her dinner, lending sympathetic ears, showing no impatience. But they tried not to overdo it.

Next morning, April 21st, 1977, they all went to Dr. Rowsell's office in Oakville. Inspector Bowles joined them but this time Dr. Rowsell wanted to see her alone. He rearranged his morning schedule, and set aside the entire morning to talk with Lisette. They arrived at his office at 9:05 in the morning. There was an atmosphere of congeniality. They were pleased to see that Lisette was in good spirits and a cooperative frame of mind.

At 12:30, Dr. Rowsell emerged from his office rubbing his eyes wearily. He reported, with resignation, that Lisette had reversed again. She was not cooperating. She was unresponsive and refused to enter into the dialogue which was necessary for him to make assessments of her recollections. There was nothing more he could do.

He gave the impression that he would prefer not to be troubled further with this matter.

The officers could hardly blame him, and were almost apologetic. The trip had not been their idea in the first place.

Inspector Bowles, always the father figure, took this turn of events in stride and talked with Lisette in a quiet, paternal way. In the course of the exchange, she categorically denied seeing or hearing anything on the morning of the 16th of November. Bowles, in passing, introduced the prospect of her taking a polygraph examination. Lisette was intrigued. She wanted to know how the polygraph worked. Bowles patiently explained it to her.

They left Dr. Rowsell's office and drove to the nearby Hearthside Steak House for lunch. In the car Lisette again expressed her interest in learning how the polygraph worked and how the examination was done. Bowles explained it again in simple, reassuring terms, and said that he could probably have the Peel Regional Police do the examination the next day if she wished. It would be up to her.

It was nearly 3:00 in the afternoon when the group settled into a table at the Hearthside. The luncheon crowd had long since dispersed and the atmosphere was warm and subdued. Lisette relaxed as she listened to Bowles' quiet explanation of the intricacies of the polygraph.

Mancuso was upset but tried not to communicate it. He did not participate in the conversation. He was watching Lisette, completely perplexed by her mercurial machinations.

Here was the single most powerful witness they had, a witness who, while not able to give direct evidence implicating George Broderick, was nonetheless capable of giving circumstantial evidence of the most probative, damaging kind. Mancuso was personally satisfied that she *had* seen George Broderick dragging Anne's body. He felt that she could not have described it with so much detail if she had not *seen* it. On the other hand, her motive for concocting the story, if such was the case, would clearly be that she considered herself wronged and abused by George Broderick in his sexual intimacies with her. In that case, she would be trying to get even. But in Mancuso's assessment she lacked the guile to accomplish this. Besides, if she wanted to "hang" George Broderick by making up a story, it was more likely that she would have said that she saw him actually committing the murder. No, there was a physical credibility about Lisette's description of what she had seen that inclined Mancuso to believe it. He wondered what other demons were tormenting her, forcing her to continually change her position and her attitude of cooperation.

It was the stuff of police textbooks.

Mancuso's reverie was interrupted when Lisette, who had been listening intently to Bowles, broke her silence with a *non sequitur*.

"The stupid bastard didn't lock the door and I walked in!"

The statement gushed as a result of something going on inside her, not in response to anything that Bowles had said. She put her head down and shook it from side to side in disbelief.

"The stupid bastard didn't lock the door and I walked in!" she repeated.

Then, on her own, she flipped over the paper placemat in front of her and took a pen from Bowles. On the back of the placemat she meticulously made a line drawing of a door. Her mouth was quivering and she fought back tears. She struggled getting the words out, but once they were out she became visibly relaxed and relieved.

On the paper she drew the location of the bathroom, a few feet away from the front door, then with equal precision she drew a line from the door to the bathroom and punctuated the line with two little marks.

"These," she said, "are Anne's feet. I saw her little feet, I saw her little feet!"

With this utterance, Lisette again became upset and tearful, falling into a fit of out-of-control sobbing.

Mancuso watched this minor drama unfold, but avoided involving himself. Lisette seemed to be re-living the event she was describing. But there it was again. The same precision. The same detail. She was speaking slowly, deliberately, as she looked down at her placemat.

"Anne was lying on her back on the bathroom floor with no clothes on. Her feet were not straight up but sideways, to the left. George was standing at her head, with his hands under her arms."

No one else at the table spoke. She was letting it out now and it would be risky to interrupt her. In ordinary circumstances, Mancuso and Bowles would both have their notebooks out and would be furiously inscribing her comments for later court use. Instead, they were committing her words to memory. They would record them later.

"I don't think he saw me. He was too busy. I watched for seconds, then ran to the car. I checked my watch. It was 10:20 a.m."

She paused, as if pondering some question.

"I thought of returning to put my watch in the closet, just inside the door, to prove I had been there, but I did not!"

There was a long silence. Finally Bowles asked her, quietly, whether she could recollect what George Broderick had been wearing at that time. She said she was not sure, but it seemed like a sports jacket and a pair of slacks.

"Not the same clothes he was wearing when I went the second time."

Bowles realized that Lisette had begun her recitation of these events at a point already well into her story, a point that obviously triggered a response from her. He decided to back her up a bit and asked her how she came to be in a position to see those things. She repeated that she was just going over to visit Anne, that she had parked the car in the drive and walked up to the steps. She had looked in the mailbox, then through the front door window into the hallway. The dog Cindy Lou was very excited and barking.

"I opened the door and stepped into the hallway. Cindy Lou stopped barking." It was then, she said, that she saw Anne on the bathroom floor, and "I just knew she was dead." This was why, she said, that when she went back the second time and George told her "Missy's had an accident," she felt like saying to him, "Bullshit, you killed her!"

This was also the reason, she said, that she told Tom Stott over at the Brookfield Garage that she thought George had killed Anne.

When she stopped speaking it was over. There was nothing more coming out and the officers knew that it would be useless to prod or probe. What she had said had been said with great certainty and as much precision as she seemed capable of. To the officers, she seemed to be scrupulous about what she said or didn't say, as to what she remembered or didn't remember. She had been suffering in her effort to be truthful and accurate.

Lisette picked up the pen and wrote on the placemat: "November 16, 1976, 10:20. I opened the front door of the house. I saw Missy, small feet, in the bathroom. She had no clothes on. Mr. Broderick, I don't think he saw me— Signed: Lisette Martineau, April 21, 1977, 3:35 p.m. Witnessed: W.C. Bowles, R. Mancuso."

Lisette folded up the placemat and handed it to Inspector Bowles.

This, without a doubt, had been the single most spontaneous and reliable description given by Lisette of her recollections. Moreover, the officers were impressed by the fact that Lisette had done it to satisfy herself, to relieve her own anxieties, rather than to satisfy the police.

Bowles drove Lisette, Mancuso, and Gordon back to the airport. During the return flight to Ottawa, Lisette confided to Mancuso that she had a solid relationship with her new boyfriend, Ryan, and that she wanted to tell Ryan about her sexual involvement with Broderick as well as what she had witnessed on the morning of November 16th, 1976. She felt, she said, that it would be better if she told him now rather than having him find out about it from the newspapers during the trial.

As a result of all this, Mancuso sent Officers McGarvey and Holland of the ident section back to 18 Beaverton to photograph exactly the view a person would have when looking through both the living room window and the front door window into the house.

With bail refused and George Broderick biding his time in the Detention Centre, the officers had time to continue to backfill their investigation and to fine tune it as directed by the prosecutors, Lindsay and Berzins.

Mancuso and Bowles flew back to Winnipeg, where they executed a search warrant at Canadian Premier Life to gain possession of original documents and the breakdown on Anne's life insurance policies. Detective Gordon re-examined the whole business regarding the purchase of the new bungalow in Kanata, through the Royal Trust Company Real Estate department. He continued to act as liaison with Lisette and made himself available whenever she wished to talk.

Officers McGarvey and Holland conducted more tests in the tub at 18 Beaverton and, at the request of the prosecutors, examined the entire house again in search of blood spatters. There were none.

In early May, Bowles and Mancuso met with Lisette at Branscombe's Motor Hotel in Ottawa. The whole situation was discussed with Lisette and her new boyfriend, as she had wished.

Tests were performed in which the blue bath oil beads were added to the same amount of water at the same temperature, progressively, and photographed until a blue was obtained that exactly matched the colour of the water as photographed on November 16th, 1976. The whole thing was turned over to professional colour laboratories for analysis and the officers went to the main Kodak labs at Rochester, New York, where, for consistency, they obtained film from the same lot to make the strip photographs.

Mancuso and Gordon made another sweep through the Quebec countryside and executed a search warrant at the law offices of the Quebec notaries regarding the Pilon complaint. Finally, they again drove the route that George Broderick had said he used on the morning of Anne's death.

This time it took just 44 minutes.

14.

With the preliminary hearing set to begin on June 24th, 1977, Mancuso and Gordon became immersed in paperwork, assembling the multitude of police reports, witness statements, medical reports, technical data and photographs into two large court "briefs" totalling over 475 pages; the briefs would enable the prosecutors to present the case in an understandable sequence. Copies were given to the defence lawyers. There are no intentional surprises in a Canadian criminal courtroom.

The intermezzo gave Mancuso an opportunity to look into another area, not of evidentiary value, but of background importance: the "Brides in the Bath" case.

The case had been documented 10 years earlier in *Readers' Digest Condensed Books* under a section entitled "The Century of the Detective." The investigation and trial of the case are well known to law students, who study it for its technical, pathological, and demonstrative evidence aspects.

In January, 1915, Detective Inspector Arthur Neal of Scotland Yard had his attention drawn to reports that recently married wives of a Mr. George Smith were being found dead, apparently by accident, in their bathtubs. The first death had occurred in December, 1913, in Blackpool; the second in December, 1914, in Highgate, the detective inspector's precinct.

There were similarities between the two deaths. In each case, the couple had been travelling; the wife complained of headache; a physician was consulted, after which the wife took a bath and was subsequently discovered, apparently drowned.

When Inspector Neal began to look into the second occurrence, he found it difficult to believe that a person could drown in a tub as described. In each case there was minimal bruising to the body and no signs of violence. He learned that the suspect had used three aliases: "Lloyd," "Williams," and "Smith." He learned that the husband in each case had shown no grief at his wife's death and had ordered the cheapest coffin. The inspector's investigation of these two cases turned up a third, in February of 1912, in Hearne Bay, a small English seaside resort. The hallmarks of the death were much the same.

The suspect, Smith, was the son of an insurance agent and the collection of life insurance was the likely motive in each case.

The deaths had been variously attributed to shock, heart problems, epileptic fit, and drowning. The inspector remained of the opinion, however, that the tubs were generally too small for the victims to have died in that manner. In the "Williams" death, the victim was five feet seven and the tub only five feet long, so that the upper part of the body would have been pushed up the sloping end of the tub far above the level of the water. There would have been violent spasms of the limbs in which the limbs were drawn up to the body and then flung outward with subsequent relaxation of the muscles. The tub was simply too small.

The pathologist in that case stated that the victim's head was under water with her legs extended and her feet protruding above the water. The investigators saw only one explanation and that was as follows: that the accused, pretending to be teasing his wife, must have grabbed her feet and abruptly yanked them upwards toward himself. This would cause the upper portion of her body to slide under water. The sudden rush of water into the nasal and throat cavities could cause shock and sudden loss of consciousness.

There would be minimal evidence of violence, none of injuries, and very little of drowning.

The inspector conducted experiments with women divers of the same size as the victims. He discovered that it was virtually impossible to force the head and upper body under water in a tub of water without a violent struggle from the potential victim. A seizing of the victim by the feet, however, resulted in the victim gliding underwater before the hands had time to grip the sides of the tub. The experiments in which the inspector and the pathologist participated disclosed a shocking truth. When this technique was tried, one of the women divers in the experiment quite suddenly stopped moving and appeared dead. She was quickly pulled out of the tub, her head falling limply to one side. The doctor and the inspector worked for half an hour to revive her.

When she was stabilized and later able to describe what happened, she remembered only that there was a great rush of water up her nose and that she had instantly lost consciousness. She had suffered a sudden and convulsive shock despite the fact that she was an expert diver, she knew what was happening, she expected the inspector to pull on her feet, and she was ready to protect herself. The shock had rendered her instantly unconscious.

Inspector Spillsbury was satisfied that this was the technique used by Williams on all of his wives. In June, 1915, Williams went on trial at the Old Bailey in London and the jury pronounced him guilty after 20 minutes' deliberation.

The researching of earlier similar crimes was considered by Mancuso and the prosecution team to be an important element in its preparation for the Broderick trial. Issues of forensic pathology that had been dealt with by the courts on other occasions would likely arise again and the prosecution would learn what evidentiary problems they would probably have to confront. How the court had resolved such evidentiary problems on other occasions could be of great benefit when Broderick's turn came.

Back in Toronto, Inspector Bowles obtained and sent the file in *The Queen v. Louis Anthony Gualtieri* to Mancuso. This case, a non-capital murder trial, had been investigated jointly by the Haldimand-Norfolk Regional Police and the Ontario Provincial Police Criminal Investigations Branch.

The parallels between the Gualtieri case and the Broderick case struck Mancuso as truly astonishing.

On December 13th, 1973, officers of the Simcoe Police Department were dispatched to a bathtub drowning. The distraught husband and ultimate accused, Louis Gualtieri, told the police that he had gone to bed at about 10:30 p.m. and awakened at about 1:30 in the morning. He noticed his wife was not in bed. He looked in the bathroom and saw her in the bathtub, lying face up in six inches of water. Water was covering her mouth but not her nose. He telephoned his mother, then the neighbours across the hall, the Brophys. The Brophys came over within minutes and found Gualtieri's wife, Diane, in the same position. The police, the ambulance service, and the coroner were called. An autopsy was performed the next day by a qualified pathologist, and the cause of death was attributed to asphyxia due to drowning and probable laryngeal spasm. There was no overt evidence of violence and nothing about the death itself to raise immediate suspicion in the minds of the police.

Six months later, in June, 1974, the deceased woman's parents complained to the police that they were suspicious about the circumstances of their daughter's death. Their suspicion was generated by several factors: a short time before Diane's death, they had noticed that she had become very frightened and, occasionally, hysterical; they had found some unexplained pills in a suitcase belonging to Louis; he had denied any knowledge of the pills; he had given a lame excuse as to why he had arrived home late on the night of the death, an excuse that proved to be a complete lie. One week before his wife's death, he had told his superior at work that Diane was dying of a terminal disease and that she would die before Christmas. To the contrary, the autopsy revealed that she had been completely healthy. After Diane's death, it was learned that Louis had a girlfriend by the name of Melanie, 21 years old, whom he had been seeing regularly. Their lovenest was a cottage in resort country near Kitchener, Ontario.

When the police decided to re-open the case, they spoke with the coroner, the pathologist, the ambulance attendants, and the attending officers, all of whom confirmed that the condition of Diane Gualtieri's body was consistent only with drowning. The police were bothered however by the fact that while they were at the scene, the bathwater was still very warm, even though two hours had supposedly elapsed since Diane had taken her bath. Also, an observant nurse at the Norfolk General Hospital stated that when the body was brought to the hospital, the backs of the legs and the buttocks had a "reddish flushing," which was consistent with the body having been in very hot water for some time. Mrs. Brophy, the deceased woman's close friend, stated categorically that the deceased would use only lukewarm water and would stay in the bathtub for just one or two minutes.

There were other anomalies: the deceased's soiled panties were found on the sink along with a folded wash cloth. This was contrary to the deceased's practice. The friend, Mrs. Brophy, noticed that Louis' bed had not been slept in that night, even though he said he had been asleep and discovered that Diane was not in bed when he woke up. The deceased woman's friend also remembered that Louis had made a strange remark to her when they came back to the apartment after being at the hospital that morning.

"If anybody asks you, say that Diane died peacefully. Don't tell them that there was any violence here."

Measurements were taken of the dimensions of the tub, the depth of the water, and the height of the deceased. The tests showed that no one could have accidentally drowned in a bathtub that small.

Chief Ontario pathologist Dr. J. Hillsdon-Smith, was consulted and, relating this back to the "Brides in the Bath" case in England, he demonstrated that Diane could have drowned by having her feet lifted up, causing her body and head to slip beneath six inches of water. But in this position her mouth and nose would not be submerged, unless force was used to push her head either to the left or to the right. That having been demonstrated with the model, it was seen just how easily the person could be drowned. Diane Gualtieri had been found with her head twisted to the left side and her lower jaw was immovable.

Further consultations disclosed that Diane could have suffered a laryngospasm when she was suddenly immersed in the water. This effect, now medically recognized, causes the larynx to close, the vocal chords to tighten up, and the jaw to lock.

He had reiterated to others that his wife was in poor health and wasn't expected to live to Christmas. The morning after the death, he called a friend and told him that Diane had passed away peacefully in his arms during the night.

Like Broderick, Gualtieri worked for a life insurance company.

Apart from the many lies, he had also spread a rumour in the autumn of 1973 that he and Diane had accepted teaching positions in Switzerland and were making arrangements for their move there. This had caused concern among his superiors at Dominion Life Insurance. They demanded to know with certainty what his intentions were.

Ultimately, when confronted with these fabrications, he insisted that he had made up the Switzerland story because Diane had a terminal disease and this had been their fantasy.

Three days before Diane's death, Gualtieri's girlfriend, Melanie, left for Europe.

Gualtieri was arrested for non-capital murder on July 5th, 1974, and was subsequently found guilty in his wife's death.

15.

Understandably, the story of the Gualtieri murder was "news" within the Canadian life insurance industry. After it was over, the case was summarized and circulated among life insurance representatives and claims appraisers. It emphasized the difficulty in ascertaining violence where purported accidental bathtub drownings occur. Accidental death triggers the double indemnity provisions of life insurance policies.

A copy of the Gualtieri commentary had come, in due course, across George Broderick's desk at Canadian Premier Life!

Malcolm F. Lindsay, son of a former Commissioner of the Royal Canadian Mounted Police, went to law school with a singular purpose: to become a Crown prosecutor. He was called to the Ontario Bar in the spring of 1968, and immediately accepted a position with the Ottawa Crown prosecutor's office under John Cassels, Q.C. Blond and bookish, with dark horn-rimmed glasses and a large, incongruous walrus moustache, Lindsay was soon labelled "Mac the Knife" by both his associates and the defence bar. The nickname was fastened on him not as a result of any crusading approach to his work, but rather because he was— in the trade— a prosecutorial "bricklayer." Even-tempered, prepared to the point of distraction, he presented his evidence to the court in a bit-by-bit, methodical manner, resulting in a wall of evidence being constructed around an accused person, often without the defendant's own lawyer having realized it. Lindsay soon developed broad experience in presenting circumstantial cases.

It was part of the incongruity of Mac Lindsay that if you looked for him on a Sunday afternoon in the summer, you would find him in full cycling leathers, bending his Yamaha 750 around the curves of Carleton County's back roads. A 10,000 mile long distance runner's certificate hung proudly on his office wall.

Lindsay believed that they had a good, solid, albeit circumstantial case, against George Broderick. John Cassels assigned a newcomer, assistant prosecutor Andrejs Berzins, to assist Lindsay.

For his part, George Broderick had chosen his defence lawyer well. Richard Bosada had been called to the bar in 1967 and was in the vanguard of the new wave of lawyers who were building practices exclusively in the criminal defence field. Immediately after being admitted to the bar, he had gone to work for the legendary defence lawyer Louis C. Assaly, Q.C., at that time one of the top four or five counsels in Ottawa. Bosada came to practice, however, during the late 1960s and early 1970s when Ottawa was in the throes of a construction boom. The government was expanding at a phenomenal rate during the Trudeau years, and every week seemed to be marked by the capping off of a new high rise office building or a new residential subdivision to accommodate the explosion in numbers of civil servants. Bosada rode the crest of this vigorous growth and established a very healthy commercial law practice parallel with his criminal practice. This dual role permitted him the luxury of accepting only a few high profile criminal defence cases. They called him "Bo."

Lindsay and Bosada had been on opposite sides before, and their presence in the courtroom on a criminal case made for an interesting study in counterpoint. Lindsay's style was to stand straight and erect at counsel table, seldom moving from his place, turning occasionally to look at the jury, and speaking and asking questions in his low to moderate even-toned voice. He communicated in a reasoned, persuasive manner, one statement building upon the next as if to say, "This is really not very complex. It is irresistibly logical, leading to only one conclusion."

In contrast to Lindsay's runner's slimness, Bosada had the thick build of a linebacker, which he put to good effect, stalking and dominating the courtroom. He moved with confidence and knowledge of the law as he addressed the court or questioned the witness in a baritone voice that filled the courtroom. You knew when Bo was on his feet, even if you were sitting in the last row.

By 1977, the grand jury system had been abolished in the province of Ontario, so the only legal hurdle to the prosecution of George Broderick was the preliminary hearing.

The preliminary hearing procedure had begun when Ontario was still Upper Canada, and was initially intended as a screening process in which a presiding magistrate (who might or might not have had legal training) received the evidence of witnesses to a crime, either *viva voce* or by deposition, in order to determine whether there was adequate evidence to send the case to trial. This function was expanded over the years until, by 1977, it purported to serve several lofty purposes: to disclose the prosecution's case in full, to give the defence an opportunity to question the witnesses, to perpetuate the evidence in the event that certain witness died or were not available at trial, and as well, to define the legal issues which might be anticipated if the case went to trial. While it is a proceeding which exists to favour the defence, the prosecution is required to satisfy a minimum test that it has sufficient evidence upon which a reasonable jury properly instructed could reach a guilty verdict. The prosecution must demonstrate the existence of *some* evidence on each essential ingredient of the charge. The defence has the opportunity to question all prosecution witnesses. The defence is not required to disclose its case or produce its witnesses. A preliminary hearing is, in other words, something of a dry run.

George Broderick's preliminary hearing began promptly on the 24th of June, 1977, and was heard by His Honour Provincial Judge R.B. Hutton. The testimony went on for 28 days. A lack of courtroom space in Ottawa at that time forced the hearing to bounce back and forth between the courthouse and a conference room at a local Holiday Inn which had been pressed into service.

When it was all over, George Broderick was committed to stand trial for first degree murder.

The hearing was significant, from the prosecution's point of view, because of Lisette Martineau's testimony— or lack of it. Her unpredictable changes of heart did not stop at the courtroom door.

At one point in the course of the investigation, it seemed that Lisette would clearly be the pivotal witness in the prosecution's case, based on her eye witness account of George Broderick's conduct as she had described it on a number of occasions. The spontaneous "placemat" demonstration at the Hearthside Restaurant had been the clincher. But her continual flip-flopping was something that Lindsay, in fairness, knew he would have to disclose to the defence. This greatly devalued her worth as a prosecution witness, but the fact remained that, on a number of occasions, she had made clear and unambiguous statements which implicated George Broderick.

Lindsay was ethically bound to call her as a witness at the preliminary hearing and make her available for cross-examination by the defence. He had decided early on, however, that he could make a case without her. He would not have gone ahead otherwise.

The preliminary hearing was adjourned a few times, so Lisette did not begin her testimony until September 12th, 1977. Lindsay began by taking her through her history and present circumstances, her present employment and social relationships. He then brought her to the morning of November 16th, 1976. Lindsay moved slowly and cautiously, not wanting to rattle the witness. By this time, he had little or no idea how responsive she would be. He kept his questions short and pointed:

Q: And on the morning of Tuesday, November 16th, you had occasion to go to the Broderick residence?
A: Yes.
Q: Do you recall what time you left your home that morning?
A: No.
Q: Do you remember when you got up?
A: No.
Q: Where were you living at the time?
A: Kirkwood.
Q: Kirkwood Avenue?
A: 1020 Kirkwood.
Q: And how far is that from 18 Beaverton, how long did it take you to get there?
A: About five minutes.
Q: Five minutes in your car?
A: Yes.
Q: Did you own a car at that time?
A: Yes, I did.

Q: And can you tell us approximately what time you arrived at 18 Beaverton that morning?

A: About 10:30.

Q: And did you park your car?

A: Yes, I did.

Q: Where did you park it?

A: I pulled up in the driveway.

Q: And did you get out?

A: Yes.

Q: And what did you do?

A: I went up to the house.

Q: How many doors are there at the front of the house?

A: Two.

Q: What did you do when you got to the front of the house?

A: I looked in the mailbox.

Q: Yes.

A: And I opened the door, the first door, and I saw the dog.

Q: When you open the aluminum door, is there a window on the inside or main door to the house you can see through?

A: Yes, there is.

Q: Did you have to climb up on anything to look through that window?

A: On the edge of the step.

Q: On the edge of the step, right. Did you look through the window into the house?

A: Yes.

Q: And what did you see?

A: I saw the dog.

Q: What was the dog doing?

A: The dog was barking and running around in circles.

Q: Did you notice any reason for that?

A: No.

Q: Had you seen the dog behave like that before?

A: No.

Q: And where was the dog barking and running around in circles?

A: Right in front of me, in between the dining room and the hallway.

Q: And how far away from you was the dog?

A: I couldn't tell you approximately.

Q: All right. Had you done that before, walking up and opening the screen door and looking in when you were going to visit?

A: Yes.

Q: And what was your reaction when you saw the dog behaving like that?

A: I was surprised.

Q: Anything else?

A: No.

Q: Did you wonder why the dog was doing that?

A: Yes.

Q: What did you do then?

A: I left and went to my car.

Q: And before leaving, did you do anything to the inside door?

A: No.

Q: Did you go in the house at any time?

A: No.

Q: Or stick your head in the door?

A: No, I didn't.

Q: Or look down the hall?

A: No.

Q: And when you were there at the door, did you see any person in the house?

A: No.

Q: You have indicated that you saw the dog barking and you turned around and went to your car. Is that what you said?

A: Yes.

Q: And how fast did you go to your car?

A: I ran.

Q: You ran to your car? Why did you run to your car?

A: No special reason.

That was it. Nothing about "Missy's little feet." Nothing about George Broderick dragging Anne's body. Nothing about seeing Anne's body on the floor by the bathtub. Nothing about Lisette's idea of leaving her watch in the closet to prove she had been there.

Lindsay, apparently unperturbed by this and revealing no surprise, continued his probing in a calm but persistent manner, trying to elicit from her what she had told the police before. She reiterated that, at the time, she was confused. The only thing she heard was the dog barking. She heard no other noise from inside the house. She heard no human voice. When asked why she had bothered to look into the mailbox, she replied that it was just curiosity.

The key prosecution witness was not going to come through.

16.

It is a universal rule of evidence that a party calling a witness may not impeach his own witness. That means a lawyer may not question his own witness in such a way as to demonstrate that the witness is giving contradictory testimony, or is lying, or is colouring the testimony. As with all evidentiary rules, however, there is an exception.

The Canada Evidence Act specifically permits that where a witness has made a previous statement outside the courtroom, and that statement is inconsistent with what the witness is now saying in the witness box, with permission of the court, the party producing that witness may be allowed to question on those inconsistencies. This may even be extended to a full-blown right of cross-examination of his own witness in special instances. This is particularly so where the prior inconsistent statements have been "reduced to writing."

At the preliminary hearing, Lindsay found himself in this position with Lisette: the inconsistency was not that she was saying something different from what she had said in her two sworn statements, but rather that she was omitting or refusing to give material facts.

It took a day and a half to hear Lindsay's application to the court to cross-examine Lisette. Lisette was excused from the witness box while Inspector Bowles testified. This necessitated a painstaking review of his involvement in the investigation, all meetings with her, their conversations and the events and circumstances surrounding the making of the sworn statements by her. Having Bowles in the witness box at this point gave the defence an unanticipated opportunity to probe into some of the more subtle nuances of the investigation. Bosada took advantage of the opportunity by cross-examining Bowles in detail. After Bowles finished testifying on the motion, Lindsay called Dr. Rowsell, the psychiatrist, who testified about his meetings with Lisette, his observations and her state of mind at the time she made her various statements.

Bosada's cross-examination of Dr. Rowsell produced an insightful characterization of the prosecution's key witness:

Q: Lisette considered Mrs. Broderick a mother figure and Mr. Broderick a father figure; her guilt and dependency go hand in hand. Would a person of Lisette Martineau's make-up intentionally disclose her anger, in testimony against a man who turned on her?
A: This is possible.
Q: You say that when Lisette is strong, she is moral and forthright. In her weak state, she tends to do what other people tell her to do,

and this did include Mr. Broderick. How does her weak state reveal itself?

A: In her strong state, she speaks loudly and positively. She is forthright and appears very open. The weak state is playing helpless, poor me, with a coy little girl's smile. She is seductive and invites a man to be the seductive rescuer himself. He gets hooked. And the strong state, with somebody like Lisette, doesn't bear much relation to their truthfulness at all. With this character disorder, you will see both, and you can get just as much hokum or truthfulness from them, whichever state such a person is in.

Q: If certain things were being suggested, I take it that she might take up those thoughts and implement the suggestion more easily than the normal person would, because of her disorder, is that correct? And in this specific case, she felt very angry because the police thought that she was holding back. Is it probable that, understanding that the police thought she was holding back, that she might have decided to offer them more?

A: It could go either way.

Q: In other words, she might offer them more and then retract it?

A: That's right. This is exactly what I understand she was doing.

Q: And this fits within her categorization?

A: Yes.

Q: Now... you talk about her having a regular dream about the incident in question. Is it possible for a person of this kind to confuse fantasy with reality and at some point establish a fantasy as a reality?

A: Give me that again? I am trying to work that out.

Q: You indicated in your report that she dreamt about certain things, like seeing Missy's feet on the night George was arrested?

A: Yes.

Q: Could that dream translate itself into something that she thought she saw?

A: I think it could, at the time of the dream, but not in the waking stage. If this occurred in the waking stage, then in my view such a person would be in a psychotic state. I am quite satisfied that Lisette has never been in a psychotic state. In my opinion, Lisette knows what she saw, if she saw something, and she is going to tell the Court or she isn't.

Q: So she said, "Now I am positive that I did not see anything. It was just a dream. I was drinking a lot, and I feel like a fool telling the inspector about her little feet, now that I know it is not true." How would you fit that comment into what you have just said?

A: I would say it is very typical, sir, of a type of doubletalk you would get from a character of her type.

Q: Now on page 12 of her police statement, the very top paragraph, she refers for the first time to Broderick, without the Mr. preceding it. We have been told that even when they were in bed she called him Mr. Broderick. The omission there of Mr. is obviously of some significance vis-a-vis her feeling towards him. Would this be an indication of anger?

A: It might be. That was the only time I ever heard her refer to him as Broderick during the hours I had with her. Just that one time.

JUDGE HUTTON: You heard, doctor? Was it not written?

A: Yes, that is correct, Your Honour. She wrote this.

Q: And she also has an exclamation mark which attaches some emphasis to what she was saying.

A: The exclamation mark is mine, sir. I like to be grammatically correct.

Q: Your deduction, then, is much the same as mine, that she was expressing anger toward him?

A: Yes.

Q: Could this be because he was no longer around to depend upon?

A: I couldn't give a confident opinion about that.

Q: Now, Lisette felt guilty about her relationship with Mr. Broderick because Mrs. Broderick was a close friend of Miss Martineau. Is it consistent with this kind of person, that they want to blame others for their predicaments, and will find and do anything to attach blame to someone else?

A: Oh indeed, yes. Particularly in the sexual exploit.

Q: Might her thinking be geared towards a way to get Mr. Broderick, or a way that she thinks she might get him?

A: It's possible.

Q: When you say, doctor, that she is a manipulator, I take it that she manipulates through her seductiveness, is that correct?

A: Very much so, but not in terms of the woman, but more in terms of being a rather child-like individual with a desire to get somebody else to look after her. This is what I refer to as leeching.

Q: So this is the leeching characteristic that you find in her?

A: Yes, the seductiveness is the hook.

Q: You said, in certain areas, she is obviously a liar. Could she be skilful at lying?

A: No, I think she is most likely an unskilful liar. In my experience, the skilful liar gets away with it and, in a psychiatric interview, very rarely tells you about the lie. He is busy telling you more lies, of the type that you can't check; usually very good ones, too, very convincing. The unsuccessful liar is one like Lisette, who says of herself, "It is the story of my life, nobody knows me." Lisette is always being confronted.

Q: So she tells people what they want to hear so that she can manipulate them, is that right?

A: She could tell somebody what she thought they wanted to hear, true, and take it back and say it was a lie. Nobody would ever know if it was the truth unless it could be proven some other way.

Q: Now, does she have what you would call a vain personality?

A: I would say so. She is very good at sex, I believe.

Q: Would she be egocentric?

A: Egocentric in the sense that she is all for getting herself looked after.

Q: And she would also be emotionally unstable, even though she doesn't suffer from psychosis?

A: I think a person with lying tendencies is...

Q: ... emotional...

A: ... fair enough, yes.

Q: And she is very definitely an attention seeking person?

A: Yes, and good at getting pleasant and un-pleasant attention.

It was a thought-provoking portrait.

Detective Murray Gordon was the last witness on the application. His evidence was largely of the nuts and bolts variety, filling in gaps where he had been able to observe Lisette from time to time.

At the conclusion of argument, Judge Hutton granted the application, which meant that Lindsay would be able to use cross-examination techniques to pry the truth from her.

Lisette was re-called to the witness stand and Lindsay began cross-examining immediately, remembering that the same witness he was now challenging would ultimately be his own witness at trial. He established that she knew that it was a serious murder investigation, that she remembered saying incriminating things to the police about Broderick, that she understood the questions, that she was not under the influence of anything and that she knew what she was doing. Lindsay went over her statements with her. He explored her fear of George Broderick and the assurances that the investigators had given her.

When Lindsay asked her about being at 18 Beaverton on the morning of November 16th, 1976, she replied with a series of "I am not sure now" responses. She was not sure about anything: whether she was there at 10:30 that morning, whether she pulled into the laneway, whether she walked up the steps. She even indicated that her earlier testimony at the preliminary hearing was not true, that she had lied to the court under oath, and that she had lied to the police when she made her statements.

Lisette's testimony was amounting to a complete retraction and, conversely, an affirmation that she had been misleading the investigators and the court.

The day ended early with Lindsay advising her that she would be wise to obtain independent legal advice before she returned to the witness stand the following day.

The spectre of perjury hung over the courtroom.

Then the bombshell. The unbelievable happened.

Mark Twain was once heard to defend truth as being necessarily stranger than fiction. "Fiction, after all, has to stick to possibilities," he said. "Truth doesn't."

What happened overnight would not be acceptable fiction.

In the culmination of a joint Capital police forces "sting" operation, Richard Bosada was arrested for conspiracy to traffic in narcotics.

Broderick's lawyer was in jail. The newspapers had a field day.

Bosada's assistant, Bill Carroll, stood up in Judge Hutton's court the next morning, pleading for an adjournment of the preliminary hearing. It was anticipated that Bosada would be released on bail and an early ruling obtained from the Law Society, the lawyers' governing body, as to whether he could continue as counsel for Broderick. If Carroll expected both sympathy and an adjournment of the case, he received neither. Judge Hutton denied the request. The preliminary would continue uninterrupted. Bill Carroll, neophyte lawyer, recently called to the bar, would have a few minutes to marshall his thoughts before standing in for the jailed Bosada. Carroll began cross-examining Lisette on November 29, 1977.

Broderick registered no emotion.

Bosada was released from custody within a few days and resumed charge of the defence, picking up the cross-examination of Lisette Martineau.

On December 19, 1977, after full argument, Judge Hutton applied the legal test for preliminary hearings: "On the evidence before me, I cannot say that I would be justified in withdrawing the case from the jury because there was no evidence on any of the essential ingredients.

"Accordingly, it is not my function to review the evidence in any way beyond saying that the evidence is, in my view, evidence that must be tested before a jury.

"And accordingly, stand please Mr. Broderick, connected with the charge of first degree murder read to you at the opening of these proceedings, I now commit you to stand trial in the next Court of competent jurisdiction, to be held in and for the Judicial District of Ottawa-Carleton at the City of Ottawa. Thank you."

Bosada now faced his own specific dilemma: his ability to properly defend George Broderick while burdened with serious criminal charges which would not be finalized for months. To put it mildly, Bosada had a lot on his mind.

He went out to the Detention Centre to see Broderick and to discuss the situation. He gave Broderick the option of dismissing him as his defence counsel and retaining someone else. A jury, after all, might be adversely disposed to a lawyer who was himself facing criminal charges. Bosada offered to cooperate fully and assist Broderick in obtaining and briefing another lawyer.

Broderick flatly refused, dismissing Bosada's offer with the simple comment, "You've stuck with me all these months, Mr. Bosada. Now I'll stick with you!"

There was nothing more to be said.

"You had to admire the man's loyalty," Carroll commented later.

17.

Lindsay was confronting a prosecutor's nightmare, and he knew it. Seldom, if ever, is a murder victim's cause of death in doubt. In most homicide cases, it is a settled issue— stabbing, bludgeoning, a gunshot. More often it is the assailant's identity that is in doubt. Identification makes cases.

But Lindsay's dilemma was fundamental and unique: if you cannot say how the death was caused, then how can you say that the victim was murdered? The conundrum had given Lindsay more than one sleepless night.

There was no legal precedent in Canada for the hot poker he was about to grasp, and Lindsay and Bosada knew it.

Was Lindsay taking the proverbial "flyer" with this case? Bosada and Carroll both thought so. Without an ascertainable cause of death pointing unequivocally to homicide, Lindsay might have simply "pulled" the charge without incurring criticism. That he chose not to was not surprising in his case.

Lindsay had great skill in putting together circumstantial cases. He assembled an evidentiary barricade around the accused that could not be penetrated by the reasonable doubt test. His quiet courtroom demeanour disguised the zealous prosecutor inside.

Lindsay opened his case on the 26th of May, 1978, before the Honourable Mr. Justice O'Driscoll at the assize sittings in Ottawa. The jury was made up of eight men and four women.

By then, George Broderick had already been held in custody continuously since the date of his arrest, 15 months waiting.

In the late 1970s, prosecutors in Canada still adhered to the traditional British approach to criminal prosecution, the principle that: "The prosecutor never wins and never loses." The role of the Crown prosecutor in those days was a "non-crusading" one, marshalling and presenting all of the facts uncovered in the investigation, whether for or against the accused person, and subsequently to argue on the strength of those facts.

It was not the tradition of the prosecutor to engage in tactics in order to secure a conviction.

Nevertheless, with the complex medical and circumstantial case that Lindsay intended to put to the jury, some planning had to be done, not only concerning the evidence that would be called in support of the prosecution's theory, but also "how" it would be called and the order of witnesses. Quite a few medical witnesses would be testifying about arcane medical concepts. There was the danger of boring or confusing the jury with a plethora of medical evidence.

On the other hand, there was a very intensely human story to be told, a story bordering on the sensational, which he knew would captivate and hold the attention of the jury. A skilful mix of the two, he decided, would be the best approach.

Lindsay kept his opening address short. The witnesses' testimony would be long enough. He outlined his case to the jury in even, convincing tones, emphasizing that they would be asked to look at circumstantial evidence pointing unequivocally to George Broderick's guilt. He spoke of the hidden side of Broderick, the financial pit he had dug for himself, his long, secret affair with his secretary, and the multitude of deceptions which were practised by Broderick. These all demonstrated "consciousness of his own guilt." All through the trial Lindsay would pound the "consciousness of guilt" theme. It would be his fulcrum.

He completed his opening address by forthrightly telling the jury that the cause of Anne Broderick's death could not be determined. But his tone seemed to say, "That's no problem."

Lindsay teed off by calling four witnesses to briefly establish background.

Rosamund Jones, the rental manager for Minto Management, the

Brodericks' landlord, testified that she received a telephone call at 9:10 the morning that Anne Broderick was found. She was precise about the time. Broderick had called her to plead for more time to pay his overdue rent. A former employee of Minto, Ron Weber, testified that Broderick had blamed his financial mess on a manufacturing partnership with someone unnamed. The business had gone bankrupt. Broderick had also alluded to several other financial deals which had gone sour. Broderick had told him about a lawyer in Nova Scotia by the name of "McRae" who would be the solution to Broderick's financial problems. When Weber tried to find "McRae," he learned that no such lawyer existed.

Carol Hudson, the credit manager with the Carlingwood Branch of the Bank of Nova Scotia in Ottawa, described a series of short term loans taken out by Broderick in the months of April and August of 1975. The April loan was to have been paid in full at the end of April from the sale of an aircraft Broderick owned in Nova Scotia. The lawyer handling the transaction would be forwarding the funds to satisfy the outstanding debt in the amount of $6,650.

This time, the lawyer was "Brian McRae."

Eventually, she confronted Broderick with the fact that she could not locate a lawyer by that name in Nova Scotia. Broderick countered by saying that he was an *Armed Forces* lawyer. When Hudson pursued it further, she learned that there was no armed forces lawyer by that name and she confronted Broderick again. This time Broderick said that the individual was an *American* Armed Forces lawyer. By this time the Bank of Nova Scotia was tired of the games and went to court, obtaining judgements against Broderick in the amount outstanding.

Broderick had told the investigators that on the morning he found his wife in the bathtub, he had arranged to meet personally with the manager of the Bank of Nova Scotia to get the money to cover the three months' overdue rent. Norman Matthew, called by Lindsay as the Crown's fourth witness in anticipation of this evidence being advanced by the defence, denied that any such arrangement had been made by Broderick for the morning of November 16th. He had had no personal contact with Broderick and had never spoken to him at all.

Having demonstrated, in a peripheral way, that Broderick was prepared to deal fast and loose with the truth with both his landlord and his bank, Lindsay then cut directly to the death scene by calling Sheriff's Officer Larry Bordeleau.

Bordeleau, probably the only bailiff in North America who did not know how to drive a car, was the first person to arrive at the scene. He reached there with his driver and assistant, Dick Poulin, at 10:40 a.m. There were no cars in the driveway at 18 Beaverton. They parked on the street to await the arrival of the representative from Minto Management to let them into the house. Bordeleau had brought the Writ of Possession and Notice to Vacate which he fully intended to execute. He said that George Broderick had called him at home at 9:15 that morning in an effort to persuade him to delay. In turn, Bordeleau had called Rosamund Jones to confirm that the eviction was to proceed. Broderick called Bordeleau back at 10:10 and Bordeleau told him that the eviction was going ahead. Bordeleau testified that he checked his watch and the time was 10:10. He testified that when Broderick called him at 9:15 Broderick said he would try to make further arrangements with Jones by 10:15. Broderick, he said, was whispering, and Bordeleau could hear a radio in the background.

When the Minto representative, Pat Landrigan, arrived, he accompanied Bordeleau and Poulin to the front door. Bordeleau testified that he entered first, using a key Landrigan had given him. He described a clean house with everything in order and no signs of violence. They had just entered the premises when George Broderick pulled into the driveway and entered the house. As Bordeleau described it: "He didn't ask me nothin' at all!" Broderick went straight to the bathroom and found the door locked. Bordeleau described Broderick obtaining an object from the kitchen, opening the lock on the bathroom door and entering.

Broderick's conduct on first entering the house was important to Lindsay. Was Broderick acting as if he already knew Anne was in the bathroom? Lindsay pressed Bordeleau:

Q: You told the jury that when Mr. Broderick came in, he said,
"Hi, Larry?"

A: Yes.

Q: Did he ask you why you were there?

A: No, he knew why.

Q: When he said, "Hi, Larry," did he stop and look at you?

A: No, he just kept on walking into his home.

Q: Did he stop at any time?

A: No, he went directly to the bathroom.

Q: From the front door?

A: Yes.

Bordeleau saw the lifeless form of Anne Broderick lying in the bathtub with her face submerged in water. Bordeleau described Broderick as cool and not excited; all Broderick said was, "If she isn't dead, I hope she doesn't turn out to be a vegetable." Broderick uttered these words on two or three occasions. Bordeleau went on to describe the bathroom scene, and the removal of Anne Broderick from the bathtub, and the attempts at resuscitation. He didn't recall seeing a radio in the bathroom. Bordeleau was quite certain that they had done nothing to cause bruising or scrapes to Anne's body.

Patrick Landrigan, Minto's representative, essentially corroborated the evidence given by Bordeleau, and had one or two additional recollections. He testified that when George Broderick entered the home behind the bailiffs, he asked, "What's going on? Where's my wife?" Then Landrigan said Broderick walked directly to the bathroom. When they entered the house, Landrigan could hear a dog barking and music playing. The music, he said, came from a radio in the kitchen and the dog left after it had barked once or twice. Landrigan did not observe the resuscitation attempts but later saw a bruise on Anne Broderick's left elbow.

It was becoming clear to the defence that the bruises and scrapes on Anne's body were going to be a problem. Bill Carroll cross-examined Landrigan, trying to raise the possibility that Anne's injuries were caused when she was removed from the bathtub and subsequently transported by medical personnel. The cross-examination was unproductive. Landrigan described repeatedly how she was lifted from the tub and "guided gently to the floor." He overheard George Broderick say, when he entered the bathroom, "Oh my God, no, my God, Anne, she is a brilliant woman. She is a nurse!"

Mac Lindsay was aware of the persuasive power of graphic and demonstrative evidence as compared with verbalized abstractions. Much of what he would be calling upon the jury to consider centred on the bathroom at 18 Beaverton. Before the trial began Lindsay had ordered a full-size model of the bathroom to be constructed for demonstration purposes, even though there was some likelihood that it would not be admitted into evidence. He knew it was a chance worth taking, even though demonstrative evidence of this type is not usually seen in Canadian criminal courtrooms.

He needed a ruling as to whether or not he would be permitted to introduce the model into evidence. The time was now, at the conclusion of the bailiffs' testimony about the death scene. It was far from certain that the model would be admitted, but it was in Lindsay's favour that there was going to be a lot of testimony centring on the bathroom. The model would help everyone understand it.

So he launched the first of several *voir dires*. Technically, the *voir dire* is a mini-trial within the main trial resulting in a ruling on the admissibility of prospective evidence. The jury is necessarily excluded so it will not be "contaminated" by hearing things which may be subsequently ruled inadmissible according to the rules of evidence. On a *voir dire*, witnesses may be called by both prosecution and defence and full argument heard both for and against.

By the late 1970s the *voir dire* process had taken on a broader meaning and had evolved to include the contesting of all objections and motions performed in the jury's absence.

This *voir dire* would give Lindsay an opportunity to overcome three separate hurdles.

Police officers are ordinarily permitted to testify using notes, if the notes were "made in the course of the investigation." Their use is limited to refreshing the memory about events that probably happened months before. The preconditions are that the notes must have been made either by the officer personally or he must have agreed with and adopted another officer's notes as part of a joint note-taking procedure. As well, the notes must have been made at the time of the investigation or relatively contemporaneous with the event. When Officer Nichol arrived at the death scene on November 16th, 1976, he believed he was simply attending at a sudden, accidental death. He did not see it as a possible murder investigation. He had conversations with George Broderick that morning, being the first officer at the scene. He did not make his notes, however, until a month later, after the investigation had turned into a homicide inquiry and after Detective Mancuso and Inspector Bowles told him to make the notes. Officer Nichol testified on the *voir dire* that although Officers O'Donovan and Gordon were present in the room at the time, and although he and O'Donovan discussed their notes, that the notes were compiled separately and independently. He did allow, however, that he merely recorded the substance of what had occurred and what had been said, not a verbatim account.

Lindsay argued that although the notes did not meet the usual criteria, Officer Nichol ought to be permitted to refer to them.

Then he called evidence on the *voir dire* establishing the accuracy of photographs which had been taken of the death scene and evidence concerning the construction of the model bathroom and the accuracy of its reproduction. Bosada objected to the use of the notes, but since it was clear that the photographs and the model bathroom would be useful to the defence as well as to the prosecution, no objection was advanced about those.

After a short deliberation, Justice O'Driscoll ruled all three points in favour of the prosecution. The court adjourned while the model bathroom was reconstructed in the courtroom, off to the left of the witness box.

The model bathroom dominated the courtroom and became the silent focal point of the trial. Except for a few minor variations it had been constructed identically to the bathroom of 18 Beaverton, complete with toilet, a bathtub 4'11" long, a vanity, and plumbing fixtures. Officer Wayne Holland, the identification officer, took the stand to give a lengthy comparison, comparing the bathroom at 18 Beaverton with the courtroom model, providing dimensions, colours, and a series of photographs from the Beaverton bathroom. The clothes hamper had been retrieved by the police and was positioned in the model bathroom in the same place where it had been in the home on the date of Anne Broderick's death. But Holland admitted to Bosada on cross-examination that the floor tiles at 18 Beaverton were in fact shinier and smoother than the floor tiles shown in the model.

Dick Poulin, the sheriff's assistant and driver, had a somewhat different recollection of what took place during those crucial few moments after they entered the house. He clearly remembered a radio playing and a dog that barked and then left. Bordeleau, he said, called out a couple of times "Hello, is anybody here?" There was no response. Poulin said that he checked the bathroom door, knocking first and inquiring whether anyone was inside. He put his ear to the door but could hear nothing. The house seemed vacant.

"I turned to Mr. Bordeleau and told him there was something funny going on. There was no answer from the bathroom, and the bathroom door was closed."

They had been in the house three to four minutes at the most, he said. Poulin, in his testimony, inferentially attributed Broderick's fast and direct walk to the bathroom door to the fact that he saw Poulin kneeling at the bathroom door as he came in. Poulin testified that he said to Broderick, "I didn't know if his wife was there or not, but the door was locked, and I couldn't get in and was not getting any answer." Broderick, he said, then got a sharp piece of metal from the kitchen, sprang the lock, and was the first to enter the bathroom.

Lindsay asked Poulin:

Q: Before he got the door open, what was his behaviour or condition?
A: He seemed nervous. He opened the door and walked in straight

136

and turned to the bathtub, and then yelled out, "Oh, my God, Anne," or something like that, and I saw Mrs. Broderick lying face down in the water.

Dick Poulin's testimony was interrupted by Lindsay, who asked Justice O'Driscoll to send the jury out during another *voir dire* concerning photographs he wanted to introduce, photographs of Donna Wallace, the civilian police employee who had been positioned in the bathtub during tests done just a week before the trial.

The *voir dire* revolved, not so much around the tendering the photographs themselves, as it did around the testing procedure. Was the prosecution not trying to simply bolster or support the recollection of the witness by creating evidence out of thin air?

Justice O'Driscoll ruled that the procedure, if conducted and recorded in a controlled manner, was valid demonstrative evidence which could be introduced through the photographs.

Richard Poulin's testimony was particularly valuable to the prosecution and not particularly damaging to the defence. His observations and recollections seemed more objective and precise than other witnesses so far.

He described George Broderick asking for assistance in lifting Anne, unconscious, from the tub. She was carefully moved but he did notice a mark on her forehead which "looked like a swollen vein" and, he said, "I noticed a bruise on her elbow." Broderick, he said, used a mirror to see if any breath was coming from Anne and said that he had warned her about using that "slippery stuff." Broderick repeated that Anne was "too smart to be left as a vegetable" and that he would rather that she were dead. (This remark would cause some concern, since, at the time, it appeared that Anne was *already dead*.) Poulin said there was nothing out of place in the bathroom. There was no water on the floor or the edge of the tub. The water inside the tub was blue and lukewarm. Anne Broderick's body felt oily and slippery to the touch.

When questioned further about George Broderick's behaviour, Poulin commented that, "If it was my wife, I probably would have acted more hurt— he took it pretty cool compared to the first time he got in the bathroom. He calmed down a bit when everything was over." Broderick, he said, "wasn't in a state of shock. He didn't remain upset for long."

On cross-examination, Bosada, rather than attempting to impeach or contradict any of the testimony that Poulin had given, conscripted Poulin into putting a more favourable dimension on some of the things he had said. Artificial respiration had been attempted on Anne several times. Even Broderick himself had tried. Bosada extracted from Poulin that he really paid no attention to the water temperature on that morning, nor had he made any particular observation of the shower curtain except to push it back. When Anne was removed from the tub she was facing upward and Poulin agreed that in removing her and performing artificial respiration he could not be certain whether any injury had been done to her. He admitted that he really could not say with accuracy what the mark on her forehead was.

Poulin confirmed to Bosada that Broderick had actually started to calm down before Anne was removed by the ambulance attendants— at a point in time when the officers were present and Broderick had left the bathroom.

This observation was ambivalent and was bound to leave a question with the jury: had Broderick calmed down because of relief at the arrival of the officers and assistance for Anne, or did he calm down because, having used the mirror, he believed she was dead and would never regain consciousness?

At the conclusion of Richard Poulin's testimony Lindsay moved for another voir dire to determine the admissibility of conversations between Broderick and Officers Nichol and O'Donovan at the accident scene.

It was the law, at one time, that only inculpatory statements made by a suspect to a person in authority must be subjected to a voir dire to ascertain their admissibility on a test of voluntariness. A statement was inculpatory if it tended to connect the suspect with the crime in some material way. In recent years, however, the rule was expanded to include *any* statement made by a suspect to a person in authority.

On this voir dire Lindsay explored the conversations between the officers and Broderick when they first went to 18 Beaverton, conversations with him while being transported to the hospital, dining room conversations after his return from the hospital, the conversations between Mancuso, Gordon, and Broderick, while in the emergency room at the hospital and, lastly, Broderick's comments arising out of Lisette Martineau's arrival at 18 Beaverton.

After protracted and intricate legal argument, Justice O'Driscoll ruled all conversations to be voluntary and admissible.

Lindsay was batting one thousand on the voir dires.

18.

Lindsay was confident that the testimony of the death scene witnesses would hold the attention of the jury almost indefinitely, so his success in the last voir dire was important. He could now tender the snippets of conversation and utterances made by Broderick in the presence of the officers at the scene.

Broderick had been under no suspicion at the time of those conversations. The police were routinely investigating an accidental death, so they had not given him the usual police warning, a necessity when an individual is under suspicion.

Lindsay would make good use of Broderick's utterances. While each one seemed innocuous enough at the time, together they had the potential to damage the defence's case.

Officer Geoff Nichol arrived at 18 Beaverton at 11:07 a.m., 27 minutes after the sheriff's officers had entered the house. He initially observed Broderick crouched by Anne's body. Nichol saw no signs of forced entry; no water on the bathroom floor; one portion of the shower curtain off its rings. He waited from four to five minutes for the Emergency Response Team to arrive, and in the meantime preserved the death scene pending the arrival of the detectives. He noticed that the water was a "bright blue."

Q: Can you recall in as much detail as possible what you overheard the defendant say?

A: As I was looking at the victim, he pointed towards the bathtub and he stated, "I told her not to put that crap in the water before. She must have slipped and fallen." He advised me he attempted to revive her. He felt the ambulance was taking a long time to arrive. He said, "She has been without oxygen for too long," and commented that brain damage could result.

After Anne was removed by the ambulance attendants, Officer Nichol engaged Broderick in conversation for about an hour. They discussed Broderick's service in the Armed Forces. He told Nichol about teaching his wife to scuba dive. Lindsay then asked Nichol if Broderick had mentioned anything about his activities that morning.

A: He told us his daughter left for school, that he and Mrs. Broderick sat in the kitchen and had breakfast and listened to the election results on the radio, and he left about 9:00 a.m.

Q: Any reference to where he went?

A: Yes, he said he drove to his office, and realized he had forgotten his glasses. He entered the Queensway downtown and followed it west, missed his exit at Merivale Road and continued on south to Meadowlands, where he stopped at a store and purchased cigarettes and had a bottle of pop, and then returned to his residence.

This description of Broderick's timetable that morning, given with obvious precision by an independent police witness, would haunt the defence throughout the trial.

Concluding his testimony in-chief, Officer Nichol told how Broderick's son, Gerry, angrily "punched out the wall" before leaving. The detectives arrived and it was shortly afterward that the young blonde woman came to the door.

On cross-examination Bill Carroll extracted from Nichol that he had observed no apparent injuries on Anne's body. Nichol described Broderick as being excited, stuttering, distraught, and pacing back and forth, all consistent with someone whose wife had just passed away.

Carroll pulled another interesting fact from Nichol, not brought out by the prosecutor, in reference to Broderick's comment to Nichol that he had stopped for a cold drink:

Q: What was your reason, sir, for looking in the car as you left?
A: I looked to see if the can was there.
Q: What did you see in the car?
A: A soft drink can.
Q: Where was it?
A: Between the seats.
Q: Did you mention that fact to Constable O'Donovan?
A: I don't believe I did.

This testimony from Officer Nichol confirmed, to some degree at least, Broderick's explanation of his travels after leaving the house that morning.

When Officer O'Donovan arrived at the house, Anne Broderick had already been removed by the ambulance. O'Donovan's observations in general were a repeat of Nichol's, but with some elaboration. He said that on at least three separate occasions while at the house and while being driven to the hospital, Broderick reiterated the comment about Anne's brain damage.

O'Donovan asked Broderick why the bailiffs were at his place. Broderick tossed it off, saying he had lost money "on the market" and other investments.

Carroll's questions emphasized that when O'Donovan was dispatched to 18 Beaverton, he was sent there to "assist Constable Nichol at a *drowning* at 18 Beaverton Avenue." Carroll established that George Broderick was genuinely distraught, but even in that condition he had offered to make coffee and lunch for the police. From his notes, O'Donovan described the meeting between Broderick and the blonde girl. He quoted Broderick as telling him, "She had a rough upbringing and looked to Mrs. Broderick as a stepmother."

As the trial progressed it was clear that two separate parallel tracks would be followed: the activities of George Broderick with the circumstantial evidence pointing to his complicity, and the line of medical evidence which would tend to demonstrate homicide.

Gordon Haye, paramedic with the Rescue Unit, was one of the few witnesses whose testimony was on both tracks. He arrived at the scene at 11:16. Anne's pupils were beady and did not respond to light. She was showing no pulse. There was nothing abnormal in her mouth, no obstruction and no blood. Haye described how she was rolled over onto her left side, face down, and the torso squeezed to exhale the lungs. At this point, he said, about three-quarters of a cup of water ran out of her mouth, and some mucous from her nose. They tried to resuscitate her with oxygen but she did not respond. He notified the hospital emergency unit that they were bringing Anne in and that it was a probable D.O.A.

In his questioning of the witness, Lindsay specifically established that in handling Anne and in transporting her to the hospital, the paramedics did not cause any injury to her.

Twice the paramedics tried to put air into her, but without success.

A: I was at the head of her and Rick was at the feet of her, and I picked her up; you grab the wrists and cross them over the chest and this gives the attendant something to hold on to. All the lifting can be done by bringing up with the arms crossed over the chest and your hands around their wrists. You are actually lifting under the armpit, and you can lift a fairly heavy person that way.

Carroll saw where Lindsay was going with this testimony; in effect, he was attempting to head off any future defence argument that the injuries to the body, so indicative of an assault, could have been caused by the paramedics. Carroll cross-examined the witness so vigorously that he was reprimanded by the judge, who excluded the jury while Carroll defended himself. The best that Carroll could obtain was a slight admission favourable to his position:

Q: It is possible in all this moving back and forth that her arms could have hit the side of the tub or the floor?
A: It is possible, but not to my knowledge.
Q: You didn't see it happen, but it is possible?
A: True.

Richard Sergeant, the second paramedic, offered more information. They had performed "compressions" on Anne on the way to the hospital and she was looking better when they arrived at the hospital than she had at the house. He did observe a mark on her elbow which "looked like she had banged it and there *was* blood, but no blood *running* at the time."

At the conclusion of Richard Sergeant's testimony, the judge called a luncheon recess. Bosada sensed that Lindsay would now launch into the "medical" phase of the trial, which would invariably involve considerable speculation and opinion as to the cause of Anne Broderick's death.

At a strategy session over lunch, the defence decided to try a motion which could be the most important defence motion in the course of the trial.

They were enthusiastic about it, but not optimistic.

19.

The indictment against George Broderick was straightforward:

George A. Broderick stands charged: That he, the said George A. Broderick, on or about the 16th day of November 1976, at the Township of Nepean, in the Judicial District of Ottawa-Carleton, unlawfully did kill Anne Broderick and did thereby commit first degree murder, contrary to Section 218(1) of the Criminal Code.

The indictment said nothing about *how* he had killed her. The *how* of a murder is sometimes stated in the indictment, but it is not a legal necessity. By now, both Bosada and Lindsay and anyone who had read a newspaper were aware that the cause of Anne's death had never been established. By the time of the trial, some of the best experts in North America had reviewed the case, and they were unable to come up positively with a cause of death.

It had taken the first half day of trial to select the jury. In 1976, a jury of 12 persons was mandatory in first degree murder cases. The jury would be the finders of fact and determine the ultimate verdict. In the event of a conviction, the sentence would be for the judge to decide, as mandated by the Criminal Code. The defence, by law, could peremptorily challenge 20 prospective jurors, that is, without giving any reason. Any number could be challenged "for cause," by demonstrating bias or pre-formed opinions about the case.

A panel of 60 prospective jurors had been summoned to the courthouse, culled from the voters' list.

When the lottery was finished, the women and men selected represented a cross-section of Ottawa's citizenry: a retiree, a business manager, a teacher, an engineer, a home-maker, a receptionist, and various civil servants.

Immediately after selection, they were excluded from the courtroom while the judge heard pre-trial motions.

A motion launched by the defence was based on a section of the Criminal Code permitting the judge to order the prosecution to provide "particulars" of the offence where it is essential to the defence's case.

The defence usually argues that without the particulars the accused is unable to defend himself. What they were arguing in this case was: if the prosecution did not provide particulars of the cause of Anne Broderick's death, the accused would be unable to meet and answer the charge. Bosada knew that Lindsay could not provide these particulars. Furthermore, it is usually the position at law that when particulars are provided in a Bill of Particulars, then those particulars form part of the indictment and must be proven.

Justice O'Driscoll, ruling against the defence, expressed it this way:

"The argument is that the indictment as framed is too bald in that there is no way of knowing when one looks at it what the Crown's allegation is. Is it alleged the accused killed his wife by shooting her, by stabbing her, by strangling her, by asphyxiation, or whatever it is the Crown is alleging?"

It seemed reasonable.

He continued: "The narrow question then is, should I, can I, narrow the Crown down to choosing or picking or delineating whether or not it was electrocution, asphyxiation or strangulation, if in fact it is any of those three? Of course, if it is not one of those three, it is no offence at all and natural causes."

In fact, the judge had just stated the theory of the defence.

The judge would no doubt be aware that to order the particulars requested by Bosada might effectively kill Lindsay's case.

"I think the narrowing down that has been done this afternoon is all that counsel for the accused is entitled to. There has been a full preliminary inquiry, 2,000 pages I am told, extending over some months. It is acknowledged that the defence has at its command full disclosure of all the Crown's evidence, and simply a situation where certainly at this point in time the Crown cannot say and all its witnesses are prepared to say that beyond a reasonable doubt or anything of that nature it was electrocution, asphyxiation or strangulation.

"During the course of the argument, I broached with Mr. Bosada the situation that would arise if there was no body and the Crown was attempting to prove its case by circumstantial evidence. Of course, in that case, there would be no post-mortem at all. I do not think under those circumstances the Crown would be stopped from laying the charge because they could not prove by what particular method the accused caused the death of the deceased.

"This is an unusual case, but I do not think that I will be doing justice if

I were to force the Crown to elect or pick or choose one of the three alternatives."

The "no body" analogy was, at best, weak, and was hardly adequate justification for denying proper particulars to the defence. It was no comfort to the defence that the judge permitted the addition of the words "by an assault" to the indictment. Murder presupposes an assault.

In effect, he gave them nothing.

Now Lindsay made two motions for the prosecution. Under the provisions of Section 7 of the Canada Evidence Act, permission of the court is needed if more than five expert witnesses are to be called by a side. This was important to Lindsay; only qualified experts may express an opinion or give opinion evidence. He followed up with a second motion asking the court for an admissibility ruling on photographs of the body of Anne Broderick taken prior to the post-mortem examination. These photographs would disclose the bruises and minor lacerations on the body before the commencement of the autopsy. Bosada argued strenuously that these abrasions and lacerations could be adequately described in verbal terms by the witnesses and that the photographs of the nude, deceased, Anne Broderick, lying full-length on the morgue slab, would only contaminate the minds of the jurors and had little or no probative value or relevance.

Both motions were ruled in favour of the prosecution. Lindsay would be permitted to call more than five experts if he felt it necessary, and the photographs would be admitted into evidence.

The defence was beginning to feel disheartened. Not a single ruling had gone its way.

Lindsay faced a major tactical problem in the presentation of the medical evidence. A large number of doctors would be testifying. Lindsay, an experienced prosecutor, knew that unrelenting, detailed medical testimony about arcane procedures and observations can be mind-numbing to the jury. Yet, the evidence had to be presented.

The medical testimony could be broken into two very distinct categories: the first being from those doctors who had some hands-on dealing with Anne Broderick, either before or after her death, and the second from those doctors who would be subsequently expressing an opinion based upon medical reports and records, but who had no direct contact with her. Lindsay tactfully decided to keep these two areas quite separate, interspersing them with a series of civilian witnesses, introducing a mix into the witness line-up to prevent jury overloading.

The three principal experts, expected to drive the case home for the prosecution, would be held until the very end. Lindsay would finish his case on a high note.

Dr. Thomas Estall was the first to treat Anne when she arrived at the Ottawa Civic Hospital emergency room at 11:25 a.m. According to Dr. Estall, she was clinically dead at that time. There was no palpable pulse, no recordable blood pressure, no heart sounds, no respiration, no spontaneous movement. Her pupils were fixed and dilated. Her skin was greyish blue. All the standard emergency steps were immediately taken and the doctors succeeded in re-establishing a normal heart rhythm. But Anne was not breathing on her own and showed no sign of regaining consciousness. Dr. Estall had been told that Anne had drowned. Dr. Estall emphasized that when he first saw Anne she was significantly cyanotic and a greyish purple colour, "not the way we see patients who are the victims of cardiac arrest while in transit." He also said: "It appeared that she might have been dead for a fair length of time."

The doctor admitted to some frank surprise that they were able to restore a normal heartbeat so quickly. The electrographic tracing, he said, "did not show any specific injury to the heart." He performed a cursory external examination and could see no evidence of trauma. There was no evidence of skeletal deformity. Significantly, he observed no dislocation of major joints and no major external wounds.

He did, however, observe a bruise to her tongue which he did not believe came from the endotrachial tube. He also observed several abrasions on the legs, superficial scrapes on the knees and shin. "They were not major injuries," he said.

On cross-examination by Bosada, the doctor agreed that they had carried out a "blind defibrillation," in which the patient is defibrillated before being given an electrocardiogram— in an attempt to reduce the time during which the heart may be fibrillating and increase the success rate. Dr. Estall confirmed that the procedures taken with Anne were not considered heroic, but were common techniques.

He did not consider that she had been temporarily restored to life, but simply that her heartbeat had been restored. In determining death, he said, a number of parameters are referred to— including brain waves and heartbeat. When Bosada cross-examined the doctor about the prospect of drowning as a cause of death, the doctor ventured that 85% of drown victims have some water in their lungs and that Anne's chest X-ray was normal. He allowed, however, that a small quantity of water in the lungs might not show up. Near the end of his cross-examination Bosada asked:

Q: What diagnosis did you make after having had this exposure to Mrs. Broderick?
A: Drowning with cardiac arrest as a primary diagnosis. The cardiac arrest I was sure of. The drowning was historical.

Bosada then concluded his cross-examination with a nice touch in George Broderick's favour:

Q: You said Mr. Broderick indicated concern, in conversations at the hospital and on the telephone?
A: Yes.
Q: Did he request that you remove the resuscitator from his wife?
A: No.

Dr. Janis Bourmanis, a haematologist, just happened to be called in to assist Dr. Estall. He confirmed what Dr. Estall had to say, but he was clearly impatient with lawyers, judges, and lay persons who could not hope to understand the mysteries of his profession.

But he introduced a few new pieces into the jigsaw puzzle of evidence. He disclosed that Anne had taken acetaminophen before her demise, and that when he last saw her at 4:20 he believed her condition to be terminal.

And he was the first to tell the jury about D.I.C., disseminated intravascular coagulation. Dr. Bourmanis testified that he had observed oozing from intravenous sites, and that later the bleeding seemed to increase. When asked about it on cross-examination by Bosada, Bourmanis responded testily, "I'm not sure what you mean. If the patient is oozing, the patient is oozing." Bosada was becoming impatient.

Q: In terms of your speciality, what does that mean? Did a red light come on and say something must wrong?
A: Yes, it made me suspect this lady had a disorder of her blood.
Q: What was that disorder?
A: The disorder would be associated with what we call consumptive coagula, D.I.C. Whatever you want to call it, they are the same.

This was the first suggestion that some pre-existing condition might have contributed to or been the cause of Anne Broderick's death. The jury's attention peaked. They leaned forward to follow this line of questioning. Lindsay squirmed uncomfortably in his place at counsel table.

Bosada continued:

Q: In layman's simple terminology, what does that mean?
A: There is no layman's simple terminology for this condition. It is a very complicated condition.
Q: Could it be categorized as the blood simply failing to clot?
A: That is one aspect of it, yes.
Q: There is more to it than that?
A: Yes, the blood could also clot more than usual.

Q: But in this particular case her blood was not clotting?

A: That is correct.

Q: Can you think of any particular reason why this was happening?

A: First of all, she had circulatory collapse. She had no reasonable blood pressure, which was allowing the blood to circulate into vital organs, and this causes tremendous changes in the body. That in itself can lead to D.I.C. She was hypoxic and that can also cause this. We were told this lady was near drowning. In near drownings or drownings, one can have D.I.C. So there were several possibilities.

Q: Were you able to determine what contributed to that condition?

A: The diagnosis of D.I.C. is always secondary after analyzing what has happened. It does not tell you what the causative insult was.

Additional testimony about the analysis of Anne's blood, on re-examination, established that all results were negative. Anne had not been taking any drugs or medication regularly. Lindsay concluded his re-examination on that note, tactfully ignoring the testimony which had been given about D.I.C. It was best not to reinforce some things with the jury.

Lindsay closed off the events in the intensive care unit by calling Dr. Robert Gannet, who oversaw Anne's transfer from the emergency unit to the Intensive Care Unit and inserted a Swan-Ganz catheter. He described Anne as being in shock and severely acidotic.

He was emphatic that at the time he observed Anne there was nothing wrong with her heart. Her ECG and blood pressure were within normal limits. But the electroencephalogram (EEG) was a flat line, indicating no brain function at all. He did not recall seeing a bruise on her right hip.

Subject to words of caution to the jury, Lindsay showed the post-mortem photographs of Anne's body to the doctor. Gannet had no explanation for the abrasions to the knee or the right ankle and left lower shin. Anticipating questions from Bosada on cross-examination, Lindsay asked Dr. Gannet whether he remembered seeing anything unusual about the fingernails on Anne's hands. He did not. Lindsay then asked, "Do you remember if anything happened, while she was in your unit, to her hands, that might have caused a couple of fingernails to be torn off?" Dr. Gannet replied, "No, I don't."

Dr. Gannet closed with a lengthy and complex technical description of Anne's condition.

At 10:24 that evening, he said, "The heart stopped completely, and we declared she was dead." Lindsay asked, "Why did she pass away at that time, and what happened?"

"I don't know. I don't know why she died. We assumed at that stage she just gradually petered out. She was continuing to lose ground during the day, and we thought she had just petered out at that stage."

Bosada's cross-examination was brief and to the point. He confirmed that the doctor could not establish a cause of death for Anne, and briefly reviewed with the doctor the bruises and abrasions which had been observed on the body. Finally, Bosada raised the question of D.I.C. He asked whether it was fair to state that when a person has that condition they would be more likely to bruise. The doctor agreed, but refused to speculate on the *degree* of trauma it would take to cause the bruising.

20.

Having concluded the medical evidence regarding Anne Broderick's condition up to the time of her death, Lindsay then began the second phase of medical evidence, the pathological observations. The jury would sympathize with the next medical witness, Dr. Egils Liepa, the highly qualified, skilled, and experienced pathologist who had performed the autopsy the day following her death. Dr. Liepa was a man proud of his skills, who had testified in many court proceedings involving traumatic deaths. Normally, he would have been told in advance whether the death was one with potential for subsequent court proceedings, since an ordinary autopsy varies considerably from one performed for forensic purposes.

Dr. Liepa had not been given any information that homicide was suspected in this case, so he performed his autopsy on a straightforward, accidental bathtub death.

Now he found himself a key witness in a sensational murder trial. A puzzled public eagerly absorbed the daily press analysis of each new tidbit of Broderick's secret life. Lawyers argued the merits of the case over their scotch and ice, debating whether Lindsay could obtain a conviction, voicing incredulity that, in the absence of a cause of death, a murder indictment had been obtained at all.

Still, Liepa's testimony would not be contentious in the usual sense. Counsel on both sides recognized that in the course of the autopsy he had made a number of important, objective observations about Anne's condition. It would be from those observations, and his report, that the opinions of the other medical experts would subsequently derive. Each side would ultimately rely on Liepa's observations in support of its own particular point of view.

Liepa began by emphasizing that he was a hospital pathologist rather than a forensic pathologist and that he approached the death in that capacity. Lindsay questioned on the point.

"When you started the autopsy, were you looking at this as a homicidal death?... What were you looking on it as?"

"Well, I understood from the notes our clinical colleagues had made that this was considered a case of partial drowning."

Liepa had noticed a number of needle marks on the body but confirmed that these were needle marks from injections that had been given to the deceased while in the emergency department. He distinguished, for the jury, the difference between post-mortem staining— a result of blood pooling in the lower extremities of the body after death— from the other observable bruises. He conducted both an internal and external examination. There were no signs of injury to the head, but he noticed bruises to the knees, ankles, abdomen and right upper arm and stomach. There were no bruises on the back. In the photographs he pointed out additional bruising on the lower arm.

During the internal examination, Liepa observed no evidence of injury or haemorrhage to the brain.

"... and there was nothing really to indicate any pre-existing disease." He brought his testimony in-chief to a graphic conclusion:

"I did not examine the mouth and tongue because the mouth was closed by rigor mortis. I looked at the hyoid bone, a small bone the tongue is attached to in the neck, which gets broken or fractured in the case of manual strangulation, and this was intact. The thyroid gland was normal, and the larynx was normal, and the windpipe as well as the lungs appeared to be entirely normal. The heart was rather small, and there was nothing wrong with the coronary arteries or valves or the heart muscle. The stomach and gut all appeared to be entirely normal, likewise the spleen, the gall bladder, liver, pancreas, lymph nodes, urinary bladder and kidneys."

Bosada could not have summarized it better himself. Finally, Liepa confirmed that he could find no evidence of drowning, but could not rule it out, since the evidence of drowning could have been removed during Anne's treatment in emergency.

"Sir, you mentioned death by natural causes. Did you find any evidence at your autopsy that she died of natural causes?"

"No, I don't have anything."

Traces of the tranquillizer librium had shown up in the analysis of Anne's blood, but it was common ground that this did not tip the scales one way or the other. Lindsay then showed Liepa a photograph of the body of the deceased and asked what observations he had made respecting the nail on the thumb.

"A part of the nail appears to be missing. It is in the process of re-growing."

Bosada's approach on cross-examination was simply to nail down the litany of causes of death which had been specifically excluded by Dr. Liepa. There was no evidence of lung damage, head injury, drowning, strangulation, dry drowning, heart trouble, cardiac problems, or electrocution. There was no evidence of trauma or foul play. Once all these considerations had been dismissed, Bosada questioned the doctor on the prospect of "heart attack" as a result of spasm. Dr. Liepa was guarded in his response.

"This has been speculated. Of course, I think there is another explanation for sudden failures or sudden deaths, but there is no way to demonstrate it. When somebody is dead, the heart muscle relaxes and the coronary arteries look the same."

Bosada left the question of spasm open in the minds of the jury, without exploring it further.

He concluded by suggesting that the doctor could not be satisfied beyond a reasonable doubt that Anne did not die of natural causes.

Liepa's response was succinct: "No, I really have no opinion on this. I can just state I don't know how she died."

Bosada looked quizzically over at the jury and sat down.

Before Dr. Liepa left the stand, Justice O'Driscoll questioned him. It was clear that the question of D.I.C. was bothering the judge and he decided to elicit Liepa's opinion. Dr. Liepa was very guarded in his response, allowing only that D.I.C. is usually associated with some other disease.

"It can be associated with partial drowning, but it is certainly not necessarily associated with this. There are infections, and quite a long list of conditions associated with D.I.C."

He called D.I.C. one type of spontaneous bleeding. Bosada was left with the impression that the judge was trying to close the door on the prospect of D.I.C. involvement. He asked the doctor whether the bruises shown in the photographs could have been associated with D.I.C. and the treatment she received at the hospital. Liepa responded only that the marks could have happened "either after or prior" to her being taken to the hospital. They might have nothing to do with D.I.C. or might all be D.I.C. dependent.

It was clear from this exchange that the judge was concerned about the spectre of D.I.C. being raised repeatedly by Bosada on cross-examination of the medical experts, and the effect that it would have on the minds of the jury.

Before taking the lunch break that day, Lindsay called Dr. Anthony

Lewis, a neuropathologist, to the witness box. Dr. Lewis testified that he had made a detailed examination of Anne's brain tissue and had observed small infarcts scattered over many areas. That meant the brain tissue had been deprived of blood and oxygen long enough to cause death.

Picking up on Justice O'Driscoll's questioning of the previous witness, Lindsay then asked Dr. Lewis about D.I.C. The doctor found no evidence in examining the brain of D.I.C.

Lindsay took it one step further:

Q: In your examination, sir, did you find any evidence that this woman died of natural causes?
A: No.

On cross-examination Bosada managed to re-establish, referring to the earlier testimony of Dr. Bourmanis, that D.I.C. is better diagnosed clinically than through later microscopic examination.

By this time, Lindsay knew that the jury had been inundated with medical evidence and could choke on it. A lot of highly technical and sometimes contradictory medical testimony had been heard and there was the danger that they might lose the flavour of the case. He decided to call one last witness to close off that second phase of the medical testimony dealing with Anne's specific condition.

Dr. Gerald Thomas was Anne's personal family physician. Lindsay's assistant, Andrejs Berzins, did the questioning. Dr. Thomas, a specialist in internal medicine, had treated Anne Broderick for several years. He described her health as being near excellent. She was in good physical condition and expressed no complaints, he said. She had no pre-existing medical problems and no history of medical difficulty, no history of fainting, spells, or falling down. He had never known her to suffer bruising and there was never anything unusual in the routine blood tests he had ordered. He had given her a complete physical examination as recently as March, 1975.

155

Carroll conducted a brief, pointed cross-examination. Dr. Thomas agreed that Anne had suffered from bad nerves and this was the reason for his having prescribed librium. He described her as having been, at that time, tense, shaky, and experiencing some tremor of the right hand. She was also something of an insomniac. On subsequent visits she had complained of indigestion and nausea, complicated by severe headaches. He had prescribed acetaminophen. The tremor had progressed to both hands, but Dr. Thomas felt that it was no cause for concern. Carroll brought out that in fact Anne had been hospitalized for a nervous condition in 1967. Dr. Thomas ended his testimony by saying that Anne was not by nature a complainer.

This concluded the medical testimony about Anne Broderick's condition both before and at the time of her death.

The jury would have ample time later to reflect on and digest the large volume of medical evidence which had been presented to it.

Tactically speaking, it was now time for Lindsay to shift gears, and to revive the jury's attention with more stimulating testimony. He decided to call Shirley Broderick to the witness box.

21.

Throughout the trial, George Broderick sat in the glass-enclosed prisoner's box, listening to the testimony attentively but impassively, imperious and unemotional as the Doge of Venice. Each day he wore a tailored, conservative, double-breasted suit and cravat, but despite his well turned-out appearance, fatigue was visible in his eyes. When his daughter ascended to the witness box, a flicker of distress broke through his equanimity for the first time. He hung his head, unable to look at her.

By the time of the trial, Shirley Broderick was 23 years old and living with her brother, Ryan, and his wife in Aylmer, Quebec. A bright student, she was completing a degree course at Carleton University, majoring in Religion and Political Science.

Lindsay was putting a human face on the case. The jury's attention rekindled perceptibly.

He began by developing background with her, the all-important home life and daily routine. What would seem to many to be relatively mundane information would later become elements in the prosecution's theory.

At the time of her mother's death, Shirley had been attending school and working part-time at a drugstore near the courthouse. She ordinarily got up around 7:00 or 7:30 in the morning, used the bathroom, then, after dressing and making-up, would eat and catch the bus to school, leaving the house around 8:00 a.m.

Her father's routine, she said, did not vary. He would be up around the same time and go into the kitchen before cleaning up and dressing. On occasion, he would drive her to the university. Her mother would not usually get up until 9:00 or 10:00 a.m., after they both had left. Anne would begin her day by having tea in the kitchen.

Shirley described the relationship between her Mom and Dad during 1976 as being unhappy. Things had not been going well, she said, for a few months before her mother's death. The situation got worse as the year went on. There were problems regarding the house and money. Her mother's nerves worsened. In the midst of this, however, she said that her father "...seemed more loving toward her... " and "... he seemed to want more love."

"How was your mother responding to that?" Lindsay asked.

"She was fed up and she didn't respond as well." Shirley agreed that the house was one of the problems. The Kanata house.

"Can you tell us about that?" Lindsay asked.

"Dad had bought a house in Kanata, and we were supposed to move into it, but the move kept on being delayed and delayed and put off, and my mother had packed some stuff, but we kept getting delayed and never moved."

Shirley was certain her mother had had no health complaints, although she did notice that sometimes Anne's hands trembled when she lifted her teacup.

Then Shirley told the jury about an unusual request that her father had made in the weeks before her mother's death. Soon after she had begun the fall semester at the university, her father asked her to write out her schedule and post it above the telephone. She emphasized her belief that this was an unusual request. At first, she complied, thinking that the idea was silly, and then she removed the schedule. George again requested that she prepare a schedule, one week at a time, and post it. She said she complied and prepared more than one but she could not say how many. Lindsay's face registered a flicker of surprise at this testimony, although he would have known it was coming. The point was not lost on the jury.

This seemingly innocuous request by Broderick pointed ultimately to the question of premeditation.

Lindsay then cut immediately to the 24 hour period surrounding Anne's death.

Shirley's alarm clock woke her up at 8:00 on the morning of November 16th, 1976. It was a Tuesday. She got ready to leave for the university.

Then she uttered something which would again cause Lindsay to register surprise. Her father was already up, she said, and she spoke to him before she left the house. He had asked her quite pointedly when she would be leaving. He sounded "nervous and hurried," she said, when he asked her. She became angry.

"From what I can recall, I was angry at the manner in which he had said it and it was sort of unusual." Lindsay pursued it, asking her what was unusual about that question that morning.

"When he asked what time I was leaving, he usually asked if I would like a ride, but his attitude was different that morning and more nosey. It wasn't usual."

She repeated that he seemed nervous and hurried. She did not see her mother before leaving at 9:15. As she was leaving, she saw her father disappearing down the hall and heard her father start the bathwater. She did not believe her mother had even gotten up yet. If her mother had run the bathwater, "She would have come out and seen me. It was unlikely for her to have a bath in the morning."

Shirley's testimony about the events of the morning of November 16th was crucial to Lindsay's case. In an effort to maintain a continuity, a flow in the narrative during this heightened area of evidence, he was tending to ask leading questions. Justice O'Driscoll stepped on him for it.

While police officers are usually experienced at giving testimony and are not rattled by the formality and decorum of the courtroom, civilian witnesses usually begin their testimony with considerable trepidation. Shirley Broderick, after Lindsay had taken her through the dynamics of the Broderick household, seemed oblivious to the courtroom and the presence of her father 20 feet away in the prisoner's dock. There was just herself, the jury, and Lindsay. She was on a roll.

Lindsay came back to the crucial events of November 16th. Her mother, Shirley said, *never* showered. She always bathed and almost always in the evening around 10:00 before going to bed. She would go into the bathroom and close the door but leave the door unlocked. She always drew a hot bath for herself. Her routine never varied. The family's little dog would sit outside the closed bathroom door and wait for her mother to come out.

Shirley could not comment on the shower curtain but acknowledged that her mother always used the same brand of blue bath beads, which she added to the water. The water would always be a light blue shade. Lindsay then produced a chart which had been entered as an exhibit in the trial and pointed to a particular shade of blue on the colour chart. The colour of the water, she said, would not be as dark as that which Lindsay pointed out.

Often, while her mother was bathing, Shirley said that she would go into the bathroom, sit on the edge of the tub, and have conversations with her mother in the bath. Her mother, she emphasized, always wore a shower cap in the tub.

Lindsay showed some apparent surprise again when Shirley said that her father would draw the bath for her mother "once in a while." But he always showered and always in the evening before going to bed. Shirley had never known her mother to use second-hand bathwater.

Anne would always take her housecoat and pyjamas, put them on a hanger, and bring them into the bathroom with her together with a little transistor radio which operated on batteries. At no time had Shirley ever observed her mother bringing an electrical cord into the bathroom.

On the morning of November 16th, Shirley testified, she left the house at 9:15 and caught the bus to Carleton University where she remained all day. Except for her father's inquiries about what time she would be leaving, there was nothing unusual when she left the house. She said that her first knowledge of the tragedy was that evening about 7:00 when her brother came to drive her home.

When they reached home about 7:20 in the evening, her father was home alone with Lisette Martineau. They all sat around the kitchen table. Her father, she said, was deeply troubled and appeared to be talking to himself and muttering.

Shirley's testimony ended for the day with that sympathetic observation of her father.

In the prisoner's box, George buried his face in his hands.

When the trial reconvened the next morning, June 9th, 1978, Shirley was more relaxed in the witness box and more expansive in her testimony. Having covered the narrative of the events of November 16th in some detail, Lindsay then started to question her about individual, ultimately important areas. These were additional "bricks" Lindsay was using to build his wall around Broderick, by painting him as deceitful.

Shirley's far-ranging recollections included that, incredibly, at the time of her mother's death, they were not aware of any rent problems nor that the bailiff might be coming to evict them. When asked about Lisette Martineau, Shirley told the court:

"She used to be my brother Gerry's girlfriend, and when he was going out with her she became a friend of the family's, but when he stopped going

ABOVE: Detective Bob Mancuso in his "office."
BELOW: The replica bathroom dominated the courtroom.

ABOVE: Detectives Bob Mancuso (right) and Murray Gordon (left) pose with Federal M.P. and justice critic Walter Baker after receiving a Kiwanis Award for their work on the case. **BELOW:** Plan of the bathroom.

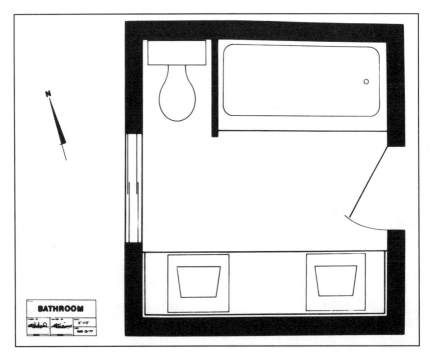

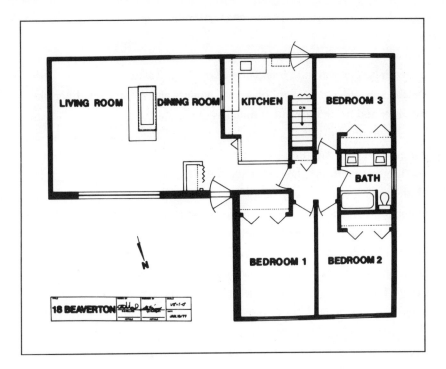

ABOVE: Plan of the house.
BELOW: "Dreemcumtru" — the hideaway.

out with her she was still a friend of the family's and a friend of my mother's." Lisette, she said, came over "once in a while," and Anne treated her like a daughter and helped her out as much as she could.

She testified that Anne inevitably turned off the electric blanket when she got up in the morning.

Lindsay questioned her about her mother's fingernails and dressing habits. Shirley had good memory of this and testified that her mother used false fingernails which she kept either in the kitchen cupboard or in her housecoat pocket. She prepared them herself and would install them over her own fingernails. She had never seen her mother leave fingernails on the bedside table. She knew that once they had been installed they would not come off easily. Then Lindsay showed the witness a photograph which had been entered as an exhibit. It showed the master bedroom with the bed and items of clothing on the bed. Shirley was asked whether there was anything unusual about what she saw in the photograph. She agreed that the bed was "tussled, and very messy" and pointed out that "mother wouldn't throw her clothes like that." This exchange then took place:

Q: Shirley, one more question concerning the photograph which shows the housecoat and the nightie on top of the bed. When your mother took her clothing off, what did she take off first, her housecoat or the nightie?
A: The housecoat.
Q: When she took it off, what would she do with it?
A: She would place it on the bed.
Q: And then she would take off her nightie?
A: Yes.
Q: What would she do with it?
A: Either place it on the bed or hang it up.
Q: We see here the housecoat on top of the nightie.
A: Yes.
Q: Is there anything unusual about that?
A: Well, her housecoat should be underneath the nightgown.

As Shirley's testimony in-chief was winding down after the better part of a day and a half in the witness box, she made more points damaging to the defence. She was aware that her father owned a cottage in Quebec's Gatineau Hills country, but astonishingly, did not know where it was. She thought it was in Quebec. She had never been invited to go there and as far as she knew her mother had never been there either.

She was aware that her father had some financial difficulties since, occasionally, she had to lend her mother money to buy groceries.

When Lindsay began to question Shirley about Cynthia Eauclaire, Bosada got ready to spring. Shirley knew Cynthia was her Dad's secretary. When Lindsay asked, "Do you know if there was any relationship between them?" Bosada was on his feet objecting to this line of questioning and demanding that both the witness and the jury be excluded while he argued his objection. Justice O'Driscoll complied and Bosada made his most forceful objection to that point in the trial, arguing that the testimony of the accused's relationship with Cynthia Eauclaire would be highly prejudicial to the accused in the minds of the jurors and was not at all probative. It would not advance the prosecution's case in any fair or logical manner but would serve only to poison the jury against his client. In counter-attack, Lindsay argued that the evidence was part of the "motivation package" by which he would demonstrate to the jury that George Broderick had reasons for murdering his wife.

Justice O'Driscoll ruled in favour of the prosecution's position, suggesting Lindsay ask the question in a more general, non-leading manner.

"Mr. Lindsay, perhaps it could be worded something like this: As of November 16th, what did you understand Cynthia Eauclaire to be?" When the jury and the witness were returned to the witness box, Lindsay put the question in those terms and received the same reply. Shirley believed Cynthia Eauclaire to be just "My Dad's secretary." She offered no elaboration.

Shirley concluded her examination in-chief by describing her mother as a practising Roman Catholic who attended church every Sunday.

She had last spoken with her father on the night of his arrest. Lindsay had Shirley look at her statement, to assist her memory.

Q: Can you tell us what he said?
A: He stressed the love he had for my mother, and he mentioned he had fallen in love with Cynthia.
Q: Had you heard that from him before?
A: No.
Q: And had you heard it from anyone before?
A: No.

Finally, Shirley described her participation in the "bathtub water test" with Detective Mancuso and Inspector Bowles at Bowles' room at the Talisman Hotel:

"They ran a tub full of water, and I was testing it to see if it was as hot as she had usually had her bath, and when they thought it was right we put a thermometer in and wrote down the temperature."

The problem confronting Bosada when he got up to question Shirley was easily recognized. She had not been "a smoking gun" witness, whose evidence described some critical event which he could attack and challenge on cross-examination. Instead, she had testified about many incidental, peripheral things, each of which might be innocuous, but in totality would assist in building a wall of evidence around George Broderick.

She was the accused's daughter. It would be difficult, if not impossible, to attack her credibility. It was obvious she was testifying with all of the anxiety and pain of a daughter testifying against a father. Probably the most damaging element in Shirley's testimony was the description of her father being agitated and "nosey" on the morning of November 16th before she left for school. He had been acting strangely and repeatedly insisted on knowing when she would be leaving the house. To that extent, the prosecution had succeeded in creating an image of someone who might be contemplating murder that morning and who was uptight at the prospect, indicating forethought and deliberation. Bosada effectively seized upon her prior testimony that she was unaware that the family was in immediate financial straits, that the rent was in arrears, and that the sheriff's men would be coming that morning to evict the family. Since Shirley had admitted that she did not know the true situation that morning, it was implicit in her testimony that she was relating her father's unorthodox conduct to the prospective death of her mother, rather than to any embarrassment and devastation that would very quickly occur when the sheriff's agents arrived.

Q: Now, my friend asked you whether or not you were aware that, on the 16th day of November, a bailiff would attend at your residence to evict your family, and you said you were not aware at that time, but you subsequently found out from your uncle, Edward Pike, is that correct?

A: Yes.

Q: And that was at the funeral of your mother?

A: Yes.

Q: When you discovered this information from him, were you surprised, shocked?

A: Well, yes.

Q: Upon learning that information, did you think back to that morning?

A: No.

Q: Did you ever ask yourself if your father's behaviour, as you described it that morning, might have been the result of the bailiff coming to the house? Did you make that connection?

A: Then, no.

Q: Did you ever make that connection?

A: Yes.

Q: When was that?

A: Now.

This would be the most salient point scored by Bosada on cross-examination, although he took Shirley through many other areas. In an attempt to demonstrate that Shirley and her father did not enjoy a close relationship—and that therefore her testimony could not be expected to be sympathetic to her father, Bosada— almost inadvertently— elicited from her that she was not the Brodericks' natural daughter but had been adopted. This disclosure seemed calculated to embarrass Shirley and did not sit well with the jury. And it did nothing to advance his case. He ended his cross-examination with Shirley describing a conversation that she had had with her mother. She said that her mother had always preferred a closed casket at any wake, and that her mother had said she wanted her eyes and organs donated to science.

Bosada asked her about the fingernails:

Q: Did you ever recall situations where your mother and father and yourself would be out for dinner and a fingernail of your mother's would fall off, and your mother would ask your father to hold it for her?

A: No.

Q: The fingernail cup was in the kitchen?

A: Yes.

Q: Was it kept for what purpose?

A: She kept it for fingernails and some glue.

Q: And she kept all of the loose fingernails in the cup, or did she keep them in other places, too?

A: In the cup, and on occasion in her housecoat pocket.

Q: Did you ever find a fingernail in the house loose, not in the cup or the coat, but somewhere else?

A: Not that I can recall.

Q: Not even on one occasion?

A: Not that I can recall.

Shirley's testimony had raised the circumstantial wall around George Broderick perceptibly higher.

22.

The prosecution next paraded an array of witnesses whose only purpose was to provide background, relate critical statements that George Broderick had made to them, and to demonstrate that the accused had lied to them regarding secondary matters. Lindsay was confronting the problem of having to plug holes in the dike before he knew precisely where they would show up or whether the defence would open a hole at all.

Thelma Roseveare was a cousin of Anne's who lived in Montreal. She met Broderick at the funeral home. He told her he was very bereaved and upset at Anne's death. He said Anne's death was very very sudden and unexpected. When asked whether she had been ill, he replied, "No, she had always been in good health." Roseveare testified that he told her about the morning of Anne's death:

"He said he left for work as usual, and they were having work done on the locks and Anne was aware that repairmen were going to come, and when the man came he couldn't get any response, and the man went to the neighbour's next door to find out what might be wrong, and they in turn contacted George at work to come home, which he did... and when he came into the house and tried to find Anne, he discovered the bathroom door locked, and at first he couldn't get the door open, and then he went and got a sharp instrument and tried to get the door open, which he did, and found Anne in the bathtub."

This version matched, more or less, what bailiff Larry Bordeleau had said earlier in the trial.

Lindsay asked whether Broderick had said anything about clothing.

"Well, he said it was very strange. Her clothing had been left in the bedroom, on the bed, and he thought it was very unusual for Anne to go into the bathroom without anything to wear coming out."

Roseveare continued. Broderick had told her that he had had Anne cremated because he had seen bodies submerged in water for months and years during the war and he didn't want her body to go through "those same conditions." Lindsay asked whether Broderick had provided any other explanation.

"No, other than the fact that when I asked him if he thought she had taken a heart attack, he said of course he didn't know at that time, but he felt that she had slipped because Anne used these water softeners that might have caused the bath to become very slippery, and in falling she grabbed for the shower curtain and it was torn."

When asked about bruises on the body, George had replied, "No, there were no bruises at all."

Thelma Roseveare's testimony about Broderick's comments was significant. Within a couple of days after Anne's death he was articulating a particular theory with respect to how Anne had died and offering an explanation for the quick cremation, as if to dispel any anticipated inquiries.

Edward Pike, Anne's brother, was called to the witness box by Lindsay's assistant, Berzins, who questioned him about the accused's business activities outside the world of life insurance. Ed knew that George was experienced in electronics from his Navy days and did not really question the story that George had told him regarding the sale of a secret electronic invention to the British government.

Q: Can you recall any particular items invented by him?
A: I had never seen them, but he told me he invented some device which had to do with radar landing which was purchased by the British government for the armed services.

Ed had first heard the story in 1972 or 1973, and believed that the invention had been sold around 1974. In 1976, George was still working on "something additional." Berzins asked him where George's centre of work was.

"Well, he told me he would go to England, and he had been to South America, but closer to home he worked quite a bit from Petawawa."

Q: Was there any connection with the military?
A: Yes, the military was involved, but he wouldn't talk about it because it was very confidential and he indicated some espionage might be involved.

Those conversations continued until the summer of 1976, Ed told the court.

George's invention had been sold to the British government for $80,000 after taxes. Ed understood that the money had been used to purchase a new home for Anne in Kanata. The story of the new home persisted "right up until the summer of 1976."

Ed described a curious event when the two couples had planned a trip to England to attend a convention. George offered to arrange the air tickets and the bookings, so Ed had sent his share of the money, $1200. Just 10 days before they were to leave, Ed still had not received the tickets for himself and his wife, and asked George about it. He was told there was no problem, but despite daily telephone calls the tickets did not arrive. George then offered him the story that his lawyer had made a mistake with Ed's cheque and put it into the wrong account, with the result that the tickets had not been paid for. Ed's suspicions prompted him to call Wardair and he was told that the tickets had been cancelled 10 days before. The refund had been forwarded to a Mr. Broderick. This was followed up by a phone call from British Airways saying that new tickets could be picked up at the airport, but instead of $600 each, the price was now $1200. Ed said he was reimbursed, indirectly, later. But the incidents did not end there.

When George went to Ed's daughter's funeral in July of 1976, in Toronto, Ed had to foot the bill. George told him he didn't have any money for either the trip or the hotel. He told Ed that the difficulty was with the tax department, and that the woman in Petawawa who had started the law suit against him had seized all his assets "and he just didn't have any money."

171

By then things were beginning to close in on George Broderick. Edward Pike, as George's superior within the Canada Premier Life corporation, was concerned about George's association with the branch secretary. He felt it was "more than it should be." At one point he called them in. He acknowledged that if he had any concrete evidence to go on, one of them would go and it would be easier to replace her than him. "I told them both that."

Q: Did you ever bring this matter up with him again?
A: Yes, I brought it up before I left, before I made the decision. I was offered the job in Toronto about the middle of October, 1969, and I didn't finally make my mind up until mid-December to take it, and one of the factors was George's relationship with his wife. Being there, I could be fairly close to my sister, and I knew the problems caused by his association with this female in the office. He told me he would change his position as far as this woman and drop her so it wouldn't distress my sister any more.
Q: What was your assessment of the situation at that time?
A: I was very provoked because I knew the thing was very unnecessary. She had been a fine wife and mother. Seeing her in this condition, knowing the way she was, was very distressful to us.

Berzins asked:

Q: Were you familiar with your sister's views on separation and divorce?
A: Yes.
Q: Can you tell us where she stood in terms of the Catholic faith?
A: Because of her religious upbringing, she would not consent to a divorce.

While other defence lawyers might have objected to this line of questioning, Bosada did not. Basically, what it demonstrated was that George Broderick was given to fanciful stories, delivered to tolerant friends and relatives with imagined credibility. The fanciful stories were a cover-up for his expanding financial difficulties. His financial difficulties had come about, at least in part, as a result of his relationship with Cynthia Eauclaire.

But a liar and a philanderer is not necessarily a murderer. Lindsay was aware of this, but the legal building blocks at the top of the wall cannot be put in place unless those at the bottom are inserted first.

The testimony of Dr. Luigi Casella, specialist in internal medicine with a sub-speciality in cardiology at St. Michael's Hospital, was called "out of order" as a necessary expedient. Ordinarily, Lindsay would have held Casella's testimony until later.

Dr. Casella was a very busy man, so Lindsay had to put him in the witness box when he was available. His testimony was short and to the point. Anne Broderick, he said, did not suffer a heart attack, nor did she suffer cardiac arrest as a result of any heart attack. There was absolutely no evidence of any organic heart disease nor of heart infarction. He used the word "definitely" in ruling out heart attack.

Dr. Casella summarized, in response to Berzins' questioning, the possible causes of cardiac arrest, generally, and what is an acceptable time for restoration of heart beat. The traces of librium in Anne's system at the time were insignificant, too small to cause death. Berzins then dealt quickly with the other possible causes.

Q: In external causes, are you referring to the lack of oxygen from asphyxia, drowning, or strangulation?
A: These are possibilities.
Q: And you also indicated electrocution?
A: Is a possibility, yes.
Q: In the event that cardiac arrest had been caused by asphyxia, drowning, strangulation or electrical shock, would you necessarily be able to tell us that from looking at the documentation, the autopsy, and the body itself, etc.?

A: No. Asphyxia may be caused in a way that doesn't leave traces and there is no trauma, for example. Electrocution, unless there is a burn, which doesn't have to be present on the body, may not be documented. It can be very difficult to document electrocution, even in industrial cases where we know electrocution has taken place. Finally, in drowning, 10% to 20% of the patients who drown suffer what is called "dry drowning," whereby there is a shutting off of the glottis and there is no water going in, so even if the patient was examined immediately no evidence might be found.

Bosada's cross-examination attempted to elicit from the doctor his opinion as to the cause of Anne's death. Dr. Casella refused to speculate. Bosada forcefully tried to relate Anne's death to the "sudden unexplained death syndrome" but Dr. Casella was not buying it on Bosada's terms.

Q: Have you ever run into situations where you cannot, for example, explain a death?
A: I have been in situations where people had conditions which could not be tested post-mortem, like asphyxiation or lack of oxygen, or other metabolic problems— the patient might be a diabetic and not sure if he had insulin or not and died suddenly; but because I am a heart specialist, in all cases we have found a pathological reason in the heart for cardiac arrest if the heart was responsible.
Q: Can we state this as a general rule, that by virtue of the existence of the category of "sudden unexplained deaths" that there are cases where people die and death cannot explained?
A: They are much less common when an expert studies one particular case. In the majority of cases where cardiac arrest is the cause of death, and cardiac arrest is a primary phenomenon, we do find abnormalities of the heart to explain it.

Bosada then tried to pry an opinion from the doctor that Anne's cardiac arrest might have been the result of a "spasm."

Dr. Casella's testimony closed the door on that angle.

Q: Is it true, doctor, that people may suffer heart attacks as a result of spasm to the arteries?

A: I see you have become quite knowledgeable in medical literature.

Q: I am far from knowledgeable.

A: Some believe that some patients with chest pain may have spasm of the coronaries, a theory that 20 years ago would have been laughed at. It has been proven that these patients usually have a history of chest pain.

Q: Or indigestion pain?

A: The chest pain might be in the chest, might be described by the patient as indigestion, and is usually distressing and not accompanied by death. In other words, this is a condition that plagues the patient but does not cause death.

Q: Is that another absolute?

A: You are trying to find the absolute truth in me, sir, and, sir, I just can't answer a question like that. From the evidence available now and our current knowledge, I find that spasm of the coronaries is uncommon and when it occurs is in a patient with other signs of coronary disease. Of course, the clinical picture is influenced by disease of the coronaries. A patient who is healthy, has normal coronaries, and has spasm of the coronary has a more benign clinical course.

Q: I am sorry?

A: Benign clinical course. "Benign" indicating they don't suffer from heart attacks, and also have symptoms if the spasm is severe enough to require the patient to go to the doctor.

Q: I take it that you are aware of cases where people have died of heart attacks attributable to spasms of the arteries.

A: Let me qualify my answer. You say you are aware of patients who have died of spasm of the coronaries. No one has documented that at the time a patient died, the patient had spasm of the coronaries. Patients with coronary disease, in other words, narrowing in the coronaries, may also have spasms. I know this very well because we always worry about operating on these patients. We may bring more blood into the circulation of the coronaries but then still have some spasm. I don't know of any case where the doctors were visualizing the coronaries and spasm was the cause of death.

After Dr. Casella left the witness box, Lindsay cut to the "backfilling" witnesses as part of his overall picture of the Broderick family.

Alice Pike was next. She was Anne's sister-in-law through marriage to Anne's brother Harold. Lindsay took her quickly to the month of December, 1975, when she had been at the Brodericks' for dinner one evening:

Q: Did something occur during dinner?
A: No, it was after dinner, between 9:00 and 10:00 p.m., and we were sitting around talking and the telephone rang. George answered the phone, and he came back and said to Anne "That was my lawyer. I have to be in court at 9:00 in the morning, and you will be in your house in Kanata on Thursday."

Half an hour later, the phone rang again and George answered it. There was a short conversation. He left, then returned. He made a telephone call and then went into the bedroom, returning quickly with his coat and a valise. He had just received a call from Uplands Airport, he said. They were warming up his airplane for him. He had to make a sudden flight to Petawawa that night. He told Anne not to expect him back before Tuesday night at the earliest. Strangely, Anne did not seem to question this.

Lindsay went directly to the events of November 16th, 1976.

At 6:00 in the evening, Alice Pike was just finishing dinner when the phone rang. It was George. Alice sensed that there was something wrong, and asked him what was the matter with his voice since she didn't recognize it. He replied, "Well, there has been an accident. Anne fell in the tub, and I took her to the hospital, and she is in intensive care and she is not expected to live." Then they discussed who should be notified.

Alice said that the call was strange. George sounded unusual. You don't call about someone dying and ask "How are you?" George had asked her, "Do you think I should go to the hospital?"

Q: Was there anything unusual about his second call?
A: If my husband were dying, regardless of how we got along, I wouldn't ask somebody if I should go, I would do it.

She then related that George said, referring to the relatives, "Tell them not to come to the hospital because there is nothing they can do for us. She is just a vegetable."

The remark was callous and a couple of the jurors shifted uncomfortably in their seats.

On cross-examination, Carroll zeroed in by suggesting Alice Pike entertained doubts about George Broderick. He asked her about the phone call.

Q: Did you believe Mr. Broderick when he told you that Anne had suffered an accident?
A: Well, I had to check it myself.
Q: In fact, you don't believe anything Mr. Broderick says, do you, and you never have?
A: Well, I wouldn't say that. We only met at social family gatherings and spoke on light topics. I had been through so many things with George that it was hard to believe a lot of things that he said.

Essentially, Alice Pike remained unshaken in her testimony. But it was clear that Lindsay had called her more to demonstrate her attitude towards George than for the content of her testimony, which had been presented to the jury before.

Jane Simpson, a close friend and confidante of Anne Broderick for many years, testified that in late 1975 she began to notice that George was changing. Where he usually had been easy going, he now seemed to be under a lot of tension and strain. He constantly blinked his eyes and seemed distressed.

She had seen Anne as recently as October, 1976, when they had met for lunch at Bayshore Shopping Centre. Anne was in good health and in great spirits. They had no luncheon plans for November 16th, 1976, since she had a dental appointment, but she had told Anne that she would call her, and did around noon. Lindsay asked:

Q: When you called on November 16th, at approximately noon, and Mr. Broderick answered the phone, what did he say to you?
A: I picked up the phone and I said, "You home, George, again?" or something to this effect, because I was surprised to find him home. The last couple of times I phoned he had answered the phone. I said, "Is Anne there?" and he said, "Oh, Jane, something terrible has happened," and I said, "What is it?" and he said, "I came in this morning, and I found Anne face down in the bathtub," and I got all upset of course, and I said, "My God," or something, and he said, "I did everything I could for her," he said, "mouth to mouth resuscitation," and I said, "I am sure you did, George," because Mr. Broderick had been a diver and I thought he would know everything to do, and he said, "I did everything possible for her," and he said they were just taking her to the hospital and he was going along and he would keep in touch with us.
Q: Did he explain what had happened?
A: I think he said she had slipped on some bath oil and had fallen.
Q: What was his tone of voice on the telephone?
A: He was very composed.
Q: Was that the only contact you had with Mr. Broderick until that night?
A: Yes, it was, but something else came up. I am a nurse. I said, "How serious is this?" and he said, "Oh, quite serious," and he said, "I hope I am not faced with the same decision that you are, Janie," and

I said, "I hope not," because my brother had had an accident about a month before and he had three brain operations, and I remember saying to Mr. Broderick that my brother was alive but not alive and I sometimes wished he had slipped away in the operating room.

Jane Simpson said George sounded very composed. She was feisty with Carroll on cross-examination and balked at Carroll's suggestion that George was merely trying to be gentle with her on the telephone. There were no problems between Anne and George Broderick that she was aware of.

When Berzins called Joan Finan to the witness box on behalf of the prosecution, he introduced unexpected fireworks into the trial. The Juliana Apartments, located at 100 Bronson Avenue in Ottawa, is a swanky building which has housed its share of government officials, diplomats, entertainers, and public figures over the years. It is a short walk to Parliament Hill. Mrs. Finan was the manager and she knew George Broderick. George, she said, had first rented a unit from her in the October, 1973, a one bedroom furnished apartment for which he had paid a total of $18,700 up until the lease was terminated in January, 1976.

The occupant of the unit was Cynthia Eauclaire. She believed Eauclaire to be George Broderick's fiancée.

Berzins' attempt to probe the relationship between George Broderick and Cynthia Eauclaire through this witness brought Carroll to his feet with one of the most vociferous objections yet raised in the trial. The witness and the jury were both sent out of the courtroom while Carroll argued his objection. This testimony, he said, apart from being rank hearsay, would prejudice the jury, delving into George Broderick's personal life, making him out to be a wife-cheater in their eyes and therefore, a person not to be trusted. This line of questioning, he argued, was not probative of the central issue of whether or not Broderick had murdered his wife. Berzins' response was simple and effective. The testimony, he argued, would go to demonstrate not only "why" Broderick had gotten into the financial mess that had already been described but would also show motivation for the commission of the offence. Justice O'Driscoll rejected Carroll's objection:

"I disagree. I think it is relevant in this case in view of all the surrounding circumstances. I think it is important the jury receive evidence as to what he was telling third parties about his relationship with this lady, Miss Eauclaire, and whether or not he was letting on to the persons who did not know any better that he was free to marry or what the situation was. I think it is relevant and important, and, therefore, it is relevant and admissible.

"Call the witness and the jury back."

With this ruling in favour of the prosecution, Berzins let Mrs. Finan tell what she had been led to believe. Cynthia Eauclaire was George Broderick's fiancee and they had planned to be married. She understood that Eauclaire had been involved in a car accident which had postponed the wedding. They had already purchased a home and George Broderick was living in it by himself. Finan described how Broderick would come into the office to pay the account each month, personally. She was not aware that he was already married to someone else. Miss Eauclaire, she said, apparently did have an accident and after she left the hospital "I never saw her again," although Eauclaire's two sons continued to live in the apartment and George Broderick continued to pay the rent. Finan had not been aware that Anne Broderick had passed away. At the time the apartment was vacated in January, 1976, there was a balance outstanding for back rent of $2,483.47. In August, 1975, Broderick had given her a cheque for $4,700 to clear the account from September, 1975 to January, 1976. She described the termination of the lease as "not voluntary." George told her that his financial difficulties arose out of a problem with airplanes on the east coast.

Joan Finan had seen Cynthia Eauclaire in the building on occasion. Berzins went to the counsel table and ceremoniously pulled a photograph from his file. He handed it to the witness. Finan identified the subject as being Cynthia Eauclaire. Berzins quickly returned the photograph to the file without introducing it as an exhibit in the case. Bosada jumped up, insisting that the photograph be filed as an exhibit for the benefit of the jury. Berzins objected strenuously and again both the witness and the jury were excluded from the courtroom during legal argument.

Usually, when the prosecution has the witness identify the subject of a photograph, it is automatically filed as part of the total court record. Only rarely does the prosecution decline to file and hardly ever does it strenuously object to it being filed. The reason for Bosada's insistence on the photograph being made an exhibit in the case, and Berzins' resistance, became obvious when the picture was handed to Justice O'Driscoll.

The witness had mis-identified a photograph of Anne Broderick as being Cynthia Eauclaire. The two women looked *that* much alike.

The court ordered the photograph to be filed as an exhibit.

Florence Harris, an employee of the diamond department of Birks' Jewellers at the Sparks Street Mall, produced a sales slip and testified that in 1975 she sold an engagement ring containing five diamonds to George Broderick. It could also be called a dinner ring, she said. The total price, including tax, was $1,338.75. George Broderick had purchased another ring from her six months before and had brought it back to have the shank changed from yellow gold to white, but it was never paid for and he never picked it up. He told her it was for his wife, who was sick in the hospital.

The defence declined cross-examination.

23.

Jack Waldron, distinguished, conservative insurance executive, would be a critical prosecution witness. As a vice-president of Canadian Premier Life Insurance, responsible for personnel, he knew George Broderick well and was aware of developing problems.

Q: In 1975, things began to change in George Broderick, is that fair to say?

A: Yes.

Q: Could you tell us, please, starting with 1975?

A: Well, it has been traditional in our company to have a managers' meeting at our head office in Winnipeg in January of each year. In January of 1975, Mr. Broderick was unable to attend that meeting, due, apparently, to illness. That, in itself, isn't particularly remarkable, but I subsequently had to go down to the Ottawa branch to convey the messages of the meeting to him in early February. I found it unusual that he managed to excuse himself three times while I was there for one day. Then, for the rest of 1975 the branch stopped making any progress. It just stopped growing, and it was becoming increasingly difficult to contact Mr. Broderick. He was out of the office very frequently, and in January of 1976 he missed the second managers' meeting in a row, ostensibly because he had to appear in court on some civil action.

After that, things continued to deteriorate. Lindsay asked:

Q: On the telephone, did he have any explanation for you?

A: Well, yes, all good salesman have explanations when they are not doing well. Mr. Broderick was a very good salesman. Presumably, everything was just about to happen.

In May of 1976, Broderick missed the biannual convention in London, Ontario, "... for what I understood was a relatively serious operation he had to beg out of going to the convention in London." Waldron was not sure of the details of the operation, but was aware Broderick "was plagued by financial difficulties."

Q: Then, sir, July 26th, 1976, you came to Ottawa?

A: Yes.

Q: And would you take us from there, please?

A: I had an all day session with Mr. Broderick and we reviewed the progress of his branch for 1975 and 1976, specifically. I indicated that I was far from happy, we were far from happy, concerning the progress of the branch. He indicated to me, and this was the first time he had so indicated, that one of the problems was that he was plagued by financial difficulties. I feel that people's financial difficulties are their own business unless it begins to interfere with their ability to handle their jobs, and certainly we had no indication from the way his accounts had been handled up to that time that there were any unusual difficulties.

There had been no requests for money other than what was due him.

I decided, if this was affecting his performance, that I should probe into what he meant by financial difficulties. He indicated to me that he had sold an invention to the British government, for about $75,000, and that he had been having considerable difficulty getting the money out of England. He had finally succeeded in doing so, and part of the money went for a down payment for a home and the rest was lost in speculative investments.

Because this money was coming he had made certain financial commitments he was now unable to fulfil. This sounded somewhat involved, to say the least, but he assured me that whatever difficulties he had had up to that point he was very capable of taking care of himself. I suggested to him that he'd better take care of them so that he could get down and do his job. I also left the very clear understanding that if there was not a turnaround in the performance of the branch by the end of 1976 I would have no alternative but to consider a change in management.

Q: Did he mention where he worked on the invention?

A: Yes, at Petawawa.

Q: Did that mean anything to you?

A: Not a thing, other than the fact that he came to us in 1966 from the Armed Forces. I believe he was a Lieutenant Commander.

Q: Did he mention any lawsuits against him?

A: Yes, he did. He indicated he had been working on some other invention at CFB Petawawa. I am a little hazy as to whether he said it was a laser X-ray or electronic beam device, he spiced his comments with a number of technical expressions and thoroughly lost me. In any event, he apparently left this device on overnight accidentally and a member of the Armed Forces died, according to Mr. Broderick. The suit was launched by the widow against the government and Mr. Broderick as co-defendants and the court, apparently, judged that the government was innocent but Mr. Broderick was attached by the widow. His assets were attached and so he was very eager to have his assets transferred to his wife's name.

After the story about the house, Waldron was becoming somewhat incredulous.

"Frankly," he continued, "I found this very hard to believe and I told him so. He reiterated that it was the truth and so I simply repeated that I still found it very hard to believe."

There was very little improvement in the Ottawa office. On top of that, Waldron had received two garnishees against Broderick's income at head office in Winnipeg. Waldron told Broderick that he would be in Ottawa during the first four days of November and while there he wanted to spend some time with Broderick to assess the situation, particularly since the garnishees had been from the Bank of Nova Scotia and Revenue Canada. He met with Broderick in November:

"Again I was assured with very positive aggressiveness that all of these things were just misunderstandings that would be cleared up very shortly... My trust was wearing thin. I made it quite unmistakeable that unless these things were resolved... we would have to discuss the fact and he would step out of management and back into sales."

Waldron was very reluctant to come down hard on a 10-year employee.

"We had invested a fair amount of money in him and he had been a darn good salesman and manager for us for a number of years, and we weren't happy about terminating an association of that length of time."

Waldron felt it was coming to a head, however, and asked his director of market administration to prepare a letter of termination.

On Tuesday, November 16th, Waldron was in Toronto with the letter of termination in his pocket.

Q: You received some information late that evening?

A: I received a telephone call from Mr. Ed Pike, the former manager of the Ottawa branch.

Q: And I believe that he advised you of what had happened to Mrs. Broderick?

A: Yes, he advised me that, unfortunately, Mrs. Broderick had died. This came as a tremendous shock not only to me but to him.

Q: What did you do as a result of that?

A: Well, it was obvious that I was not going to terminate a man whose wife had just accidentally died and I immediately destroyed the letter of termination and instructed Mr. Hunter to destroy the copy. I did not want it in the files if his wife had just died. We had to give him some time to recover his composure and get over this tragic thing.

At this point in Waldron's evidence, Lindsay interrupted the testimony and announced a prosecution *voir dire*.

Lindsay had recognized he was approaching an area of controversial testimony, and in fairness, wanted a court ruling before going into it.

Lindsay was hoping to present evidence to the jury on two issues. The first was about the fraud and theft committed by George Broderick against Kaspar Stauffacher. The second centred on the policies of life insurance George Broderick had maintained on Anne's life over the years and which would pay double indemnity.

On the Stauffacher affair Lindsay's argument was simple: he wanted to demonstrate Broderick's crushing financial situation as being so bad that it drove him to commit the theft. Bosada argued equally strenuously that by now, from previous witnesses, the jury must be more than well aware that Broderick was in serious financial straits and that the theft from Stauffacher would only serve to inflame the jury and could add nothing more to the prosecution's case.

Bosada's argument against the introduction of the insurance policies was less tenable. It was obviously quite relevant, going to the question of motive.

The jury was entitled to know whether or not George Broderick stood to gain financially from Anne's death.

Justice O'Driscoll ruled in favour of the prosecution on both questions.

Jack Waldron was then recalled to the witness box and Lindsay had him detail the life insurance policies which George Broderick had taken out on his own life. The first policy was in the amount of $15,000 and had been purchased on August 24th, 1966. Anne was the beneficiary. A second policy, a 25 year reducing term policy, in the initial amount of $10,000, was purchased on the same date. Anne was also the beneficiary. In addition, there was a group life insurance policy in the amount of $50,000— for a total of $75,000. Waldron testified that George Broderick had been maintaining the premium payments on his own policies and they were all up to date. Those policies were on George Broderick's own life.

Waldron was then questioned about the Kaspar Stauffacher affair. In June of 1973, Canadian Premier had received an application to borrow the sum of $6,380 against Stauffacher's policy. A cheque was issued to Stauffacher the same month. Waldron produced the relevant documents in court, including the "Policy Loan Agreement," purportedly signed by Stauffacher and his wife. There was also the signature of a witness. Lindsay showed the application to the jury and filed it as an exhibit in the case. Waldron then produced the cancelled cheque, which had been made payable to Kaspar Stauffacher and endorsed on the back by both him and George Broderick. The cheque had been cashed and cleared. Ultimately, he said, in May, 1975, the Stauffacher policy lapsed because they had not received the premium for that year. The premiums had been forwarded to the company by Broderick in the past.

Finally, Waldron described the insurance policies which had been taken out by George Broderick on Anne's life. The first policy, in the amount of $3,000 ordinary life, had been purchased on November 3rd, 1966. George Broderick was the beneficiary. The policy included an additional accidental death benefit in the amount of $3,000. This was the double indemnity policy. The next policy was in the amount of $12,500, also ordinary life, and had been purchased on November 11th, 1970, on Anne's life. George Broderick was the beneficiary. It was also double indemnity and would have paid $25,000 in the event of the accidental death of Anne Broderick. There were some minor loans outstanding against these policies. The third policy was a group policy taken out July 1st, 1974, for $2,500. George Broderick had taken out the policy on Anne's life, naming himself as beneficiary. Premiums were paid by payroll deduction.

All policies were paid up at the time of Anne's death and shortly thereafter a cheque for $5,000 had been forwarded to George Broderick on the second policy.

Jack Waldron was a highly credible witness who testified to facts which would be hard for the defence to dispute. Not surprisingly, Carroll treated him with kid gloves on cross-examination when the jury returned after the voir dire, and limited his questioning to points of clarification and elucidation rather than attempting to contradict him. Any other approach might have antagonized the jury. Carroll managed to elicit from Waldron a favourable description of Broderick at Anne's wake:

Q: Can you tell the jury Mr. Broderick's disposition at the wake?
A: Well, he was a very distressed man. He had difficulty holding back tears on numerous occasions. My conversation with him was not lengthy, but he was gracious enough to introduce me to other members of his family and friends who were at the wake whom I had not met before. It was a very difficult period. I thought he was an extremely emotionally wrought individual and, obviously, in great distress.

So ended the testimony of Broderick's boss.

24.

Lindsay was on the move. Now he would score rapidly with the jury by calling single-point witnesses whose testimony was virtually incontrovertible. The jurors would hardly have time to digest what one witness had to say before another would be on the stand. It was very effective, sustaining a high level of attentiveness and interest.

A special investigator with the security branch of the Canadian Armed Forces, Ross Carruthers, testified that George Broderick had terminated his career on January 22nd, 1966, and was no longer on the payroll of the Canadian Armed Forces in a civilian capacity or otherwise. He said that Broderick had had no connection with the Armed Forces since 1966. During 1970, some laser trials on 105 mm Howitzers gun sites had been going on at Petawawa but Broderick had no connection with those. The only airplane crash that had taken place in the area was a helicopter accident in early 1972, during training manoeuvres. Broderick was not involved. Military records disclosed no lawsuit in which George Broderick was being sought to pay thousands of dollars to a soldier's widow. The witness did agree with Carroll that it was remotely possible that Broderick could have been connected with the military in some other capacity.

John Jansen testified that since Broderick's retirement from the military, the only income paid to Broderick had been his military pension. There was no income from secret electronic inventions or counter-espionage duties.

Anne was not employed outside the home. The house that George said he was buying for Anne would have been beyond the family's financial means.

Sheila Kaszas was a real estate agent with Royal Trust and held the listing on the Kanata house. It was owned by a dentist. To the best of her knowledge there were no structural problems with the house and the owner's wife was never ill. Kaszas was not aware of any lawsuits involving the house which, she said, was purchased two months after it had been listed for $71,000. She had received no offer and no down payment from George Broderick. She had never heard of George Broderick.

Kaspar Stauffacher might be described as the type of individual George Broderick wished he had been. No longer a young man, he earned his living in the adventuresome and dangerous profession of flying fireman— he repeatedly flew huge bombers heavy with water into the smoke and heat of forest fires. With skill and luck he might make his drop into the heart of the blaze and extinguish it. As of June 14th, 1978, the day he took the witness box, he was employed in the Canadian north at Great Slave Lake, under contract to the Alberta government.

Originally from Switzerland, he had embraced the Canadian north with considerable appetite. Despite the fact that Stauffacher's prospective evidence had already been the subject of a *voir dire* and despite Justice O'Driscoll's ruling in favour of the prosecution, Bosada was on his feet strenuously renewing his earlier objection to Stauffacher's testimony being heard by the jury. Bosada reiterated his argument that the testimony would show the questionable character of the accused and would contribute nothing to the advancement of the prosecution. It would only contaminate the jury and was not at all probative to the central issue of murder. He pointed out that there was no solid evidence that Broderick was a forger.

Again, the court ruled that the evidence would be admitted.

Stauffacher was also an air maintenance engineer, an A.M.E., and during the off-season, when he was not flying the forest fire patrol in the north, he would return to the Ottawa area and work as an aircraft engineer. In 1972 he had met George Broderick, who sold him a life insurance policy in the amount of $8,000. He had extended the policy for an additional five years. He testified that in September of 1976, Broderick had brought him a document which he signed over the printed word "Insured." He was shown the document, now a court exhibit, which was the application for a loan against his policy. He acknowledged his own signature but said he had no idea about the other signatures. He had had no intention of applying for a

189

loan and had been left with the impression he was signing a document in the routine administration of his policy. When shown the cheque, he was emphatic. He had neither endorsed it nor received the funds.

Stauffacher was difficult to cross-examine. The noise from the "big engines" of the aircraft had dulled his hearing and he had difficulty with Bosada's questions. Bosada, for his part, seemed to be having some difficulty with Stauffacher's thick Swiss accent. Bosada questioned him closely about his life insurance policy and the loan application. Could the witness be mistaken?

Stauffacher flared up at any suggestion that he was aware of or party to the application, and he bristled perceptibly at the suggestion of it. Bosada took him through, again, his conversations with Broderick and the $10,000 loan that he had made to Broderick in late 1976. Stauffacher adamantly stated that he could recall the conversations with Broderick in great detail and told the police "my exact story."

Bosada could not shake the very credible Mr. Stauffacher— the hard-working bush pilot who was supporting two sons in a Swiss school by flying into the middle of forest fires in the Canadian north. The jury was very impressed.

The surreptitious tape recording of conversations, without warrant, would undoubtedly have resulted in the contents being ruled inadmissible in evidence, (whether "voluntary" in law or not), after the proclamation of the Charter of Rights. In 1978, however, such was not the case. The only test then was the test of voluntariness and relevance. Lindsay wanted a ruling on the conversations between the accused and Inspector Bowles, Detective Gordon and Detective Mancuso which had been secretly recorded using Bowles' ubiquitous briefcase.

The conversations, while perhaps not in and of themselves damaging to the defence, might prove useful later. Lindsay had no way of knowing whether George Broderick would take the witness stand in his own defence or not. If he wished to cross-examine Broderick on the statement he had made to the detectives, it was imperative that they be subjected to a *voir dire*.

So Lindsay called for a *voir dire* to test two broad issues: the voluntariness of those recorded statements, as well as the question of admissibility of the bathtub tests performed using the police employee. Lindsay, in argument, described Broderick as being "loquacious" on both occasions, eager to speak, knowing nothing about the fact that he was being recorded "live" on either occasion. Justice O'Driscoll, after announcing that he had long been a proponent of tape recording interviews with accused persons, said he could find nothing wrong with what had been done.

"Consequently, without any hesitation, it is my ruling that all of these conversations with the accused either before or after he was arrested are voluntary and admissible, if the Crown chooses to tender them to the jury."

The bathtub tests presented a more thorny problem. They had not been performed in what one might call a "laboratory setting," and the control factor was very limited. Nevertheless, the court ruled that they were relevant, probative, and admissible.

Lindsay was still batting a thousand on the rulings.

25.

The prosecution, having called substantial medical evidence to disprove that Anne had died from any natural cause, now turned its attention to the "hardware" in an attempt to preempt any argument that she had died from accidentally slipping in the bathtub.

Albert Moyse, the owner of Trend Notions and Novelties Inc. in Montreal, identified the shower curtains from the death scene and testified that his company had made them. At the request of Inspector Bowles, he had examined the curtain, and, using identical material, had reproduced another set of curtains identical in weight, material, and stitching. The new set, he said, was now on the model bathroom which dominated the courtroom.

The testimony of Yash Kahnna, about the shower curtain hooks, was similar. He was production manager at James B. MacGregor Company Limited, the principal Canadian distributor for the hooks. He identified the shower curtain hooks on the courtroom model as being identical to those from the death scene.

Detective Murray Gordon took the stand. He immediately had the full attention of the jury; he was the first member of the plainclothes police team to testify. Only 28 years old at the time, he had covered the death scene with Mancuso and described how he had observed a tear in the top portion of the shower curtain. Three of the metal rings, he said, were off the runner and the third hook from the end had been bent almost straight. The stitching behind that hook had ripped. When he viewed the scene, the shower curtain was out from the wall "a little bit" and definitely outside the tub.

Gordon left the witness box for a few minutes, walking over to the model bathroom to demonstrate the position of the curtain as he saw it on November 16th, 1976. He pointed out that closing the door against the tub would in effect block the curtain. He showed the position of the tear in the curtain and described it as being between two and six inches long.

The prosecution immediately moved on to Ontario Provincial Police Officer James Hobbs, who had been in charge of videotaping the various tests. He identified the tapes, described the camera angles, and outlined the steps taken to insure accuracy.

By now the centre of attention in the courtroom had shifted to the model bathroom against the wall opposite the jury box. It dominated the courtroom like a silent accuser, threatening to bring justice with the same authority as the everpresent chandelier in *Phantom of the Opera*.

When Inspector Bowles had come up with the idea of reconstructing the bathroom and performing tests in which an accidental fall would be simulated, he was well aware that this procedure would be subject to intense courtroom scrutiny and that controlled conditions must prevail if the evidence was to be admissible. His master stroke was having the tests performed before the trial, as part of the investigation, and videotaped beforehand, rather than attempting to perform the tests during the trial itself.

Bowles had solicited the assistance of Eric Kruger from the Centre for Forensic Sciences, who held a master's degree in engineering and metallurgy and belonged to the Association of Professional Engineers. Kruger had tested the rings from the death scene and had supervised all subsequent testing. The curtain rod, he said, was the same curtain rod from the death scene at 18 Beaverton. He used a female model, Julie Seto, whose weight at 105 pounds and height at five feet, approximated that of the deceased. She simulated three falls onto foam cushions in the test bathtub. On each test a fresh set of curtains was used and a new series of hooks. Kruger described the purpose of the tests:

"The objective was to simulate a fall and have the fall broken by the person executing the test by grabbing the curtain with one hand and trying to prevent a full fall into the tub."

This, he said, involved an application of the full body weight to the curtain and to the hooks close to the position of the third hook. There would be a deliberate application of body weight with a pulling motion. Kruger then demonstrated that in the first test the model was standing inside the bathtub when she simulated the fall and the grabbing of the curtain.

Berzins asked him, "And what are your results as far as the first test is concerned?"

A: There is no damage to either the curtain or the hooks from those three tests.

The court took a recess while Kruger set up the shower curtain to demonstrate the second test, which was performed in a similar manner to the first, "except that the first two hooks were taken off the rod." On this occasion the model stood outside the bathtub to cover this contingency. In the simulated fall she grabbed the curtain fairly close to the third hook and slowly applied her weight to the curtain. Kruger emphasized that this was not a simulated fall. Instead it was a deliberate pulling against one hook, after the other two had been detached. The video of the tests showed that when Julie

193

Seto was holding onto the shower curtains below the third hook and applied a steady and gradual continuous pressure with her weight, all four hooks straightened out one after the other.

The third test was performed with the model standing inside the tub and using both hands to apply her full weight to the shower curtain while again simulating a fall. This demonstration showed that none of the curtain hooks would be dislodged from the shower rod. Kruger emphasized that the only way the hooks could become dislodged was by force applied to the hook from underneath. He did allow that if the fall was broken by the application of a firm grip, it was likely that one hook might stretch slightly. But it was impossible to dislodge them as they had been at the death scene.

The court adjourned for the day with the prosecution leaving this thought with the jury:

Q: Can you account for the death scene result without the deliberate unhooking of these first two hooks?
A: Well, from my attempts to dislodge them, as it were, accidentally, I find it extremely unlikely that this would happen. In my opinion, the only way they could have come off is if somebody removed them.

When court resumed on the morning of June 16th, 1978, the trial had been going for three and a half weeks.

Court was late starting. The brightly lit courtroom was a melange of lawyers, court staff, and police officers, milling around waiting for the morning's face-off. Ten minutes passed with nothing happening. Then the court clerk entered to announce that the jury was not quite ready to continue the trial. The toilet in the jury room had quit functioning and this was disrupting the routine of the tightly sequestered jury.

Just as everyone was beginning to wonder how long the disruption would last and how quickly the services of a plumber could be obtained, to the amazement of everyone in the courtroom, the toilet in the model bathroom inside the courtroom began to flush. Everyone turned to look in disbelief at this hitherto silent apparatus. How could this be possible? The toilet in the model bathroom was not connected to anything. The courtroom broke into a fit of laughter as Detective Mancuso, in his capacity as licensed plumber, went over to investigate. He discovered a small tape recorder, secreted behind the unconnected toilet bowl in the model. The tape recorder had been activated and was intermittently broadcasting rude flushing noises. Mancuso did not have to investigate much further to determine the author of the prank. Joe Finn, legendary crime reporter, who was covering the case for the tabloid *Ottawa Today*, was at the back of the courtroom shaking his head in unconvincing denial. He maintained his innocence until his retirement.

The clerk said drily that His Lordship was not amused.

Bosada's cross-examination of Kruger emphasized that simulated testing of the type conducted by him could, at best, only approximate what had actually occurred. There were a number of variables which entered into the equation— the fact that the deceased would be aware that there was water in the tub and, that the tub was slippery and that the model, in the simulation, *knew* she would be falling on foam. When people *know* something is about to happen, they anticipate and prepare for it. Also, because of the absence of foam, the deceased would have fallen approximately one foot farther than the model.

Kruger countered by pointing out that the purpose of the test was not to re-evaluate the entire "accident" but only to test the shower curtain and the hooks. For example, no tests had been conducted with a person sitting in the tub and grabbing the curtain for assistance in getting out. Bosada did get out of Kruger that if the individual had grabbed the curtain under hook number three, then more force would be applied to number three and it would be the first to bend.

Officer Wayne Holland was recalled to the witness box in his capacity as photographer and identification officer at the death scene. He said that he measured the water in the bathtub to be seven inches deep and took samples in vials both at the centre and at the surface. He said the water texture was "fairly slippery," and so was the bottom of the tub, which had no skid protection. By the time he felt the water, it was slightly cool. He could locate no fingerprints on the bathroom wall or from the bathtub itself. He did find the blue bath oil beads in a vanity cupboard. Again, there were no fingerprints.

He said he observed pieces of the false fingernail on the nightstand to the right of the clock in the master bedroom. He did not touch or remove them. The master bedroom was undisturbed. He showed photographs to elucidate. He recovered the plastic wrapping from the floor by the bed and described it as being very thin and flimsy, a wrapper of some sort. He then corroborated that the locking mechanism on the bathroom door could be secured from inside but an instrument was needed to open it from the outside.

When Holland started to describe the bathwater tests which he had orchestrated with Shirley Broderick at the Talisman Hotel, Carroll objected. The jury was excluded from the courtroom when the debate erupted.

Carroll argued that the tests would be worthless since Shirley had last felt her mother's bathwater at least two years prior to 1976. This had already been established in the evidence. In addition, he said, Anne Broderick would not normally have taken a bath with the water temperature at 105 degrees, which he knew to be the temperature at which the tests were conducted. The witness Poulin, the bailiff's driver, was also expected to say what he believed the water temperature to be.

Lindsay countered, not by saying that Carroll's objection had no merit, but rather by asserting the legal position that Carroll's argument addressed not the admissibility of the evidence but its weight. And weight was a question for the jury. Carroll, in turn, countered, "What I say is that the evidence may well be admissible but the prejudicial effect on the accused, as my friend intends to use it, far outweighs the probative value and the assistance this jury can benefit from or gain in making a determination of what actually happened..."

After a long argument, the Court ruled the evidence to be admissible, even though he allowed that "The jury may conclude that it is of little or trifling weight or significance. That is their province, not mine. The evidence may be adduced if you see fit to call it."

So Lindsay called it.

Holland continued detailing how the test was conducted using a tub with seven inches of water with a starting temperature of 105 degrees fahrenheit. The temperature was taken every 20 minutes for four hours. The police had been very thorough. The same test was later repeated at 18 Beaverton Avenue. Carroll went over Holland's testimony in cross-examination, item by item, confronting, challenging, emphasizing the complete absence of fingerprints at the death scene or any sign of violence. He brought out that after Holland had completed the fingerprint testing of the plastic bag with negative results, he merely threw it away, suggesting that a valuable piece of evidence was now gone.

Holland and Sergeant McGarvey had driven the route described by George Broderick as part of the investigation on May 9th, 1978. The round trip from 18 Beaverton— to and back— was 16.8 miles and was covered in 35 minutes. He confirmed that on March 31st, the date that Poulin was taken to 18 Beaverton for the bathtub test, Mancuso found the false fingernails on the floor in the master bedroom. Carroll did not pursue it beyond that.

Later, it would be difficult to see how the next witness fit into the prosecution's scheme, but Lindsay wanted to touch all bases before heading for home plate. The "electrical connection" was tenuous at best. Lawrence Crawford was a licensed electrician who had examined the electrical system at 18 Beaverton. He found that the fuse controlling the bathroom electrical outlet was "over standard" at 30 amps. It should have been 15 amps. A 30 amp fuse would take longer to blow, he said. While sinister inferences may have been drawn from this fact, the prosecution had never alleged that Anne's death had been caused by electrical shock, nor that the defence was going to allege electrical mishap. Again, the prosecution seemed to be attempting to close doors before the defence had even opened them.

A question by the prosecution about the consequences if an extension cord was plugged in and tossed into the bathtub resulted in another objection from the defence. The jury was retired again.

The defence argued that the witness was not qualified to state an opinion on this subject. The court ruled in favour of the prosecution but limited the extent of the question and the response. Crawford was permitted to testify that if the electrical cord were immersed in the water, the electricity would take the shortest route to ground. This would be through the tap or drain and ultimately the fuse would blow. A 30 amp fuse would theoretically take twice as long as a 15 amp fuse to blow. There would be no sign of a burn at the wall outlet because no arcing would occur there. Carroll, on cross-examination, managed to neutralize some of the testimony by getting Crawford to admit that in fact most of the fuses in the house were "over standard."

Next, Donald Watson described the workings of the blood gas analyzer, known as the "Corning 165." His testimony was taken in conjunction with Nancy Vandenbeek's, who used the machine to analyze Anne Broderick's blood. She described the results as abnormal, but left their interpretation to the physicians.

Dr. Frances Smith, a specialist in haematology, had received the readings taken by Vandenbeek. She described Anne's blood as being strongly acidic, in the "grey zone," in a range "nearly incompatible with life" and where recovery might not be anticipated. In a word, Anne had suffered from anoxia, that is, her tissues lacked oxygen.

All of this was by now obvious, but Lindsay wanted it on the record in technical terms, anticipating his later medical experts.

26.

Curiously, the low man on the police totem pole, Detective Murray Gordon, would give the bulk of the testimony about the police investigation. Not Bowles. Not Mancuso.

He was recalled to the stand and examined in-chief by Berzins. His testimony was both specific and wide-ranging, beginning with his arrival with Mancuso at the death scene and culminating with the circumstances of George Broderick's arrest. Most of the same ground had already been covered by other witnesses. This was the first precise police perspective, however.

He described the bathroom scene in graphic detail, pointing out that there was no water on the floor or the sides of the tub. There were no items of women's clothing in the bathroom, just Anne's slippers near the toilet. When Gordon saw Broderick at the hospital later that day, Broderick told him that he had gone to the bank to get money for the landlord, Minto Realty. He said he didn't make it on time even though he had phoned the bank. Broderick, he pointed out, had hedged on the time he left the house, first stating it was between 9:05 and 9:10 and then saying it was about five minutes after his daughter Shirley had left.

He confirmed the conversation when Mancuso asked Broderick if he was "pigging around." Then, back at the house, Gordon himself asked Broderick if he had a girlfriend. Again Broderick denied the suggestion.

At this time, at the house, Broderick related the bizarre story about the police killing in Mexico.

Broderick, Gordon said, could not come up with a copy of the credit card slip for the gas he claimed to have stopped to purchase. On the whole, he described Broderick as being cooperative and providing a written statement the next day. This time however, Broderick said that he left the house around 9:55 or shortly after 10:00.

That was three different versions, so far.

Then Gordon described an exchange with Broderick about the mysterious arrangement of Anne's clothing on the bed:

A: We indicated to Mr. Broderick the clothing on the bed in the master bedroom. We explained to him that when one undresses, he or she takes off the housecoat first, then the nightgown, and puts them down the same way on the bed. They were the opposite. He

199

said he might have moved them, looking for something to cover his
wife.

Q: Okay, I just want to get this clear— in the bedroom you found
the nightie on the bottom and the housecoat on top?

A: Yes, sir.

Gordon described the layout of the house and the location of the master
bedroom. He found the control to the electric blanket in the "On" position,
a curiosity in light of the "Energy Saver" signs around the house. He related
George Broderick's version of how he found Anne's body submerged, her
routine when bathing and use of the distinctive blue bath beads, and finally,
when asked about insurance policies, Broderick had cooperated by producing
the two policies immediately.

Then he described the following exchange and the "Columbo" com-
ment which kept Mancuso awake:

"Mr. Broderick advised us that he was a skin diver and had trained Mrs.
Broderick to dive as well. She was very religious, a very religious person.
They were a close-knit family. There were no problems marriage-wise. No
problems sexually. He had had a testicle removed some time earlier and was
presently on Corax. Because of a slight nervous problem, his wife had been
sharing the Corax with him.

"At this time Sergeant Mancuso got up and went to the washroom. Out
of the blue, Mr. Broderick commented to me that because of the strangeness
of the death, it would be a good case for Columbo. It was after this that he
gave the written statement."

Gordon had been troubled by the missing gasoline receipt. When a search
was finally conducted of the house, he found a batch of copies. There were
none for the date of November 16th.

Bosada's cross-examination of Detective Gordon was equally far-ranging
and probing. He re-examined each bit of critical evidence given by Gordon;
but on the whole since Gordon's testimony was straightforward and factual,
it remained relatively unscathed. At one point Bosada challenged the methods

which the police had used to establish the all-important time of George's departure from the house.

Q: What occurred on the 16th?

A: We interviewed neighbours until about 10:05 p.m.

Q: And how many people did you interview?

A: Three neighbours, best of my recollection.

Q: And is this a normal thing for you to do when you are conducting your investigation into a sudden death?

A: I would say I have done it once before.

Q: Mrs. Broderick had not even died at that time. Why would you investigate to that extent then?

A: We just went around to see if anybody had seen what time Mr. Broderick had left.

Q: Why was that a point of some concern to you?

A: He had told us first about the two hours, and there was some curiosity on our part in regard to that.

Q: He was doubtful about the time he left?

A: Yes, sir.

Q: So why was that such a big thing?

A: One of the neighbours might have been able to clear the point up for us.

Q: Why wouldn't you have gone straight to Shirley?

A: We did go to Shirley. Mr. Broderick answered the questions for her.

Broderick answering for his daughter? It was a damaging response.

If Bosada wanted to score points about the police perspective, the investigation or the lack of direct evidence, he would have to do it through cross-examination of Gordon. He started by attacking Gordon's testimony regarding the conversation in the emergency unit, Broderick's time of departure from the house, the dining room conversation, and in particular Broderick's "big lie":

Q: Why did you ask him again the question about whether or not he was having an affair?
A: You would have to ask Sergeant Mancuso. He asked that question.
Q: You know why he asked the question about the time. Do you know why he asked that question?
A: No.
Q: Did you really expect to get a truthful answer to that question from a man whose wife was in hospital?
A: Yes.
Q: You thought he might tell you about an affair he was having?
A: He was not asked if he was having an affair. He was asked if he had a girlfriend.
Q: "Were you, are you, pigging around?"
A: Exactly.
Q: That was an appropriate question to be asking him at that time?
A: I felt we should have gotten an answer from him.

Usually, the investigating officer or officer in charge of the case is presented to the jury last, as the witness most knowledgeable about the case, the "wrap-up" witness. The investigating officer is usually seen by the jury as "the star of the show" and it is an effective tactic to leave that testimony until the end.

Lindsay decided against this. He put Mancuso and Bowles on the stand in the normal stream of testimony as just two more witnesses unfolding a continuing narrative. If the investigators have done a thorough job, there is usually very little left for them to say. Other witnesses have already said it all.

So Mancuso had very little to say. Berzins took him through most of the investigation which the jury, by now, had already heard, confirming minor points here and there and backfilling the testimony of the previous witnesses. It was almost dreary. He did hit on two points that would strike a chord with the jury:

> Q: Could you tell us about Mr. Broderick's attitude?
> A: Mr. Broderick was reluctant to let us speak to Shirley. We pressed the issue and he finally agreed. We did speak with Shirley in her bedroom, briefly, with respect to the time she left, and Mr. Broderick appeared to have assisted her with her memory as to what time she left...
> Q: While this search was being conducted, what were you doing?
> A: I was sitting in the living room. Mr. Broderick was there quite often. The television was on. Mr. Broderick commented that television had a lot of violence on it and he said, you know, some people could watch television and enact some of that violence.
>
> He stated to me that he frequently saw older fellows with young chicks, as he put it, in downtown Ottawa, and he said it was disgusting; their wives in all probability were sitting at home with the supper in the oven, waiting for them to come home.

Bowles' testimony centred on the conversation with George Broderick which had been surreptitiously recorded during their interview at Branscombe's Motor Hotel. Again, the point was fought over on *voir dire* by Lindsay and Bosada, resulting in the ruling that the one hour and 10 minute interview would be admitted in evidence.

This was a cagey tactical move from Lindsay's point of view. He did not know whether George Broderick would be testifying and this was a method of having Broderick say his piece in open court, almost like forcing him to testify for the prosecution. Bowles described the interview as very low key. It was not a "hot light" grilling, with the suspect sitting in a bare room. The conversation was free and casual in a cordial atmosphere. It was clear from Broderick's tone that he was attempting to allay the suspicions of the investigators. His responses were quick and easy. And he had a response for everything. He even ventured his own theory as to how the accident had occurred.

"Many's the time I've seen her stand up in the bathtub to wipe off little marks on the tiles or to adjust the curtain and I've always given her hell for it because the tub stays slippery. She must have gotten up to do something of this nature and just slipped and fell and hit herself and then dazed herself and she went under the water. When I found her, it looked as if she'd tried to save herself from falling and grabbed hold of the curtain, because it was torn down and she just seemed to be lying in the tub as if she had been trying to save herself and just hadn't succeeded."

At the conclusion of this sequence, Bowles produced a map to demonstrate for the jury the 16.8 mile route Broderick said he had followed on that day. This route would take approximately 41 minutes.

Bowles described how, on February 10th, 1977, the date of Broderick's arrest, the tape recorder was activated both in the car and at the police station.

This time Bowles avoided the free and easy conversational tone which had prevailed during earlier discussions with Broderick. With heavy seriousness he administered the standard police caution and told Broderick he would be charged with first degree murder. Broderick's response: "I'm not interested in that, Bill, because I'm innocent."

Despite being cornered, Broderick then continued to patronize Bowles by repeatedly saying that he had been trying to reach *them* (the police) all this time. From the tape:

BRODERICK: I have phoned Murray (Gordon) for the last three days running and I've kept my days open the whole damn time for him to call me. I've given him all my phone numbers and he promised to phone me and he has never done it. And yesterday and the day before I phoned him because I had two phone calls from Lisette Martineau...
BOWLES: Uh hum.

BRODERICK: And it was pretty disturbing what she told me...
BOWLES: Uh hum.
BRODERICK: ... and she phoned my son and said exactly the same thing in a different context. That really disturbed me and I wanted to speak to him so badly and he didn't phone me and tonight I went out for supper. My daughter knows nothing and Murray promised Cynthia that he'd give her time to let my daughter know and all of a sudden you chaps are here. I thought you'd give me some time..."

Then he began to prattle:

BOWLES: ... Let your daughter know what?
BRODERICK: Well, God, Bill, she doesn't know that I'm under suspicion of this. She knows her mother is dead but she doesn't realize that this investigation is going on. I've got nothing to hide, Bill, nothing...
BOWLES: Ah, Mr. Broderick, it's now 10:30. We'll be leaving and driving to Nepean Police Office. At that time, I'll read you a caution again so that you're sure that you understand your position. If you wish to make a statement then that's fine. It's entirely up to you. Do you understand?
BRODERICK: I'd like to make a statement tomorrow. I've had three or four drinks tonight... I've asked Murray to let me talk to you. I did not lie to you at any time but I did not tell you everything that you wanted to know because I was afraid of letting you know about Cynthia. Now, Lisette told me things the other night that I was not aware of.
BOWLES: I see.
BRODERICK: And I'm really concerned about it.
BOWLES: What did she tell you?
BRODERICK: Well, this is why I'd like to talk to you tomorrow, Bill, because my mind is a little bit fogged. Lisette phoned and told

me that she wanted to tell the truth to the police... did you get my coat and scarf?

GORDON: This is where you're sitting.

BOWLES: Okay, Murray, we'll stay here.

GORDON: Okay.

BRODERICK: Lisette told me that she'd gone up to my house at 10:30 and she said that she'd heard an argument. She had not knocked or pressed the bell...

BOWLES: Um hum.

BRODERICK: And, she left. So then the next night she phoned me and she said that she was going to tell the police the truth, and I said, Lisette, the only thing you can do is tell the truth and then she said that she heard Anne scream and I said well that might be a... I don't know, Lisette, and I said just tell the truth. She was frightened. Then she phoned my son and she said that she'd heard Anne scream many times. And my son asked her, "Was my Dad's car there?" and she said, "I don't know." So I don't know what the hell she's doing. I really don't know. It seems to me that I'm being put into a position by my friends that is giving me a hell of a... I don't know, Bill, I really don't know.

BOWLES: Did you and Mrs. Broderick have an argument that morning?

BRODERICK: No... not any way. We talked about the election with that clown in Quebec. We listened to the radio. We had breakfast. She did her flowers and I got dressed and left and that was it. Now, Lisette said she saw all the pictures that you people showed her and the bathtub was clear. But the pictures you showed me, Bill, showed... blue colouring in the tub...

BOWLES: Okay, we can discuss it further...

Broderick then said he wanted to phone Cynthia.

BRODERICK: Hello, Cynthia? I just want somebody else to listen to this conversation. Listen, sweetie, they picked me up for first degree murder— I don't know what the hell we're going to do— now, you spoke to Murray and Murray promised you a couple of hours to speak with Shirley— now we don't have the money to have a good lawyer, I don't know what we're going to do— I have no intention of speaking with them tonight because I've had three or four drinks. I have nothing to hide, as you know, and so I'll speak with them tomorrow. I really feel bad because they haven't spoken to me other than the once I spoke with Bill Bowles. I don't know what they have on me, sweetheart, I think it's pretty well the evidence, what this Lisette said, I don't know... listen, sweetheart, I have nothing to hide— they— I can't be convicted of loving you, I can't be convicted of being in debt, and you know as well as I do I had nothing to do with Anne's death, so I'm not worried... yes, I'm up in the Nepean Police Force. Bill Bowles is on the other line. I insisted he listen to this... all right, sweetie... Bill, answer that, please...
BOWLES: Until bail can be arranged... Mrs. Eauclaire... yes, Mr. Broderick has been charged with murder as he told you and he should get a lawyer as soon as possible... he'll appear in court tomorrow morning... he'll be remanded in custody, yes.
BRODERICK: No, sweetheart, you can't do that— get hold of Mike Deslaurier and get him into the office. I've got 12 appointments, sweetheart, and you know Canadian Premier Life has to go ahead. So get Mike in and get him on the phone... Don't tell him what the score is, just tell him that I've been detained and I can't get into the office...
BOWLES: It's entirely up to you, George.
BRODERICK: I've been pretty cooperative with you people all the way along the line, and I expected you to cooperate with me, to call me back and ask me questions so I could tell you things I didn't tell you the first time. I've not lied to you. Everything I've told you is

the truth. But I have not elaborated on certain debts that I have and I'm willing to tell you anything that you want but I only wish that you had called me in the last two or three days so I could talk to you. The thing that bothered me was those bloody phone calls I got from Lisette Martineau.

27.

All eyes in the jury swung to Cynthia Eauclaire as she was ushered in from a side door to take her place in the witness box. She was neither a happy nor a willing witness. She was there under subpoena. She was sworn in. Thirty-nine years old, divorced since 1969 and an employee of Canadian Premier Life Insurance. She had three grown children.

As she answered Berzins' questions, she looked directly at George Broderick sitting in the prisoner's dock. Yes, she had been in love with him since the fall of 1969. Yes, they had exchanged rings. Yes, George had helped her financially and set her up at the Juliana Apartments. Yes, they had a cottage together on Lac Sheridan. Yes, she had named the cottage "Dreemcumtru." Yes, George spent weekends there with her. Yes, he was good to her kids, like a father. Yes, George had given her daughter away when she was married. Yes, yes, yes.

George Broderick looked at her from the prisoner's dock with a confusion of pride and dispiritedness.

Remarkably, Cynthia testified that she had never bothered to ask George where he had been on the morning of Anne's death, even after he had been charged with Anne's murder. Cynthia was not, she protested, a nosey person.

She described George as being in good physical condition, and strong. At the cottage he liked to rough it up and put "holds" on people jokingly. She suspected he had taken judo at one time.

Berzins questioned her again about the rings. She agreed they were expensive.

He questioned her about Annie Frew, the Scottish woman who had invested $15,000 with George. Cynthia had seen the correspondence from Annie Frew, demanding to know where her money was. Cynthia had asked George about it and he had replied that it was his problem and nothing to worry about. "Nothing illegal," he told her.

On cross-examination Bosada had a friendly witness. He pitched slow balls and Eauclaire batted them across the courtroom. Her replies were animated.

The rings, she pointed out to him, were nothing more than friendship rings. While George had assisted her in moving into the Juliana, he was not part of her family and did not try to be. She had no idea why he was always going to Camp Petawawa. (He had given her the same story.) George was a generous person, always helping others. He seemed to have lost a lot of his stamina after his operation. During their time together at the cottage there were always others there. She was last there with him in 1975. She described, in response to Bosada's questions, her fantasy of marriage to George.

Q: But it was a fantasy?
A: Right.
Q: Did you ever feel that it could be accomplished?
A: No, sir.
Q: Did you ever do anything to accomplish it?
A: No, sir.
Q: Did he ever indicate to you that he would do anything to accomplish it?
A: No, sir.
Q: So it was just a hope?
A: That is right.

Q: Now, in the matter of marriage, did you ever consistently or perpetually remind Mr. Broderick that you wanted to marry him?
A: Never.

Eauclaire was clearly reading Bosada's questions very well and providing appropriate answers. No doubt they were truthful. She was adamant that George Broderick was never a violent person and, talking to her on the phone on the day of Anne's death, he was crying.

Q: Did you ever find Mr. Broderick to be a violent person?
A: Never.
Q: Are you still prepared to marry Mr. Broderick if the opportunity arises?
A: Yes, sir.
Q: And do you have any reservations at all about doing that?
A: None whatsoever.

In the prisoner's box, George Broderick was beaming.

Then a Quebec farmer, Dave Gowan, testified that Broderick had purchased the cottage near his farm around 1970. He knew Cynthia Eauclaire, as he had seen them together and George had introduced her as his wife. He said that George told them they had been married about three months. He was so convinced they were husband and wife that when Broderick's son, Gerry, told him his mother had died, Gowan assumed that it was Cynthia who had died.

Following Gowan's testimony, the prosecution and the defence went into a huddle resulting in an agreement: the defence agreed to admit the amount of Broderick's indebtedness at the time of the death. From the defence point of view, it would be unwise to have a parade of prosecution witnesses coming through the witness box, each describing how much money Broderick owed them. Why emphasize the indisputable? From the prosecution's point of view it saved a lot of time and bother. Lindsay read the list of creditors into the record: the Bank of Montreal, the Bank of Nova

Scotia, TransCanada Credit, Household Finance Corporation, Lewis Motors, General Motors Acceptance Corporation, and Revenue Canada. The total Broderick owed was just under $42,000.

Constable Rod Williams was identified as an intelligence officer with the Ontario Provincial Police who specialized in electronic interception. He had been conscripted by Inspector Bowles and was called by Lindsay to the witness box to establish the technical details of the wire-taps which had formed part of the investigation.

Lindsay snapped on the tape recorder and played part of the intercepts between George and Cynthia for the jury. Everyone in the courtroom felt as if they were eavesdropping.

MR. LINDSAY: We are ready to play it.
UNKNOWN MALE: Hello.
BRODERICK: Hi, Dee Dee, how are you?
UNKNOWN MALE: I'm pretty good.
BRODERICK: Ah, good. Everything coming along fine?
UNKNOWN MALE: Yeah, no problems.
BRODERICK: Is Mum there?
UNKNOWN MALE: She's in bed. Would you like to speak to her?
BRODERICK: Oh... is she asleep?
UNKNOWN MALE: Well, I'm sure she'd like to talk to you.
BRODERICK: Okay.
UNKNOWN MALE: Okay, just a sec.
EAUCLAIRE: Hello.
BRODERICK: I'm sorry to wake you up.
EAUCLAIRE: No problem.
BRODERICK: How you feeling?
EAUCLAIRE: Rotten.
BRODERICK: What's the matter?
EAUCLAIRE: Oh, what's the matter... just... you know... it's getting a little bit...
BRODERICK: I can't hear you.

EAUCLAIRE: Nothing... you just can't... you know, the whole thing, I guess, it's sort of worn me down— I don't know...

BRODERICK: I know how you feel— I'm worried sick about it and I can see you... dropped... dragged into it...

EAUCLAIRE: Right.

BRODERICK: I didn't bring you into it in the first place because, you know, I just didn't want you brought into it.

EAUCLAIRE: Yeah, right.

BRODERICK: You shouldn't have told them as much as you did.

EAUCLAIRE: Right, what do you mean?

BRODERICK: Oh, about how close we were and things like that, but I guess there's nothing else you could do.

EAUCLAIRE: Oh, there was absolutely no way I could lie.

BRODERICK: Yeah, I know what you mean...

EAUCLAIRE: Because they had the pictures and everything... (sniffs).

BRODERICK: Yeah, I know. I just hope I can keep you out of it. I don't want you in it at all.

EAUCLAIRE: I don't know, but I think we're both going to be visiting...

BRODERICK: Visiting what?

EAUCLAIRE: Jail.

BRODERICK: Aw... don't be silly...

EAUCLAIRE: No, I'm not trying to be smart— really.

BRODERICK: Well, why do you say that?

EAUCLAIRE: Well, just the way it's going...

BRODERICK: Well, we'll find out when I come back...

EAUCLAIRE: Yeah, right...

BRODERICK: You won't be there, that's for damn sure.

EAUCLAIRE: Oh, there's not too much you can do about that now, I don't think...

BRODERICK: Oh, yes, there is... the thing is that it's circumstantial evidence, you know what I mean?

EAUCLAIRE: Yeah, right...

BRODERICK: It's unfortunate everything came out like this... when I come back, I'll just tell them the complete story and I'll just have to go on from there. That's all.

EAUCLAIRE: Yeah, right.

BRODERICK: But I try not to worry about it, because, shit, there's nothing I can do about it.

EAUCLAIRE: Yeah...

BRODERICK: I'll just have to explain things when I get back... in the meantime, I'm just so sorry for you.

EAUCLAIRE: Oh, well, don't worry.

BRODERICK: I love you very much, you know...

EAUCLAIRE: Oh, I know what, and I love you, too...

BRODERICK: I'm just so sorry that you're dragged into it... they went through my desk...

EAUCLAIRE: ...

BRODERICK: My nerves are pretty shot...

EAUCLAIRE: I guess so... no, I still say that's where it comes from.

BRODERICK: Eh?

EAUCLAIRE: I mean, I know where it comes from.

BRODERICK: Well, I don't know. I haven't talked to him about it. I don't want to, you know, in case they don't know. I just want to keep it quiet.

EAUCLAIRE: Yeah, right.

BRODERICK: Just say a few prayers to Uncle George, I guess.

EAUCLAIRE: I've been doing that, but it's the only way that I can see it.

BRODERICK: Yeah.

EAUCLAIRE: They just can't hit the jackpot like that, there's just no reason for it.

BRODERICK: Yeah.

EAUCLAIRE: Anyway, thank you very much for calling— I was wondering how you were doing and all that... things don't look too good, but then... (laughs).
BRODERICK: Well, as long as I've got you, I couldn't care less.

It was, on the whole, good tabloid stuff.
Court adjourned for the day after the tapes were played.

That night the prosecution team met, as they had each night since the beginning of the trial, to determine the order of battle for the following day.

A major decision now confronted Mac Lindsay. The meeting that night between Lindsay, Berzins, Bowles, Mancuso, and Gordon, went over the pro's and con's of calling Lisette Martineau to the witness box. It was a lively discussion.

On the morning of June 26th, 1978, the court was called into session but the jury was not brought in. Proceedings began immediately in the jury's absence to hear argument about Lisette's testimony, part of which had been obtained from the wire-taps.

Knowing that it was facing an uphill battle, since it had not yet won a single ruling in the trial, the defence tendered its most vociferous argument yet: Lisette should not be allowed to testify. She had changed her story back and forth, including at the preliminary hearing. She was a demonstrably unreliable witness. In any event, the defence argued, her testimony was not probative to the central issue of whether or not Broderick murdered his wife. Her testimony would only prejudice the jury against the accused. The court, in a somewhat curious ruling, ruled that her testimony would be allowed:

"The matter of the tape I have already ruled on. The Crown may play it to the jury and tender it as it sees fit.

"As far as Miss Martineau is concerned, in my view, it is open to the Crown to show what the accused has said in statements to the police and to other persons and if there are lies contained therein. I do not see it as irrelevant evidence but relevant evidence in all the circumstances. Consequently, the Crown may ask Lisette Martineau about her relationship with the accused over the years.

"Are we ready for the jury?"

Lisette's testimony began with a potpourri of details about her relationship with the Broderick family and her ultimate involvement with George.

She had last seen Anne just a week before she died and it was the first visit with her in three months. On the day of Anne's death she had returned to see her, by car. The police were already at 18 Beaverton when she arrived and she was there less than five minutes. George had embraced her and said, "Missy had an accident." She described him as being very upset and he was a person who was not easily upset but was usually "calm and collected."

She saw blue marks on George's face; spots of some sort on the right cheek. She had never seen these before. She left and drove to see Tom Stott.

At this point, Carroll objected. Lisette should not be able to testify as to what she said to Tom Stott in her distraught condition. Lindsay, recognizing the legal point was against him, quickly withdrew the question.

Lisette continued with her story.

She returned to 18 Beaverton late that afternoon and found George downstairs doing the wash. The police had dirtied the bathmat with fingerprint powder. George told her that Anne had slipped and fallen in the tub, but said there were no marks on her and no bleeding. Those were his only comments to her.

George suggested that Anne may have been washing the tiles, standing up when she slipped. George called her the next day to tell her that Anne had died. They went out for dinner and a drive and then he took her home. After the funeral they went to Ryan's house in Aylmer, Quebec, where they had lunch. Lindsay asked her:

Q: Was it just a family gathering?
A: Well, there were friends there, too.
Q: And after the party where did you go?
A: Straight to Mr. Broderick's home.
Q: Is that to 18 Beaverton?

A: Yes.

Q: Did you stay there that night?

A: Yes, I did.

Q: Did you sleep with Mr. Broderick that night?

A: Yes, I did.

Q: Did you have sex with him?

A: Yes.

Q: And once he was asleep you went into Shirley's room to sleep?

A: Yes, I did.

Q: Did you stay through the night at Mr. Broderick's home?

A: Yes.

Q: Miss Martineau, was that the first time you had had sex with Mr. Broderick?

A: No.

Q: Can you tell us about the other occasions? How long they were before, for instance, or where?

A: I don't remember.

Q: Can you tell us the number of times before that night?

A: I don't remember.

Q: Was it more than once?

A: Yes.

She then told the court how they cleaned the bathroom and disposed of some of Anne's personal belongings.

Lindsay then pursued this exchange:

Q: Up to and including that Sunday, did Mr. Broderick at any time propose marriage to you?

A: No.

Q: Or suggest it?

A: No.

Q: Did he mention anything to you about the two of you being together thereafter?

A: Not that I remember.

Q: Or mention having a child with you?

A: Yes, he did.

Q: He said that?

A: Yes.

Q: What did he say?

A: I don't remember the exact words.

With that, the dirt was in the minds of the jury and it was impossible to assess its impact. Like the proverbial feather in the wind, it could not be pulled back nor could they ever disabuse their minds of it.

From the looks on the jurors' faces, they were not happy with this young woman and clearly they were not impressed with George Broderick. Neither were they impressed with Lisette's testimony that when they were cleaning up the house, George threw out Anne's precious memento, the wedding announcement of his marriage to her.

When Carroll cross-examined, Lisette broke down and cried.

He brought out that she had no real family of her own. The Brodericks were her only family. She was very close to Anne. The stories of George being involved in espionage and being a karate black belt, she had not taken seriously. Carroll continued, point by point, to dilute the somewhat extravagant evidence that she had given in-chief. Lisette's tears in the witness box had a good effect. Carroll managed to relate this to her feelings for Anne and her guilt over bedding down with George on the day of Anne's funeral.

Q: You have ever had a child by Mr. Broderick?

A: No.

Q: Now, the sex you had with Mr. Broderick caused you great guilt feelings, is that not true?

A: Yes.

Q: In fact, when we began this examination this morning, and you started crying, it was in relation to your feelings for Mr. Broderick, is that not true?

A: Yes.

Q: I know this is difficult for you, but you have to answer the questions as best you can. You were surprised when you saw the police cars there that morning on the 16th, is that not correct?
A: Yes.
Q: And subsequent to the 16th, you had a number of interviews and talks with the police officers, is that not correct?
A: Yes.
Q: And all this time you were feeling guilty about your sexual relationship with Mr. Broderick, is that not true?
A: Yes.
Q: And, in fact, in part you blamed Mr. Broderick by transferring your guilt to him, as well for having hurt Missy, because he had intercourse with someone close to the family?
A: Yes.
Q: And do you remember that in early February, you were at the Talisman Motor Hotel, in Inspector Bowles' room?
A: Yes.
Q: And do you recall making certain telephone calls to Mr. Broderick?
A: Yes.
Q: And some of the questions that you asked Mr. Broderick on those telephone calls were written out for you by the police, is that not correct?
A: Yes.
Q: And you indicated in those telephone calls you felt it was possible that Missy did not have an accident?
A: Yes.
Q: And Mr. Broderick responded, "Don't be ridiculous," or words to that effect?
A: Yes.
Q: And he was very upset that you would even consider that?
A: Yes.
Q: And all of this time the sexual relationship with him was troubling you, wasn't it?

A: Yes, it was.

Q: The questions that the officer made up for you were based on stories that you had told the police officers?

A: Yes.

Q: Were those stories true or false?

A: False.

Not surprisingly, she concluded her testimony by saying that she had not spoken to George since and had not visited him in prison.

28.

Lindsay was rounding third base and heading for home.

He entered the closing phase of his case, hoping to conclusively demonstrate to the jury that Anne Broderick had not died of natural causes.

The opinions of three medical specialists would be called to establish that negative feature, and to offer their views about how she *might* have met her end.

Among the prosecution lawyers, these specialists were referred to as the Three Wise Men.

When the National Aeronautics and Space Administration was preparing for the first tentative voyages of Americans into outer space, they selected Dr. Jerome Modell as physician to the Project Mercury astronaut recovery team. He was a member of the ground crews for the first manned space missions and was there to receive both Alan Sheppard and John Glenn after their historic flights.

Dr. Modell was a medical doctor of incredible accomplishment. He had been in practice since 1957 and was a member of the staff at the University of Florida and the College of Medicine. He was professor and chairperson of the Department of Anaesthesiology, responsible for anaesthetic services, critical care and intensive care units. He had been chief of anaesthesiology at the United States Naval Base at Pensacola, Florida, and had developed a sub-specialty in critical care and pain treatment. Ultimately, funding from the National Institute of Health freed him to spend 80% of his time on research.

He was *the* acknowledged expert in the entire United States on drowning. He had published more papers on the subject than any other researcher in the United States and probably the world. In 15 years he had published between 120 and 130 papers in recognized medical journals, half of which were on drowning or the intensive pulmonary support applicable to drowning victims. In 1970, he had published a book on the subject and had spoken extensively throughout the United States and Europe on the topic. In May, 1978, a week or two before the commencement of Broderick's trial, he had addressed the World Life Saving Congress on drowning.

In 1977, when he agreed to consult with Mancuso and Gordon about the Broderick case, he adopted a very objective, credible approach. He would base his opinion exclusively on *medical* facts. He specifically directed that the detectives give him no information whatsoever about Anne's death, the death scene or anything developed in the course of their investigation. He had access to and reviewed all of the documentation prepared by Doctors Estall, Bourmanis, and Liepa.

The jury leaned forward in unison, listening to what this remarkable physician had to say.

First, he discoursed on the possibility of Anne Broderick having drowned:

Q: And what I would like to discuss with you are the various possibilities as to how a person could end up in that position in the bathtub, dealing, first of all, with the possibility of an accidental fall— that is, standing up and losing footing and falling into the bathtub and subsequently becoming submerged in the bathtub. Would you comment on that possibility in relation to the medical background in this case?

A: In the situation that you have postulated— if one slipped and fell into the bathtub, but did not lose consciousness during the process— then I would not expect to see the individual die of drowning but rather to be able to lift her head up from the water.

Then, one would have to go one step further, and say that if indeed the final event was the drowning episode, then what could have rendered the patient unconscious?

If someone were normal and healthy immediately prior to this, I would have to postulate that the individual fell, struck her head and suffered a concussion, which would cause the individual to lose consciousness. I would expect, in that situation, to see some evidence of external trauma to the skull and/or a bruise to the subcutaneous tissue. In other words, damage to the tissue right underneath the skin, the fat and the connective tissue, or even a small collection of blood or discolouration or what we call a haematoma, in the muscle that overlies the skull. However, it is possible to have a concussion without having any noticeable effect on the brain.

So, I think a concussion in this case would be unlikely. It is my understanding that an examination externally and right under the skin in the skull did not reveal any areas that might be compatible with trauma sufficient to cause unconsciousness.

Next, Dr. Modell dismissed the prospect of epilepsy because there was no history of it in Anne's case. He considered cerebral-vascular accident, or stroke, but this would disclose a clot or an area of cerebral ischemia where the blood flow to the brain was cut off.

He considered heart attack, or myocardial infarction, whereby the blood supply to a specific part of the heart is compromised. He considered electrocution, severe metabolic disorder, such as an overdose of insulin, and drug overdose.

"These possibilities come to mind, but I might say one other thing in relating all of this to drowning— if any of these things had happened, then it would be extremely unlikely that this victim died of drowning. I make that statement because drowning is defined as suffocation by submersion in liquid in the broadest sense."

Dr. Modell expressed the conclusion that many things indicated that there had been no aspiration of water by Anne Broderick. There was no evidence of aspirated fluid in the lungs.

After giving a highly complex medical analysis involving the chemical considerations attendant upon drowning, he then finished his testimony in-chief:

"Therefore, I have to conclude that this patient did not die of drowning with aspiration. If this patient indeed did die of drowning the patient would have to fall into the overall 10% of people who drown without aspiration, who, in other words, suffocate in water. In a situation of an adult in a bathtub— although we don't have any nation-wide statistics or international statistics— but based on what I have seen, I would have to conclude that the incidence of near drowning in a bathtub without aspiration by an adult without any previous significant medical history would be considerably less than 10%."

Berzins knew he had struck gold with Dr. Modell, and was reluctant to let him go:

Q: Can you assign any percentage of chance that Mrs. Broderick slipped and fell in the bathtub?
A: I think it extremely unlikely. If you are asking for a number, I would have to say that based on the medical knowledge we have it would have to be significantly less than 10%.
Q: What would you say about the likelihood that Mrs. Broderick suffered a convulsive disorder such as epilepsy and ended up as she did in the bathtub?
A: The answer would be 10% or less, and that is based on the fact

that in all experiences of proven drowning, only 10% drown without aspiration, so that would be the maximum figure.

The possibility of concussion without any sign of concussion is slim. The possibility of a convulsive disorder without any previous history of it is slim. A drug overdose, without the finding of drugs in her system, would be virtually impossible, provided the tests were carried out properly. The possibility of a stroke, without any evidence of it, is extremely unlikely, and so on.

Q: And a heart attack?

A: A heart attack would be the same thing. Electrocution without any evidence of any current source would again be extremely unlikely. I can't really attach any other numbers.

What I am saying is that if all those things were extremely likely, the maximum possibility would be 10%. In light of the fact that all of them, as we look at them individually, are so extremely unlikely, we have to decrease that figure from 10% down towards zero.

Berzins got into the question of vagal-vagal reflex, death by pressure on the vagus nerve. Dr. Modell considered the possibility:

"Some individuals have a very, very sensitive carotid body and carotid sinus, and if you press on them they will undergo a vagal-vagal reflex which can actually give you what we call a vagal arrest of the heart. The vagus is a nerve that tends to slow the heart when stimulated, and there are sensitive people. This is not usual, but unusual, but it does occur."

Q: Is this what is called reflex cardiac arrest?

A: That would be one type of reflex cardiac arrest. I think the term "reflex cardiac arrest" is almost a wastebasket category for any reflex that causes cardiac arrest, but this is a specific one, and stimulating the vagus nerve and causing a cardiac arrest on that basis would be what I would consider a classic definition of reflex cardiac arrest.

Q: Is this something that could be done with one's hands?

A: Yes, sir.

Q: And is it something that would leave signs on the body afterwards?

A: Probably not. You don't have to press very hard. There are some patients whose heartbeats go very, very fast, and one of the medical treatments for this is to try to produce a vagal-vagal reflex to cause acute slowing of the heart, and in these cases we as physicians might compress the eyeball, which in some cases might do that, or compress the carotid body area in order to be able to do that, under complete medical monitoring.

Q: What is the term you described with respect to the pressing of the nerve?

A: It has been described as a vagal-vagal reflex.

Ultimately, the whole question was reduced to percentages.

Q: If the chance of the first category of possibilities was significantly less than 10%, does that mean in your opinion that the possibility of asphyxiation, suffocation, electrocution, the vagal-vagal reflex, as a group was significantly more than 90%?

A: I think I can make that statement, yes.

On cross-examination, Bosada challenged the method by which Dr. Modell had arrived at his conclusions. The doctor rejected Bosada's challenge unequivocally:

Q: Doctor, do you then agree that some of the findings in this particular situation that you reviewed may not necessarily be as accurate as they could have been, and that this could ultimately affect your opinion?

A: No sir, I do not think that conclusion is justified.

Q: Why not?

A: Because the findings that I have reviewed and the opinion that I have given you is based on laboratory tests, and it is based on analysis of calculation of blood gas exchange, it is based on the literature on the percent probability of people drowning with or without aspiration, and items of that sort. I don't think that comes within the same category as whether a patient's pupil was up or down during a cursory look.

Bosada led him, item by item, testing each possibility the doctor had rejected: concussion, aspiration of water, choking, cardiac arrest, asphyxia. He asked whether the diatom analysis method of determining drowning victims is conclusive.

Any cross-examiner would have been over his head with this expert. Bosada was particularly careful not to offend the jury by challenging the doctor's good faith. At one point he attempted to turn the question of vagal-vagal reflex to his advantage, with minor success.

Q: Is it not the result of pressure on some area of the neck?
A: All you have to do is push in the vicinity of the carotid sinus and carotid body.
Q: Do you have to be medically trained to induce that kind of reflex?
A: No.
Q: It is as simple as having a hand pushed against someone's throat?
A: Yes. If you go into the lateral side of the throat where the carotid... (He then indicated with gestures.) Some people's reflexes are very sensitive. They either respond that way or they don't. The majority of the population doesn't respond that way, but there are patients who do, and when they do it is very, very dramatic, as you might expect.

A small point for the defence.
Bosada eventually wound up his cross-examination by attempting to turn the doctor's entire body of testimony in favour of the defence. The result was not successful.

Q: Knowing everything that you do about the history of Mrs. Broderick and of her medical chart and so on, you are stating there is a possibility, and you have put it into percentages for us, that Mrs. Broderick could have become unconscious as a result of concussion, been unable to raise her head out of the water, subsequently reflexed, and gone into a larynx spasm, preventing the aspiration of fluid. Is that a fair assumption?

A: No, sir. I think you have taken my words and turned what I testified to as a negative statement and turned it into a positive statement.

What I have testified to is that the chance is at least 90% that the victim did not die of drowning, and that I believe the possibility of suffering head trauma and a concussion is certainly less than 100% in this patient, and therefore that probability would also have to be taken into consideration when calculating a percentage; so that the probability of the individual slipping and hitting her head and suffering a concussion without any external signs whatsoever, and on top of that, a final event of drowning without aspiration, would have to be a multiple of the possibility of suffering a concussion by hitting one's head without any evidence of it at all, which is one number, and multiplying that probability by a probability of less than one in 10 of possibly drowning without aspiration; so I have testified that it is very unlikely that this occurred, and that I believe, in medicine, one can never give 100% of everything. What you are suggesting, I would consider as a remote possibility, but if you are talking about percentages of one in a 1,000 or one in a 1,000,000, I could not say that is not a possibility.

Dr. John Henry Deck had been retained by the police exclusively and specifically for the purpose of examining Anne Broderick's brain. His specialty was pathology with a sub-specialty in neuropathology. He practised at Toronto Western Hospital and was an assistant professor at the Faculty of

Medicine, University of Toronto. He continued as a guest lecturer at Stanford University in California.

He told Lindsay that he had been asked to examine the brain for "pathological process," or any process of abnormality occurring before death. In the final analysis, he could find no evidence of injury to the brain. The blood vessels were normal, he said, and there were no localized abnormalities, bruises or contusions. No evidence of trauma could be seen. There was no indication of any pre-existing disease.

Having established these conclusions at the outset of Deck's testimony, Lindsay then took him in more detail through the prospect of post-traumatic epilepsy, that is, *after* any injury to the head. Again, no indication of it. He then discussed anoxia, the deprivation of the brain of oxygen.

"Systemic anoxia results in unconsciousness, which would generally be the earlier event, and then cardiac arrest which would be a slightly later event."

Q: What is the time space we are talking about between the two, sir?
A: We are talking about a matter of a very few minutes to the loss of consciousness. It is possible for people to hold their breath for a couple of minutes, perhaps, but if they haven't taken a breath and are struggling and using up oxygen as would be the case, with smothering, for example, then the oxygen in the body would be consumed relatively quickly. The amount of oxygen remaining in the blood and available to the heart after five or 10 minutes would be insufficient to keep cardiac action going.

Lindsay anticipated Bosada raising the issue of D.I.C., disseminated intravascular coagulation. He decided to preempt this possibility by raising it himself with Dr. Deck.

The doctor agreed with what other witnesses had said. It was not really a disease but a "process." If it had been present, he said, he would have expected to find it upon micro-examination, but he found no evidence of it.

It was the first thing that Bosada got into on cross-examination. Bosada challenged him with the proposition that D.I.C. could not be ruled out in the case of Anne Broderick.

Dr. Deck agreed, "... from the very limited evidence that has been presented to me."

Bosada then asked him:

Q: And also from a review by you of the slides containing the brain tissue?

A: That is correct.

Q: Taking everything you know about the case in general, as well as the photographs that have now been shown to you, you cannot exclusively rule out the condition of D.I.C.?

A: I can't rule it out.

Bosada had scored a point, particularly when taken together with later questions he asked Dr. Deck about the bruising and abrasions.

Q: The spontaneous bleeding, or the bleeding that could not effectively be controlled, and the bleeding that started upon the insertion of the I.V. tubes, were alarming to the doctors attending Mrs. Broderick, and they attributed that to D.I.C. You do not rule that out as possibly existing in Mrs. Broderick, is that correct?

A: No, I don't rule it out.

Q: The bruising or abrasions that you can see in the photographs would not necessarily be caused by D.I.C., is that what you are saying?

A: I am saying more than that. I am saying they could not be caused solely by D.I.C.

Q: Could D.I.C. be a contributing factor?

A: I said it could.

When Dr. Deck dispelled any suggestion that Anne Broderick had died of a heart attack, Bosada scored a second point.

Q: Doctor, can you think of any situations, other than cardiac arrest, that cause a sudden drop in blood pressure?

A: I can think of lots, but you would like me to think of some that might be relevant to this case?

Q: Yes.

A: Well, the one that has been repeatedly alluded to is the possibility of some anoxic process occurring, and this can result in loss of blood pressure within a relatively brief period of time as I indicated earlier. There is one example for you of a relatively sudden loss of blood pressure occurring in an otherwise healthy person.

29.

To cap off his case, Lindsay called his star medical witness. Dr. John Hillsdon-Smith, the chief forensic pathologist for the Province of Ontario, was the 51st and final witness. Not unexpectedly, his credentials were highly impressive, lending a powerful credibility to the opinions he would deliver. Educated at the University of Birmingham in England and becoming ultimately a lecturer in forensic medicine at the University of Edinburgh, Scotland, he testified that he had performed over 5,000 autopsies. These included 250 cases of drowning, in which between 20 and 25 were bathtub drownings.

Dr. Hillsdon-Smith was *capo di tutti capi* and advisor to 280 pathologists in the Province of Ontario, as well as several dozen coroners scattered throughout the province. He was equally at home in the courtroom or the laboratory and being examined and cross-examined by lawyers was part of his job. He did not seem to take exception to being "grilled" by non-medically trained people, as did many other specialists. In fact, he seemed to enjoy it.

For the Broderick case, since he had no body, he had relied exclusively on the material which had been turned up in the investigation, the medical reports which were then available and an examination of the organ tissue.

Together, he and Lindsay dissected the profusion of medical testimony, piece by piece.

First, the drowning.

"I formed the conclusion that Mrs. Broderick had not in fact drowned, but I also felt I could not absolutely exclude drowning, so I was somewhat comforted to read Dr. Modell's report. I think he came to the same conclusion I did, and he has, as you have heard, a vast experience in drowning deaths over 20 odd years; so, in conjunction, I think one can rule out drowning as a cause of death."

Then, the possibility of cardiac arrest. In Hillsdon-Smith's opinion, Anne was already in that state when she found herself in the water. Lindsay asked him about the causes of the cardiac arrest. He said there was no evidence of any disease process in the heart, and that being the case "... one has to look elsewhere, and such things as electrocution, asphyxia by suffocation, can cause it and leave no outward signs. And, thirdly, the phenomenon called reflex cardiac arrest, sometimes called vasovagal inhibition, which simply means under certain circumstances the nerves' impulses are shut off from certain areas in the body and relayed from the brain down to the heart and stop there, and the heart goes into ventricular fibrillation."

He discounted any prospect of electrocution. Lindsay wanted him to elaborate further on the question of reflex cardiac arrest, and, like a good jockey who knows his horse, gave him the lead and let him run flat out:

Q: Sir, to clarify a matter, in your opinion, is it possible for pressure to be applied to the carotid artery or sinus to stimulate it without marks being left?

A: Yes, it is possible, and has been documented. The case I am very familiar with through the literature is one which occurred in London during the Second World War. A soldier and his girlfriend were dancing, and she was seen by 250 other people to drop— and she was dead. His comment was, "I simply tweaked her neck playfully." He had tweaked it right over the carotid sinus, and Professor Keith Simpson, who carried out the autopsy, found no bruising in that area but offered this mechanism as the mechanism of death, and this was accepted, and since then there has been quite a build-up of literature on this topic, and I think it is now established as a possible but rare cause of sudden death.

Dr. Hillsdon-Smith was being expansive.

He next described asphyxiation as being "a general mechanism of death" involving deprivation of oxygen. He reviewed some of the accidental ways in which this could happen. One of the more common homicidal methods is to hold a soft plastic bag forcefully over the victim's nose and mouth. The only things that will turn up on an autopsy are the general signs of asphyxia "and they are so general they are not of any distinctive or diagnostic importance."

"It is the third named mechanism whereby somebody could die and leave no signs at autopsy, a pathologist's nightmare."

In contrast with the testimony given by the hospital pathologist, Dr. Liepa, earlier in the trial, Dr. Hillsdon-Smith, a forensic pathologist and the most highly qualified in the province, was permitted to express opinions in a far broader range, unrestricted specifically to medical matters. This became evident when Lindsay asked him whether Anne might have died accidentally in the bathtub. His response was reasoned and credible:

"From the medical point of view, I find it impossible to reconcile a previously healthy, fit woman falling into the bathtub from standing height and not causing any splashing of water outside of the bathtub, or knocking some articles over: bottles, face cloth, a brush. The whole thing looked too tidy under the circumstances of a fit person suddenly collapsing into that bathtub, and I understand and I have been told the only water around the outside of the tub was, in fact, placed there when the body was removed from the bathtub, so I assume that prior to that there was no water on the floor and no water had been splashed out at some previous time."

Since this was a critical part of Lindsay's case, he had the doctor elaborate on that response, providing more detailed reasons for the opinion. Bruise by bruise, abrasion by abrasion, Hillsdon-Smith ponderously distinguished each and how they might have been caused, the absence of marks in particular locations, all the while relating his comments to the configuration of the bathtub and the bathroom.

Lindsay was aware that Bosada would be raising the spectre of disseminated intravascular coagulation, D.I.C., again. Lindsay went for the preemptive strike by raising it with Hillsdon-Smith himself. The witness was deferential to the earlier testimony of Dr. Bourmanis, but commented that this was a clinical diagnosis made by the physicians in the emergency room "which was not substantiated by any laboratory tests. In fact, one test was carried out which would, in my opinion, exclude it, and that is that it is reported that thrombin, which is a clotting agent, was added to the blood and it still would not enable the blood to clot... And this doesn't normally occur in D.I.C."

He provided this elaborate peroration, designed to eliminate any notion that D.I.C. played a role in Anne's death:

"Examination of the microscopic preparations showed no evidence of D.I.C. But, in regard to what I was saying earlier, the absence of bruising over the chest or haemorrhage under the skin over the chest, and in particular over the back of the body, bearing in mind that there is evidence that some form or other of artificial respiration had been carried out at the scene and during the transmittal of Mrs. Broderick to the hospital, and there was quite considerable pressure placed on her back; now, if she was suffering from D.I.C., as it was thought in the hospital, in terms of drowning, then I would have expected the back to have a lot of bruising, and also when external cardiac massage was being applied during the trip to the hospital, which is a very forceful procedure, and if there was any tendency at that stage for D.I.C., I think we would have seen bruising over the front of the chest, particularly over the left side of the front of the chest and the back of the body."

Q: One of Dr. Deck's tests was to determine if D.I.C. was evidenced in the tissues of the brain.

A: Yes.

Q: And did you receive a report from him?

A: Yes, I did.

Q: Does it help you in your opinion today?

A: Yes, it does. He found no evidence of D.I.C. in the brain tissue. I found no evidence of D.I.C. in the kidney, or the heart, or the spleen, or the other organs that I examined, and my opinion is that D.I.C. was not present.

Lindsay was clearly concerned about the prospect of D.I.C. being an "out" for George Broderick.

When court resumed on the morning of June 28th, 1978, Lindsay returned to the question of intentionally caused asphyxia, specifically the idea of murder by plastic bag. Dr. Hillsdon-Smith gave this graphic illustration:

Q: Doctor, what mechanically happens to a person who is the victim of suffocation?

A: The idea of the use of a plastic bag in this regard is to block off the nose and the mouth simultaneously, thereby preventing any air reaching the lungs. If the plastic bag is maintained over the face, occluding the nose and mouth, consciousness is lost within 60 seconds, and often a little earlier than that. During that process, the lack of oxygen affects the brain and probably the heart at about the same time, and the victim dies within a matter of four or five minutes, or possibly even within a shorter period, from the combined effects of lack of oxygen to the brain and cardiac arrest.

Again, near the conclusion of Dr. Hillsdon-Smith's testimony, Lindsay decided to preempt the anticipated defence position.

Q: Sir, I believe you have found no cause of death or specific cause of death in this case. You heard from Dr. Liepa, and you have read his report?

A: I have.

Q: And is that generally your comment in this area?

A: Yes, there is no definitive cause of death.

Q: And considering that, have you taken into consideration the possibility of death here by natural causes, disease?

A: Yes, I have. There is absolutely no evidence in the findings of the pathologist, in the examination I made, that Dr. Deck made, and all the medical witnesses have made, to indicate any significant degree of natural disease, and on that basis I think I would exclude natural disease as a possible cause of death.

The doctor excluded suicide absolutely before summarizing for the jury:

Q: Sir, that leaves you with your fourth category.

A: Taking all the circumstances into consideration, from the pathologist's point of view, this case has all the hallmarks of a homicide, complicated by the fact that there is no known cause of death. And, as I said yesterday, this raises three possibilities: one is death from suffocation, an asphyxial process as opposed to any other type of asphyxia, suffocation; secondly, what you might call a wet electrocution; and thirdly, the reflex cardiac arrest with the trigger zone that I described yesterday.

I may say that numerically, statistically if you like, that suffocation in a homicidal setting is by far the commonest of the three, by far the commonest.

Bosada had his work cut out for him. He was aware that his cross-examination of Dr. Hillsdon-Smith could be very dangerous. The doctor had testified in-chief with great authority and credibility and with the unarticulated nuance that he spoke for the entire Province of Ontario. He had given his opinions with confidence, but had not overstated them. He had provided cogent reasons.

Bosada decided not to be confrontational, but rather to review with the doctor these complex matters which were often subject to interpretation. Some neutralization was the best that Bosada could hope for in the circumstances. On the other hand, if he simply had the doctor repeat all of the opinions he had expressed in-chief, this would simply reinforce these opinions in the minds of the jury. Bosada zeroed in on very specific issues.

The suggestion that the bruises on Anne's body were caused by the rescue team's handling was immediately killed by Hillsdon-Smith. It was not possible at all. She was already clinically dead. The doctor was quick to demonstrate how he could turn a proposition of the cross-examiner against him:

Q: Do you agree that all of this handling could explain some of these bruises that were noticed on the body of Mrs. Broderick?
A: It is not the presence of those bruises which concerns me. It is the absence of those that should be there, sustained by the activity you have just described at length: they are not there: so what goes for one circumstance must go for the other.

Then Bosada returned to probing, again, the prospect of D.I.C., referable to the findings of Dr. Bourmanis and the opinion of Dr. Deck. The issue of D.I.C. had become a window of opportunity for the defence.

Q: Did you confirm or deny, at the very early stages, the existence of D.I.C.?
A: In the early stages, I think I said in my report the diagnosis of D.I.C. was a clinical one and was not supported by laboratory tests. The doctor subsequently followed that up.
As I said yesterday, this was not a case of D.I.C. D.I.C. itself is not a disease process; it is always the result of some other disease, and no other disease was found. Drowning, in my opinion, has been excluded. So, I think we are in a very tenuous area to suggest that D.I.C. was here at all. The alternative explanation of post-mortem fluidity of the blood is a very tenable and attractive one.

Q: In April, 1977, you did not think that to be the case?
A: No, I hadn't had time then to research this area. I mean that D.I.C. is not in my area.

Next, Bosada raised the prospect of "dry drowning" and referred to the testimony of Dr. Modell.

Q: We also learned that he did not like the term dry drowning, which, I take it, is a result of the reflex of the glottis in the throat, which prevents the finding of water in the lung passages?
A: Yes, that is correct.
Q: And this is the 10% or less that you are talking about?
A: That 10% are dry drownings, yes.
Q: There is no fluid or water aspirated into the lungs with dry drowning?
A: This very small percentage of dry drownings was related to dry drownings in a bathtub with water 70 degrees fahrenheit or warmer, as opposed to dry drownings in large expanses of water. There, I think, the figure is 10%. He is bringing that 10% down considerably only in relation to deaths in the bathtub.

Bosada shifted direction, suggesting to the doctor that it was the position of Anne's body in the tub, on her left side facing inwards, that had propelled him to his "no accident" opinion. Hillsdon-Smith forcefully rejected this idea.

"No, no, no way. I excluded a fall in the bathtub on other grounds. First, as I said, it is a very small bathtub, and there are plenty of things for a conscious person to grab if they are falling. If they have fallen and subsequently gotten into a position where they are lying on their side, face down, or on their back, it doesn't matter, you have to have some head injury."

On each and every subsequent proposition put to the doctor calling for an explanation, he became increasingly adamant in countering the proposition. The only area where the defence made some progress was in speculation about electrocution. The doctor agreed that subjecting someone to 110 volts of normal amperage would be enough to put them into cardiac arrest, particularly if they were in a tub of water, and that the longer the current was applied to the body the less chance of survival there was.

Dr. Hillsdon-Smith's opinions about Anne's death were wide-ranging, definitive, and spoken with the confidence of unequalled personal experience and the authority of the Centre for Forensic Sciences. Credibility permeated the courtroom during his testimony. He had not been mauled on cross-examination and had given up nothing important.

Lindsay tossed a few "clean-up" questions on re-examination which Hillsdon-Smith, his final witness, handled with finesse.

For Dr. Hillsdon-Smith, it had been a testimonial *tour de force*.

Lindsay's case had now reached its critical mass.

He had demonstrated motive, exclusive opportunity and consciousness of guilt. He had negated death by natural causes and raised possibilities, a smorgasbord from which the jury could select its cause of death.

But he had not proven cause of death.

There was a brief lull as Lindsay conferred quietly and quickly with Berzins and Bowles.

"That's the case for the Crown," he announced, and sat down.

It was now time for Bosada to come out of the dug-out.

30.

In a murder trial, an overnight adjournment at the end of the prosecution's case is a welcome protocol. It gives the defence a breather, an opportunity to adequately re-assess its position, and a last chance to block strategy.

Dick Bosada and Bill Carroll went out to the jail that night to meet with George Broderick. They had a lot to discuss, but just one thing to decide: whether or not George Broderick would testify.

It is risky business for an accused person *not* to testify in a murder case. The jury members want to hear words of denial spoken by the accused. They want to hear the protestation of innocence. They want to hear the tone of outrage. They want the accused to expose himself to cross-examination. It is an atavistic throw-back to the days of trials by battle and ordeal.

Failure of the accused to take the stand in a serious charge is likely to be seen by the jury as suspect. Of course, that is not the *law*. The accused is entitled to stand silent and the judge must instruct the jury that it is his right. The jury must not draw an adverse inference from his silence.

But that is not the psychological reality. In a serious charge like murder the jurors tacitly wonder: if he has nothing to hide, why doesn't he get in the witness box and say so? It is something that hangs over every jury case like a dark but transparent mist. You can't see it, but you know it's there.

Defence lawyers sweat over it.

Just as Lindsay had confronted his own dilemma— the absence of any definable cause of death— Bosada now confronted its counterpart: Broderick's lies and lifestyle. If Broderick took the stand to deny involvement in Anne's death, Lindsay would likely hang him out to dry on his lies and obfuscations. They weren't proof of his guilt, but they would destroy his credibility. And if he had lied to his wife, his mistress, his superiors, and his clients, then why should the jury believe his denials of murder?

"Consciousness of guilt," Lindsay had repeatedly argued.

It was a tough call.

Ultimately the final decision would be left to the client, after he had been fully advised of the consequences of either route.

Broderick asked Bosada a perceptive question.

"If I testify, can Lindsay question me about *everything*, or just the stuff I testify about?"

"Everything."

"Cynthia?"

"Yes."

"Lisette?"

"Yes."

"The house deal?"

"Yes."

"What about the Petawawa stuff?"

"That, too!"

Broderick reflected on this last item. He was rapidly getting the picture.

Yet, once all the legal dust had settled, Bosada still did not believe the prosecution had demonstrated a *prima facie* case. There was still no specific cause of death.

All Broderick's mischief, Bosada reasoned, taken together, did not prove murder. With no cause of death, there was no proof of murder, and no case to answer.

Bosada argued this line of reasoning first thing next morning before Justice O'Driscoll on a motion asking for a directed verdict of acquittal. In effect, he asked the judge to *direct* the jury to find George Broderick "Not guilty," because no minimum case for murder had been presented.

O'Driscoll refused, then put Bosada to his election. Would the defence be calling any evidence or not?

Another thorny tactical question confronted Bosada. In Canadian criminal procedure, if the defence calls *any* witnesses at all, it must make its closing argument to the jury first; the prosecution argues last. The defence will have no right of reply. If the defence does not call any witnesses, however, then it has the advantage of arguing last. The jurors retire, after the judge's instructions, with the defence argument freshest in their minds. If closing arguments are long, this can be a decided benefit.

In that case, not only must the prosecution present its own position, but it must anticipate the defence arguments and respond in advance.

"Defence evidence, Mr. Bosada?" Justice O'Driscoll was waiting.

"The defence elects to call no evidence."

The words echoed through the packed courtroom like the crack of a bat in a ball park. O'Driscoll looked up sharply from his notes, to see if he was hearing right. Reporters made quick, stabbing bows to the court and hurried out to the hallway phones.

Broderick would not be testifying.

His story, his denials, his protestations, would never be heard in open court. The jurors' faces reflected obvious disappointment. Lindsay leaned over and conferred *sotto voce* with Berzins.

Justice O'Driscoll, all business, ordered the closing arguments to begin right away.

Mac Lindsay went first. He was not a pacer. He spoke to the jury in his low, even, logical manner for two hours from behind a lectern— like a university professor lecturing his pupils. He reviewed all the salient testimony, methodically tying one piece in with another, brick by brick, until he had erected his wall around George Broderick.

Broderick's affairs, the lies, the $50,000 debt, the apartment for Cynthia, the engagement rings, "Dreemcumtru"— taken together, constituted a smouldering volcano that erupted on the morning of November 16th, 1976. With the impending eviction Anne would learn everything, and George would stand exposed.

"She would have found out about the problems he had and he would have been unearthed as a liar," Lindsay said, driving the point home. The inevitable arrival of the bailiffs was "the last straw."

Lindsay advanced the prosecution theory that when Broderick realized he could no longer hold off the eviction, or "protect" his wife from all the lies, he planned to kill her. It was, he said, easier for Broderick to kill his wife than to face the "guilt and humiliation of having his secret life exposed to her."

Broderick's conduct throughout the investigation pointed to "consciousness of guilt."

Dealing with the prosecution's dilemma— the inability to prove any specific cause of death— Lindsay used a two-pronged approach, eliminating specific natural causes, then presenting the remaining options. He reminded the jury that the experts, particularly Doctors Modell and Hillsdon-Smith, had no trouble discounting death from natural causes and had both pointed to the specific possibilities: electrocution, suffocation, or the application of pressure to the vagus nerve to cause heart stoppage. Broderick, he argued, then placed Anne's body in the bathtub and arranged the room to feign a slipping accident. Broderick timed his return to 18 Beaverton to coincide with the arrival of the bailiffs. Together, they would "discover" the body.

A "timely coincidence," he called it. It was Lindsay's only uncharacteristic use of sarcasm.

His summation was all good, straightforward stuff, delivered without histrionics, one logical step at a time, one proven fact hooking onto the next, driving toward one inescapable conclusion: George Broderick had murdered his wife.

While speaking, Bosada strode back and forth in front of the jury, involuntary gesticulations punctuating the air as he delivered point after point— a restrained pugilist fighting for his client.

George Broderick had no reason to murder Anne. He loved her.

Bosada hammered this theme home to the jurors. Broderick, he argued, was in a position to shield Anne from knowledge of his debts, and in fact he was in a position to pay off all but $6,000 of it (a dubious argument unless the jury accepted that money would be coming in from the secret invention or sale of the non-existent airplane).

Broderick, he argued, could easily have shielded Anne from knowledge of his love affair with Cynthia Eauclaire. He had shielded her from these unhappy realities for years and could continue doing so.

People do not murder someone they love for these reasons. He termed the prosecution's suggestion "preposterous," saying, "Life is surely not that cheap!"

Bosada was tacitly appealing to the experience, reasonableness and collective knowledge of the jury. Many men get into debt, many get involved in affairs, many tell fantasy tales and act foolishly. But they don't kill.

George Broderick, he argued, was on trial for *murder*. Not for his morals. Not for his lifestyle. The jury should not be influenced by the testimony that he had made love with his son's former girlfriend the night of Anne's funeral.

And it was impossible for a sane man to murder his wife merely to "stave off eviction."

Bosada cut to the weak link in the prosecution's case, the absence of any cause of death.

No cause of death, no murder! He accused Lindsay of using a "shotgun approach" and of inviting the jury to indulge in pure speculation and "guesswork." He had never seen a case last so long that had "proved virtually nothing." Bosada argued with the conviction that he was, in law, correct. No *murder*, he said, had been proven. The cause of death had not been demonstrated and certainly not beyond any reasonable doubt.

By suggesting three *possible* causes, the prosecution was reduced to merely speculating. The jury must not speculate. The prosecution was asking the jury to do something it could not do in law, that is, to select a single cause of death from among the possibilities.

Even the prosecution's medical experts had conceded that there was a small chance Anne died of natural causes. Heart attack, spasm to the arteries of the heart, and epileptic attack had not been *conclusively* ruled out. And then there was the prospect of D.I.C.— disseminated intravascular coagulation. The doctors had specifically recognized this possibility with Anne. Even so eminent an authority as Dr. Deck admitted he could not rule it out.

Chances of Anne dying from natural causes had been placed by the experts at "less than 10%." But there was still that 10%.

It left plenty of room for reasonable doubt, Bosada urged.

In summation, Bosada tried to turn Lindsay's "timely coincidence" comment against him. If Broderick really planned to murder his wife, why wait until a time when officialdom would be at the door? It was the worst possible time to do it. He had known of the eviction notice for several days and, in fact, had expected the bailiffs the day before.

And then Bosada argued the practicalities.

Even accepting the prosecution's theory at face value, Broderick would be left with a mere 15 minutes to murder his wife, place her in the bathtub, re-arrange the rooms, fake the damage to the shower curtain and hooks, and get out of the house before the bailiffs arrived. Nor, he said, was the prosecution's theory consistent with the evidence of witnesses who described Broderick's legitimate concern and attempts to revive his wife with artificial respiration.

"This trial has been reduced to guesswork," Bosada urged. "It has been turned into a... game show!"

He thanked the jurors and sat down.

He had been speaking, stalking the courtroom, pleading, for three hours.

The facts are for the lawyers and the jury; the law is for the judge. The jury must take their law as the judge gives it to them. But the judge has a wide discretion to comment on the evidence, suggesting to the jury how they should assess it and expressing his own opinion about its strengths and weaknesses. He must, however, remind the jurors that they are the sole arbiters of fact.

Justice O'Driscoll began his instructions to the jury promptly next morning, July 6th, 1978. The courtroom doors were under guard. No one was permitted to enter or leave while he gave his instructions. He spoke most of the day, going over the jury's obligations and role in the process. He analyzed the charge of murder, what it meant and its ingredients. He outlined the principles of circumstantial evidence, the fundamental doctrine of proof beyond a reasonable doubt, and the burden of proof upon the prosecution.

He discussed the meaning of "planned and deliberate" in relation to murder. He emphasized that they and they alone were the sole judges of the facts, including the ultimate fact— whether or not the accused was guilty. He instructed on assessing the credibility of each witness and how to test the evidence:

"Rephrasing the matter, are you convinced beyond a reasonable doubt that Anne Broderick's death was neither from natural causes, nor from accident? If your answer is 'No,' the matter ends and the verdict is not guilty. If your answer is 'Yes,' you next ask yourself, are you convinced beyond a reasonable doubt that Anne Broderick's death was caused by George Broderick? If your answer to that is 'No,' again your verdict is not guilty. If your answer is 'Yes,' you then ask yourself, are you convinced it is caused in circumstances that render it murder? If your answer is 'Yes,' are you convinced that it was both planned and deliberate so as to render it first degree murder? If 'yes,' then your verdict is guilty as charged."

He characterized the case itself.

"This is a perplexing case. It is a case which, so to speak, has no middle ground. If George Broderick did not cause his wife's death, then his arrest, detention and trial have all heaped mounds of injustice upon him. If George Broderick did cause the death of his wife, then you have before you a very crafty, cunning killer who almost pulled off the perfect crime."

The defence would later complain that this statement by O'Driscoll was intemperate and inflammatory.

He then went through the wealth of medical testimony, attempting to make it more comprehensible to the jurors but leaving little doubt that *he* believed the expert testimony left no doubt. In a few sentences he virtually removed from the jury two of the arguments of the defence.

"It is for you to say, but it is my view, again my view and disregard it if you think otherwise, that D.I.C. is a total 'red herring' in this case."

The defence was dismayed by this comment.

Who would disagree with the view of a Supreme Court judge? Then he posed rhetorical questions about the bruises on Anne's body, questions which the defence would allege indicated partiality.

"I ask you, how could all those bruises have been caused? By the paramedics and the doctors? There is not one bruise or mark, back or front, from the cardiac massage, which the doctors say sometimes causes broken ribs.

"Are you not convinced that those bruises were sustained by the deceased at 18 Beaverton Drive after Shirley Broderick left, and before the cardiac arrest or death occurred?"

He examined in some detail the lies and motivations attributed to Broderick, by inference connecting them with the prosecution's "consciousness of guilt."

"Why did she die? Did anyone have a motive for killing her?

Crimes are more likely committed by someone who has a motive than one who has no motive, but it is not always possible to discover the motive. There is a great difference between absence of proved motive and proved absence of motive. If the prosecution can prove that the accused had a motive for committing the crime, it may do so, because the existence of a motive makes it more likely that the accused did, in fact, commit the crime, but a person may be convicted of a criminal offence even if he has no motive.

"Counsel for the Crown submits that the accused was having and for some time had been having an affair with Cynthia Eauclaire. She had her divorce papers and her certificate of freedom. He had purchased rings for her and she for him. He was married to a woman who did not believe in divorce and would not facilitate his divorce. He was locked in. He was getting into debt more and more each day and more and more each month: $18,000 plus for the Juliana Apartments, and Cynthia Eauclaire was not even living there through most of it. He was going to be evicted from his house. The Crown also says there was $31,500 in life insurance available on Anne's accidental death. The Crown argues that by arranging an 'accidental death' he freed himself up to marry Cynthia, and he could pick up the $31,500 to alleviate his financial dilemma."

There, in a nutshell, was the theory of the prosecution.

Later, O'Driscoll posed another rhetorical question: "If the Crown has satisfied you beyond a reasonable doubt that some person caused Anne Broderick's death by culpable homicide and murder, who was that person?

"Counsel for the Crown submits to you that the evidence points to one person and one person only, the accused, George Allan Broderick, the husband of the deceased.

"The Crown submits to you that: (1) the accused was the only person who had a motive to kill her, and (2) the accused had the exclusive opportunity to kill her."

He returned to Broderick's lies and falsehoods, and Lindsay's "consciousness of guilt" argument, obviously supporting it.

"Counsel for the Crown submits that there is evidence before you which shows that statements the accused made to the police, to Cynthia Euclaire, to Lisette Martineau, to Shirley Broderick, to Mrs. Simpson, after the death of Anne Broderick, that he knew were false, and that since the evidence demonstrates that such statements were false, such recourse by the accused to such falsehoods leads fairly to an inference of guilt."

He then went on to review some of the lies in detail and discuss their value as evidence. For Cynthia Euclaire, whom he described as testifying "with some degree of reticence," he reserved special remarks. Referring to her testimony upon learning, in the witness box, that her conversations had been taped by Inspector Bowles:

"It was only then that this demure woman turned tigress and bared her claws... I carry no brief for Inspector Bowles. I never recall seeing him before the start of this case. I suppose it is not really what you call select judicial language, but I can think of no other phrase for what she did other than to call it a 'cheap shot.' It is the act of someone who obviously has been cornered."

In general, he asked many rhetorical questions which seemed to leave little doubt about his view of the evidence. He reminded the jurors, however, that it was their view which mattered, not his.

One of Carroll's later complaints was that the judge had spent four and a half hours explaining the theory of the prosecution and about four and a half minutes explaining the defence position. The court summarized that position:

"I have explained to you the position of the defence that the Crown has not proved its case. Indeed, the Crown has not proved what the cause of death is. If you have not got a cause of death that is homicide, then there is no way you can have murder, let alone a first degree murder."

It was late in the day when Justice O'Driscoll finished. The jurors filed out to the jury room. If they needed to deliberate overnight they would be sequestered at the historic Albion Hotel across the street. The courthouse caretaker, Al, was already swabbing the terrazzo floors with his bucket and string-mop as the jurors passed by.

When the door closed behind the last juror Bosada jumped to his feet, barely able to suppress his rage.

"With respect to the direction that your Lordship gave to the jury, my remarks, and notwithstanding a long list of items that I have considered perhaps not properly part of the charge should not be mentioned, I say this: that the charge effectively amounted to a misdirection."

Emotional and convoluted, but to the point.

Bosada complained that the judge had advanced a *third* theory for the prosecution, one not even advanced by Lindsay himself.

Bosada complained further about the judge's presentation of the respective theories to the jury.

"… and having done that, and having reviewed the highlights of that evidence, entirely favourable to the Crown, and not once, in my submission, mentioning any evidence on which fair and reasonable inferences could be made in cross-examination or qualifications of that evidence, dealt with the theory of the defence in approximately three minutes."

He took particular exception to the reference to Broderick as a possible "crafty, cunning killer who almost pulled off the perfect crime," the characterization of Cynthia Eauclaire as "the tigress exposing herself…" and the D.I.C. reference as being a "red herring." The latter reference, he complained, left the jury with the inference "… that the defence attempted to raise red herrings for the purposes of covering up something else…"

Additionally, the jury, he said, should be made aware that lies by an accused do not fill the void in situations where the prosecution cannot prove its charge beyond a reasonable doubt. In other words, being a liar did not, *ipso facto*, make Broderick a murderer. And finally, the court had inadvertently told the jury that Broderick had been seen washing the *bedclothes* the morning after the death, rather than the bathmat. A small matter but it could be unfairly damaging.

Justice O'Driscoll recalled the jury and re-instructed them, admitting his error about the bedclothes, and apologizing. He re-instructed on the D.I.C. remark, and the fact that there was no "third" prosecution theory.

Again the jury retired and George Broderick was led away to the holding room to await his fate.

On his way he stooped to pick up a piece of string that had come loose from the floor cleaner's mop.

To some lawyers, waiting for a jury is the most stressful part of a trial; others it flushes with euphoria. Nothing more can be done. The cards have been played, and it is out of their hands. Nothing to do but wait. It could take hours or it could take days.

George Broderick's jury was out four hours and 20 minutes, not very long for 26 days of testimony.

For the defence, this was a bad sign.

Court was re-convened and Broderick was brought in, passing by Mancuso on his way to the prisoner's dock. Broderick held up the piece of string and swung it back and forth. He had made it into a noose.

The rest happened fast. The clerk asked the jury whether they had agreed on a verdict. They had.

"We, the 12 members of the jury, unanimously find the accused, Mr. Broderick, guilty of first degree murder as charged." Again, the crack of the bat in the ball park.

Mac Lindsay would dispute it later, but some spectators would say that he was the most surprised person in the courtroom.

When asked if he had anything to say before sentence, George Broderick answered with resignation, "No, just to reiterate what I have said all along, that I am not guilty of the charge."

The sentence was quickly pronounced by Justice O'Driscoll.

"The sentence that I pass is that you be sentenced to imprisonment for life without eligibility for parole until you have served 25 years of that sentence."

It was over.

Mancuso and Broderick exchanged parting glances as the custodians led George Broderick away. There was no rancour in Broderick's eyes, just resignation. Even relief, some said.

George Broderick, after all, had been right. Columbo only investigates murder cases!

Epilogue

George Broderick is confined in maximum security Joyceville Penitentiary. He has a small cot, toilet facilities, and a little desk with a goose-neck lamp, a few books and a bible. A crucifix hangs over the desk. During the day he works in the prison machine shop. He is a model prisoner.

Soon after his conviction an appeal was filed with the Ontario Court of Appeal alleging 58 errors made by the trial judge, mainly in his charge to the jury. The appellate decision, written by Justice Arthur Martin, acknowledged that errors had been made, but dismissed the appeal, saying there was no substantial miscarriage of justice.

"Notwithstanding the errors that we have mentioned, we think that they were comparatively minor in the context of the total evidence against the appellant. They occurred during the course of a charge which, apart from these defects, was a model of clarity in a case involving complicated medical evidence. The errors which we have found related to the judge's charge with relation to evidence going to show who the killer was. We think that the jury could not reasonably find otherwise than that the death was not due to natural causes, suicide or accident. Once the jury came to that conclusion, since the accused had exclusive opportunity to kill the deceased, and a strong motive to do so, we think that a properly instructed jury would inevitably have convicted on the evidence."

On April 6th, 1981 the Supreme Court of Canada refused to hear an appeal from the Ontario Court of Appeal's decision.

In October, 1992, under new parole amendments, Broderick was permitted to have his parole application considered by another jury. He was represented by Felicity Hawthorn, barrister. The Crown's opposition to the application was handled by Louise Dupont, assistant Crown prosecutor, and Mac Lindsay, now a Queen's Counsel. Evidence was presented to Justice Dan Chilcott and the jury that Broderick was in all respects a model prisoner, energetic and hard-working, and had advanced himself to positions of trust and responsibility within the penitentiary. The main negative assessment came from Dr. Ralph Serin, prison psychologist, who had worked with Broderick over the years, dealing with Broderick's application to go into minimum security. Serin referred to Broderick's "exemplary performance in the institution" and said "he impresses very well in an interview, very skilful, very conversant, humorous— you know, very appropriate." But the psychologist was not satisfied. He reported that when confronted with the facts and evidence emanating from the police investigation into Anne's death, Broderick "felt that they were either incorrect or an exaggeration and a distortion of what had actually occurred."

Serin felt he could not recommend Broderick for minimum security, because, despite his stellar institutional performance, he was still denying the facts.

Broderick himself testified. Age was catching up with him. The hair was silver; the hands trembled. He still loved Cynthia Euclaire; he still hoped to marry her some day.

In the final result, the jury recommended that Broderick be considered favourably for parole in 1994. He will then be 72; he will have been in prison for 19 years.

After living under a cloud for two years himself, charges of conspiracy to import and traffic in narcotics against lawyer Richard Bosada were dismissed on a directed verdict of acquittal— essentially, for lack of evidence.

In 1987, nearly 10 years after Broderick's trial, *The Fifth Estate* and *Newsline*, both television documentary news programs, had the relevant material reviewed by a number of prominent medical experts in the United States and Canada.

Dr. David King, forensic pathologist at the Hamilton General Hospital, described the medical evidence in the case as being "very weak" and observed that, at the trial, the "expert evidence was given quite forcefully." As to how Anne Broderick died, he replied, "I'm baffled." He expressed relief that he did not have to decide the issue.

After reviewing all of the medical records in the case, another pathologist, Dr. Laurel Gray, said, "It is more likely that this woman died of natural causes than from any of the *un*natural causes discussed... I'm surprised it got as far as it got... (It's) a castle of cards built on the basis of this report... All the experts in the world can't come to any real conclusion based on this amount of information." She went further. "There is absolutely nothing," she said, "in the autopsy report to indicate foul play... If you have to play numbers, I would say it is a 75, 85, or 90% chance she died of natural causes— on the information we've been provided."

Dr. Gray is the deputy forensic pathologist for the province of British Columbia.

Dr. James Farris, chief forensic pathologist for British Columbia, had been interviewed by Mancuso and Bowles in the course of the investigation. Based on the information they showed him, he was of the opinion that there was insufficient evidence to proceed with criminal charges, pointing out that with a negative autopsy report such as Anne Broderick's, the *presumption* is death from natural causes. Speaking to *The Fifth Estate*, he said, "I can't recall a case where the autopsy was totally negative where there was a subsequent trial and successful prosecution of the case... You cannot presume a death is unnatural based on a negative autopsy. Generally speaking, if the death is unnatural the evidence of injury or the unnatural event is not difficult to detect and we do know that there are very many natural causes of death, perhaps involving the electrical system of the heart, which can cause sudden death and leave nothing to find."

Dr. Joel Morgenroth, a cardiologist specializing in sudden death, is also head of the Sudden Death Prevention Program at Haniman University, Philadelphia. He mentioned that there are half a million sudden deaths in North America every year which leave inconclusive evidence as to cause. He studied one of Anne's earlier ECG tracings.

"The electrocardiogram, while not conclusive, suggests she may have had an abnormal electrical system in her heart... My educated guess would be that she had a natural death from a cardiac arrhythmia, possibly due to an abnormal by-pass track in her heart. That's what the evidence suggests to me is most likely... That kind of electrical abnormality is possible, not definite, in this particular patient. One would have to see previous ECGs to be certain."

Finally, Dr. Charles Petty was consulted. Head of the Institute for Forensic Sciences in Dallas, Texas, Dr. Petty is considered the dean of American forensic pathologists. He reviewed the medical records and the court transcripts before being asked his opinion. Was there a 90% chance of murder, the percentage alluded to at the trial?

"(The) percentages are twisted. It's probably the other way around— a 90% chance she had some natural disease process or an accident, 5% or 10% chance homicidal." He listed things that he believed should have been examined which were not, e.g., the coronary arteries, to find out "... what they *really* looked like, were they other than normal?" He attributed the lack of conclusiveness in the case to "disjointment," an absence of coordination between the investigators, the pathologist and the Centre for Forensic Sciences.

The case has broader implications, however, since the legal principles and tactics employed by the prosecution in securing the conviction are now being questioned and bear upon other persons convicted in the same way. The Crown's presentation presaged recognition of what has now come to be known as the "Meursault Syndrome," which, according to *The Toronto Star* (September 11th, 1992) "pervades the Ontario justice system," and was evidenced in the Toronto cases of Susan Nelles, Rui-Wen Pan, and Guy Paul Morin.

In each of these cases, as in Broderick, the lack of a correct emotional response to the death was waved before the jury as evidence of the murderer's identity and proof of guilt.

Ultimately, the case of George Broderick is left to legal history and law students. Having broken new legal ground in the "consciousness of guilt" area, Mac Lindsay is often called upon to lecture law students about the case. The question inevitably comes up: would the outcome have been different if Broderick had testified? And, why didn't he testify? A gossamer answer surfaced when it was rumoured, around the courthouse, that Broderick had adamantly refused to testify when he learned that Lindsay would be able to cross-examine him about the Petawawa business. George never did reveal what had been going on there. He said it was in the interest of national security for him to say nothing and he would never reveal it!

To the end, like one of Columbo's villains, he remained silent and cryptic.